Intrinsic
Motivation

PERSPECTIVES IN SOCIAL PSYCHOLOGY

A Series of Texts and Monographs • Edited by Elliot Aronson

INTRINSIC MOTIVATION
By Edward L. Deci • 1975

In preparation

SCHOOL DESEGREGATION
By Harold B. Gerard and Norman Miller

Intrinsic Motivation

Edward L. Deci

Department of Psychology
University of Rochester

PLENUM PRESS·NEW YORK AND LONDON

Library of Congress Cataloging in Publication Data

Deci, Edward L
    Intrinsic motivation.

    (Perspectives in social psychology)
    Bibliography: p.
    Includes index
    1. Motivation (Psychology) I. Title. [DNLM: 1. Motivation. 2. Behavior. BF683
D295i]
BF683.D43   153.8   75-17613
ISBN 0-306-34401-7

© 1975 Plenum Press, New York
A Division of Plenum Publishing Corporation
227 West 17th Street, New York, N.Y. 10011

United Kingdom edition published by Plenum Press, London
A Division of Plenum Publishing Company, Ltd.
Davis House (4th Floor), 8 Scrubs Lane, Harlesden, London, NW10 6SE, England

Printed in the United States of America

Preface

As I begin to write this Preface, I feel a rush of excitement. I have now finished the book; my gestalt is coming into completion. Throughout the months that I have been writing this, I have, indeed, been intrinsically motivated. Now that it is finished I feel quite competent and self-determining (see Chapter 2). Whether or not those who read the book will perceive me that way is also a concern of mine (an extrinsic one), but it is a wholly separate issue from the intrinsic rewards I have been experiencing.

This book presents a theoretical perspective. It reviews an enormous amount of research which establishes unequivocally that intrinsic motivation exists. Also considered herein are various approaches to the conceptualizing of intrinsic motivation. The book concentrates on the approach which has developed out of the work of Robert White (1959), namely, that intrinsically motivated behaviors are ones which a person engages in so that he may feel competent and self-determining in relation to his environment.

The book then considers the development of intrinsic motivation, how behaviors are motivated intrinsically, how they relate to extrinsically motivated behaviors, and how intrinsic motivation is affected by extrinsic rewards and controls. It also considers how changes in intrinsic motivation relate to changes in attitudes, how people attribute motivation to each other, how the attribution process is motivated, and how the process of perceiving motivation (and other internal states) in oneself relates to perceiving them in others.

The book assumes that there is personal knowledge (i.e., that persons have access to their own internal states in a way in which

v

others do not). However, it also shows that these internal states are changeable and that cognitive processes represent one means by which they change. The emphasis of the book is on cognitive processes, and the reasons for this are simple: Not only do cognitions affect internal states such as attitudes and motives, but, as this work shows, individuals choose what behaviors to engage in on the basis of their cognitions about the outcomes of those and other behaviors.

This work is intended as a source book on intrinsic motivation; it has attempted to draw together from many areas of psychology all of the available literature related to intrinsic motivation. Different aspects have been the subjects of varying degrees of attention, and this is largely a reflection of my own interest. The book is appropriate for use as a textbook for upper-level courses and seminars in human motivation, social cognition, and social psychology. In Chapter 8 some of the applications of research and theory on intrinsic motivation are considered, especially as they relate to the areas of education and organizational motivation.

Throughout the book I have employed the referent pronoun "he" in the generic sense, i.e., to refer to such nouns as "person." I have done so, despite the current criticism of this usage as sexist, because there is to my mind no really satisfactory alternative available to the writer. The use of "they" to refer back to "person" is grammatically incorrect, and the use of "he or she" is rather cumbersome for repeated use throughout a work of this length.

I originally began investigating the area of intrinsic motivation about five years ago when I was a second-year graduate student in the Psychology Department at Carnegie-Mellon University. At that time Vic Vroom was very supportive and helped me begin to formulate my ideas on the topic. I began writing the book about two years ago while working as a part-time research associate in the Management Research Center at the University of Rochester. Bernard Bass, director of the Center, provided the financial support which enabled me to begin this book, and Wayne Cascio and Carl Benware were at that time working actively with me on the research reported in Chapters 5, 9, and 10. To all these people I acknowledge my gratitude.

I wrote most of the book during the 1973–1974 academic year, with the financial support of an interdisciplinary postdoctoral fellowship at Stanford University granted by the National Institute of Mental Health. I am grateful to both Stanford and the NIMH for providing me with a stimulating (and sunny) environment for working on this project.

Elliot Aronson read the entire manuscript and made many useful suggestions. I appreciate his help and his friendship.

I would also like to acknowledge the aid of Daniel Berlyne, who commented on the entire manuscript; Ralph Haber and Zur Shapira, who read several chapters; Edward Walker, who contributed to Chapter 2; Doug Stern and Ned Dwelle, who made suggestions about Chapter 1; David Elkind, who offered feedback on Chapter 3; and Eileen Zucker, who reviewed Chapter 10.

Charles (Skip) Lowe helped enormously by making extensive comments on an early version of Chapter 10, and David Landy worked with me in developing some of the ideas presented in Chapter 7. I appreciate the intellectual and personal companionship of both these colleagues very much.

During the first few months that I worked on this book, I was living in a commune with six other psychologists: Drs. Harold Bernard, Ken Cohen, Sandy Ehlinger, Judy Krusell, David Landy, and Allan Schwartz. Their love and support was at times distracting, nonetheless it provided me with energy to live and work enthusiastically. To them, and to the rest of the "extended Canterbury"—Nancy Wickens-Thies, Lou Morrice, Amanda Morrice, Louise Sheinman, and Mitchell Bernard—this book is affectionately dedicated.

Stanford, California   *Edward L. Deci*

Acknowledgments

I would like to thank the following publishers for permission to reprint quotations of copyrighted material:

Academic Press, Inc: de Charms, R. *Personal causation*. New York: Academic Press, 1968; and Pritchard, R. D., Equity theory: A review and critique. *Organizational Behavior and Human Performance*, 1969, *4*, 176–211.

American Association for the Advancement of Science: Copyright holder of Berlyne, D. E. Exploration and curiosity. *Science*, 1966, *153*, 25–33.

American Psychological Association: White, R. W. Motivation reconsidered: The concept of competence. *Psychological Review*, 1959, *66*, 297–333; McClelland, D. C. Toward a theory of motive acquisition. *American Psychologist*, 1965, *20*, 321–333; Hebb, D. O. Drives and the c.n.s. (conceptual nervous system). *Psychological Review*, 1955, *62*, 243–254; Kagan, J. Motives and development. *Journal of Personality and Social Psychology*, 1972, *22*, 51–66.

Columbia University Press: Woodworth, R. S. *Dynamic psychology*. New York: Columbia University Press, 1918.

Crown Publishers: Applied Psychology from Ausubel, Nathan (Ed.), *A treasury of Jewish folklore*. New York, Crown, 1948, pp. 440–441.

Hart Publishing Co: Neill, A. S. *Summerhill: A radical Approach to child rearing*. New York: Hart, 1960.

Harvard University Press: Bruner, J. S. *On knowing: Essays for the left hand*. Cambridge, Mass.: Harvard University Press, 1962.

McGraw-Hill Book Co: Tolmon, E. C. Principles of purposive behavior. In S. Koch (Ed.), *Psychology: A study of a science*, Vol. 2. New York: McGraw-Hill, 1950, pp. 92–157.

Pitman Publishing Corp: Copyright holders for Holt, J. *How children fail*. New York: Pitman, 1964.

University of Nebraska Press: Hunt, J. McV. Intrinsic motivation and its role in psychological development. In D. Levine (Ed.), *Nebraska Symposium on Motivation*, 1965, *13*, 189–282.

John Wiley and Sons: Heider, F. *The psychology of interpersonal relations*. New York: Wiley, 1958; Young, P. T. *Motivation and emotion*. New York: Wiley, 1961.

Contents

I

THE NATURE OF INTRINSIC MOTIVATION

1

Some Comments on the "Why" of Behavior

The most frequently asked questions about human behavior are undoubtedly "why" questions. "Why is Ken playing tennis?" "Why did Judy fail her exam?" "Why does Sandy keep touching everything?" People seem particularly interested in knowing the causes of behavior. They want answers to "why" questions.

"Why" questions fall within the field of motivation, and psychologists working in the field have provided various kinds of answers to these questions. Psychoanalytic theorists, for example, have concentrated on unconscious processes, asserting that people's behavior is determined by a complex interaction between their unconscious drives and the environment. Cognitive psychologists believe that people *decide* what to do, so they have concentrated on thought processes. They consider the way people process information and make choices about what to do. Humanistic psychologists, like cognitive theorists, believe that humans are active organisms making continual choices about what to do. Unlike cognitive theorists, however, humanists have been less concerned with thought processes and more concerned with the "wholeness of a person," that is, the inner force and phenomenological experience of people. Still other psychologists have concentrated on the affective component of behavior, postulating that people develop patterns of behavior and hierarchies of responses as a result of the affect associated with their behaviors. Finally, behaviorists are concerned with the mechanistic associative links which develop between stimuli and responses through reinforcement of a response in the presence of a stimulus.

Very little attention will be given to the psychoanalytic view of motivation. Instead, we will consider the various approaches to motivation which are based in experimental research. We shall begin by briefly contrasting the passive or mechanistic approach of behaviorists with the more active or organismic approach of cognitive, affective, and humanistic psychologists.

Although we will be attempting to answer "why" questions by looking at experimental psychological research, it is both fascinating and important to note that much of the answer to "why" questions lies not in psychology, but rather in philosophy or metapsychology. Only the details and specifics of the answer lie in experimental psychology. Therefore, we will begin by looking at some metaissues as we briefly contrast the mechanistic approaches with the organismic approaches.

Each approach to psychology is based on certain assumptions which it makes about humans. That is, the investigator begins, either implicitly or explicitly, by answering questions such as "Do humans have free will?" or "Can they make choices about what to do?" or "Do thoughts cause behavior?" One cannot answer these questions scientifically. One cannot "prove" whether or not humans have free will. The questions are philosophical, and the set of answers to these and other such questions is the starting point for psychologists. These assumptions about humans are what we begin with when we try to answer "why" questions. In some sense, they represent the heart of our answers. To say, for example, that one can decide what to do is to go a long way toward answering "why" questions. This is an assumption—a starting point for research and theory. When based on this assumption, a psychologist's research and theory will look quite different from that of another psychologist who begins with the assumption that people's decisions do not cause their behaviors.

Once psychologists have made assumptions, they can get down to the business of scientific psychology. They can gather data and develop theories to answer the specifics of "why" questions. In so doing, they will be building a network of findings which make sense in light of their assumptions.

Intertwined with the assumptions are the methodologies which are used for studying behavior. Certain methods are appropriate for studying behavior when one set of assumptions is made, whereas they would not be if others were made.

For example, the advent of behaviorism was primarily a set of statements about what kinds of methods should be used to study behavior and what kinds of evidence or data are admissible to that study. So, the methodology in some sense determined the approach. However, the methodology actually derived out of some underlying assumptions about humans (whether or not the assumptions were explicit), and will be appropriate only within the framework of those assumptions. Similarly, other schools of psychology use methodologies which reflect their assumptions about the nature of humans and about the acceptability of certain kinds of data.

Lest I get caught in my own trap, let me make clear that my assertion about the centrality of assumptions about the nature of human beings is in itself an assumption. I am therefore presenting a particular point of view, based on my assumptions.

Mechanistic Approaches

Mechanistic theories of psychology view a person as a machine which is being pushed around by various forces. Behaviorism, for example, falls within this category, and although there are substantial differences among behaviorists, their approach focuses on links or associations which are built up between stimuli and responses and which "drive" the organism. Behavior is assumed to be initiated by stimuli and determined by the mechanistic bonds which have developed between those stimuli and various responses.

Early psychoanalytic theory was also mechanistic in its assumption that humans were driven by the interplay of id forces and environmental forces. However, since we will not be considering psychoanalytic theory, we will discuss the mechanistic approach in terms of behaviorism.

As is the case with most areas of psychology, the experimental study of motivation has been dominated by behaviorism. This study has been characterized by objective techniques to the exclusion of "subjective" data. Strong emphasis has been placed on the objective descriptions of observables such as stimuli, responses, and reinforcements.

Some behaviorists have virtually ignored internal processes, pointing out that such processes cannot be observed or measured and therefore should not be part of scientific psychology (e.g., Watson, 1913). In its most extreme form, behaviorism does not allow for constructs. Consequently, many behaviorists have failed even to recognize the construct "motivation," asserting that it is not necessary to formulate constructs in order to understand behavior. With the emphasis on stimulus–response bonds, learning was the primary content area, and "motivation" was subsumed by the study of learning.

There are great differences among the various behavioristic theories. Skinner (1953, 1971) is perhaps the best known behaviorist, yet his work is somewhat atypical of behavioristic and neobehavioristic thought in that he virtually ignores inner processes. Other behaviorists, such as Hull (1943), paid great attention to inner processes which mediated between the stimulus and response. Still, they were mechanistic in their approach. The important distinction, then, between the mechanistic and organismic approaches is not that one considers inner processes and the other does not, but that one attributes behavior to stimulus–response associations (the behaviorists' approach) and the other, to *choices* made by the person (the approach of cognitive and humanistic theorists).

Since Skinner's views are extreme on the question of inner processes, we shall look first at his approach. In large part we shall do this in order to contrast extreme positions. We will, however, also consider the work of Hull, which has been extremely influential in the behavioristic school and out of which has come the important work of N. E. Miller (1959), Mowrer (1960), Osgood (1953), and others.

Watson (1913) and Skinner (1953) in proposing theories and methods were also adhering to a set of assumptions about people. We look now at those assumptions:

Skinnerians assume that one's behavior at any given time is fully determined by his reinforcement history and the contingencies in his present environment. This implies, of course, that people do not have free will and that their behavior is not caused by their choices. While they may have thoughts and may make choices, these thoughts and choices do not cause their behavior; they are epiphenomenal to the causes of behavior. When one assumes, as Skinner does, that people have no free will, that behavior is controlled by reinforcement histories and contingencies in the present environment, and that cognition and affect have no causal relationship to behaviors, then the theories and methodologies of behaviorists like Skinner and Watson make eminently good sense. Their theories tend to be internally consistent, and they predict certain kinds of behaviors quite well. Further, the research tends to support their theories. But the research does not substantiate the assumptions which underlie the theories; it is simply interpretable in light of these assumptions. This distinction may seem a nit-picking one; however, it is very important. If one were to begin with assumptions different from those of, say, Skinner, one's theory would be different, and therefore, one would interpret the experimental findings differently.

Consider this example: A person happens to look down one day and finds a $10 bill on the street. After that, he spends more time looking down. A behavioristic interpretation of this behavior would be that the response of looking down was reinforced by the $10—with the result that the response recurs more frequently. The person does not decide to do it; it happens because of the strengthening of associations between stimuli (e.g., presence of the street, etc.) and the response (i.e., looking down). A cognitive interpretation, on the other hand, would be that the person values money, and he decides, because of finding the $10, that he may find money more often if he looks down more. So he *decides* to look down more, and the behavior follows the decision. The data can help to substantiate either theory, but they cannot prove that a person's decisions affect, or do not affect, his behavior. They do not really help give us the essence of the answer to why the person looks down more.

So, experimental data help us build theories and derive comprehensive frameworks to account for behavior. And, indeed, this is the goal of scientific psychology, to be able to account for behavior in a comprehensive and systematic way. The goal is not, as people often think, to discover ultimate truths about what makes humans work. Those ultimate truths are not discoverable, they are only assumable.

Skinner (1971) dealt in some detail with the assumptions which underlie a behavioristic approach, though he did not always make it clear when he was presenting assumptions (metapsychology) and when he was presenting empirical findings (psychology). For example, in Chapter 5 Skinner asserted that if someone fails to control another person, he does not give control to that other person, but rather to some other aspect of that person's environment. That statement is not psychology; it is metapsychology. It is a direct corollary of the assumption that man's behavior is totally determined by reinforcements and contingencies in his environment.

The most critical assumption made by Skinnerians, then is that all behaviors are determined by past reinforcements and the contingencies in the present environment. There is no need to consider "will," thoughts, motivation, etc., they say. If one knows a person's reinforcement history, and the contingencies in his present environment, one can, using behavioristic principles, predict his next response with certainty. Of course, since both the reinforcement history and the present contingencies are infinitely complex, it is never possible to know these fully. Therefore, the best that one can do is to make probability statements about the likelihood of certain responses. In practice, then, Skinnerian principles are stated in terms of probabilities, but in metatheory, they are stated as absolutes.

At any rate, according to this approach, one has no choice about what he does. A person's thoughts or cognitions are irrelevant to the causes of his behavior. One does not decide to do X in order to get Y, but rather he must do X (that's determined by reinforcements and contingencies), so his desire for Y is irrelevant to the causes of X.

Skinnerians, therefore, attempt to explain behavior in terms of the observable environment. Skinner (1971) claimed that to understand behavior we should look only at the behavior and the environment and ignore inner processes. This means that we cannot answer a question, such as, "Why is Harold playing his guitar?" with "Because he likes to play; it makes him feel good." Nor would, "Because his friend Allan asked him to play and he has always enjoyed playing guitar with Allan," be an acceptable answer. Rather, the only acceptable answer would be, "Because his guitar playing was reinforced in the past and there was an eliciting stimulus present when he began." It is very important to note that this statement is quite different than the following statement, which is frequently (and mistakenly) believed to say the same thing: "Because when he has played guitar in the past he's had a very enjoyable time, so he's decided to do it again." In both cases there is reference to the fact that the behavior was "reinforced" in the past; the important difference is the reference in the latter version to his having made a *choice* to play because it was enjoyable before and presumably would be again. This is not a behaviorist's account of the behavior; it is a cognitive interpretation. It implies that his thought processes play a causal role in his behavior. The mechanistic interpretation bypasses thoughts. It states that associations are built up between stimuli and responses as a result of reinforcements, so that current behavior is determined by these associations and is not voluntary behavior under the control of the individual.

Taking this approach, the psychologist is interested in such things as how schedules of reinforcement compare to each other in terms of the rate of responding, what extinction patterns follow what reinforcement schedules, how reinforcement of one response generalizes to others, and so on.

The Role of Thoughts and Feelings

Thoughts and feelings are not determiners of behavior, according to Skinnerians. They are either concomitant with behavior or consequences of it.

The notion that thoughts and feelings follow behavior, rather than cause it, is not a new one. Two of the first psychologists to be concerned with the notion were William James (1884, 1890) and Carl Lange (1885). Although these two worked separately, their work, which was published at about the same time, was sufficiently similar for the theory to become known generally as the James–Lange theory of emotion. In essence, the theory proposed that stimulus inputs to the central nervous system initiate changes in the viscera and muscles which are then perceived as emotions. So, for example, a stimulus such as a growling bear is presented to a person. The person becomes tense, his heartbeat increases markedly, adrenaline is secreted, and he runs away. He then experiences fear because of the changes and behaviors. He did not run away because he was afraid; he became afraid because he ran away.

Using a mechanistic approach, one could view thoughts or feelings as behaviors and could then analyze them in the same way that he would analyze eating or throwing a ball. In doing this, one gives up the fundamental policy of dealing only with observable behaviors, and in fact this is being done more frequently by advocates of the mechanistic approach.

Thoughts or feelings then can be viewed as behaviors which are initiated by some set of contingencies (e.g., the growling bear, the flight from the bear, etc.) and will be likely to recur if they are reinforced.

In sum, internal states such as emotions and cognitions are believed by Skinnerians to be concomitant with or to follow from behavior, rather than to precede and cause it. They are epiphenomenal, and focusing on them, according to Skinner (1971), interferes with rather than adds to the understanding of human behavior.

Skinner's position is based heavily on the *law of effect* (Thorndike, 1913), which says in essence that if an organism emits a response, and that response is followed by reinforcement, the probability of the response's recurring will be increased.

For persons concerned with motivation, the notion of reinforcement is the critical aspect of the law of effect. (Thorndike actually spoke of satisfiers and annoyers, though reinforcements and punishments have replaced those terms.) A response is strengthened when it is reinforced, so the answer to motivational questions (i.e., "why" questions) must come in terms of reinforcements. This then raises the important question, "What is a reinforcer?"

This question is sometimes answered empirically, "A reinforcement is anything which increases the probability of a response." However, as Postman (1947) pointed out, this answer runs into great difficulty because of its circularity. It leaves us with "A reinforcer increases the likelihood of the recurrence of a response which it follows" as the definition of the law of effect, and "A reinforcer is anything which increases the likelihood of the recurrence of a response which it follows" as the definition of a reinforcer. To make this law testable or useful for deriving hypotheses, it is necessary to define reinforcement independently of the recurrence of a response. To do this would take one "inside the person", leaving him with a kind of hedonistic position. Reinforcers become things which satisfy, and one is left with motivational notions. It is not my intent to evaluate the law of effect. Anyone interested is referred to Postman (1947, 1962), Meehl (1950), and Greenwald (1966). I have raised the point simply to consider the motivational aspects of the Skinnerian approach.

The way that reinforcement is typically operationalized is through deprivation. The reinforcements most often used are food and water, and these will, of course, be more or less effective as reinforcers, depending on the state of deprivation. However, degree of deprivation is not a variable which has been incorporated into the theories. Rather, an ammial is simply deprived sufficiently to make food or water a salient reinforcement. Nonetheless, degree of deprivation is really parallel to some aspects of the construct motivation, even though Skinnerians do not consider motivation and do not acknowledge motivational concepts such as thirst or hunger. They simply use water and food as reinforcers and ensure that they will be effective reinforcers by depriving the animal for a certain number of hours.

Hull was much more concerned with inner processes of the organism than was Skinner. He did not, however, focus on cognitions or thought processes, but rather on internal, associative links between chains of stimuli and responses. He concentrated on how organisms develop those links (or habits) and how they are activated. It is the latter question which is of concern to us, since that is a motivational question, whereas the former one is a question of learning.

Organisms learn habits (i.e., they acquire associative links between stimuli and responses) when responses to given stimuli are reinforced. Reinforcement involves the reduction in a drive stimulus, that is, it involves returning one of the organism's tissue needs to equilibrium. Drives, therefore, are the motivational aspect of physiological needs. Drives activate habits, and the reduction of drive stimuli strengthens habits.

We see then that drives are the motivational component of Hull's system. Drives develop when needs such as hunger or thirst have not been satisfied, and they activate responses which are linked to the drive stimulus.

In addition to drive stimuli there are two other kinds of stimuli in Hull's system. External stimuli which are in the organism's environment and proprioceptive stimuli which are in the organism's musculature can also be linked to responses.

Learning consists of the development of links among any of the three kinds of stimuli and responses. These typically occur in the form of chains of associations. Since the organism's response can become a stimulus, it can learn to emit a long sequence of responses (e.g., running a complicated maze) from a small number of external stimuli. This process of redintegration provides the basis of what Hull (1930) referred to as foreknowledge. Through these stimulus–response chains, an organism can react to a stimulus not yet presented because of its position in a learned chain.

Although responses may be elicited by any one of the three kinds of stimuli, they will only be elicited in the presence of a drive. However, Hull also explained that stimuli other than tissue deficits can become "secondary drives" when they are paired with primary drives.

Hull's theory which has been elaborated by many of his colleagues and students, was the first elaborate conception of motivation and has had the greatest impact on the field of motivation. At the heart of this work are the concepts of drive and drive reduction. Drives activate stimulus–response associations, and drive reduction strengthens stimulus–response associations.

In fact, drive reduction is so important in the theories of Hull and his followers, such as Miller and Dollard (1941), that the theories are often referred to as drive-reduction theories. We have not even begun to scratch the surface of the Hullian position here, nor will we do so in this book. Anyone interested in that work is referred to Hull (1943), N. E. Miller (1959), or Brown (1961).

Our purpose here was to look very briefly at the way motivation is treated by mechanistic theorists. We saw that behaviorists place heavy emphasis on the notion of reinforcement. Some have dealt with the meaning of this quite explicitly (e.g., Hull), and in so doing have postulated about internal states such as drives. (See Berlyne, 1967, for a discussion of this.) Others such as Skinner have more or less ignored the concept of motivation, looking instead only at observables such as schedules of reinforcements, and so on. The commonality among mechanistic behaviorists is their emphasis on stimulus–response bonds which are developed when a response is reinforced in the presence of a stimulus. Organisms behave because of these bonds rather than because of thoughts or feelings about what they want to do or what rewards they want to obtain.

Organismic Approaches

The organismic approaches differ from mechanistic ones in that they consider humans to be active organisms. Whereas the mechanistic approaches assume that humans are passive and under the control of the environment, organismic approaches assert that they act on their environment. In their continual interaction with the environment, humans will be acting to bring about changes in the environment, and they will also be adapting to the environment. (See, for example, the work of Piaget, 1951, 1952.) The organismic approaches differ from those of behaviorism by placing primary importance on cognitive and/or affective processes as determiners of behavior. Humans act on their environment in a lawful and ordered way, as determined by their thoughts and feelings.

Affective Arousal Theories

Consider first the approach which focuses primarily on affect, namely, the affective arousal theories. For an affective arousal theorist (e.g., McClelland, Atkinson, Clark, & Lowell, 1953), affect is the basis of motivation; it precedes behavior and energizes and directs the behavior.

McClelland (1965) has defined motives as "affectively toned associative networks arranged in a hierarchy of strength or importance with a given individual" (p. 322). In other words, behavior is motivated when some cue redintegrates an affective stiuation. The person experiences affect when a cue is presented, and he then engages in the behavior in anticipation of a recurrence of an affective state previously experienced.

Young (1961) also stressed the importance of affect in motivation by stating, "From every point of view the affective processes must be considered motivational in nature" (p. 166). Young proposed an experimental hedonism which suggests that all stimulation has an affective component and that organisms behave so as to increase positively affective arousal and decrease negatively affective arousal. This affective arousal, if positive, orients an organism toward a stimulus object, or, if negative, away from it. It is therefore a motive. Motives can be acquired through the association of a stimulus with an affective arousal. McClelland (1965) took a similar position and went further to suggest that all motives are learned. He stated, "Not even biological discomforts (as from hunger) or pleasures (as from sexual stimulation) are 'urges' or 'drives' until they are linked to cues that can signify their presence or absence" (p. 322).

The strength of a motive depends, according to Young, on the intensity, duration, frequency, and recency of previous affective arousals. For McClelland, the strength is determined by the position of the affective cluster in the person's hierarchy of clusters. McClelland's position would agree with Young's notion that the strength of a motive depends on the magnitude of the arousal.

To return to the example question, "Why is Harold playing his guitar with Allan?" the affective arousal answer would be, "He is playing because the cue of Allan's asking redintegrated an affective experience and led him to anticipate that positive affect would be associated with the guitar playing."

The affective arousal approach differs from the behavioristic approaches in that it explains the causes of behavior in terms of affect, though, as is true of behaviorism, affective arousal theories pay little attention to the role of cognitions in the cause of behavior. Further, affective arousal theories tend to be mechanistic in that they assert that behavior is not voluntary (i.e., that a person does not make choices about what to do), but rather that behaviors are determined by affectively toned associations. So although I have categorized these theories as organismic because of the importance they place on affect, they are more mechanistic than the other organismic approaches.

Cognitive Theories

A cognitive approach to motivation places primary emphasis on a person's thought processes. It assumes that people decide what to do on the basis of their evaluations of the likely outcomes of their behavioral alternatives. Then they behave in accordance with their decisions. This means of course that cognitive processing is an important determinant of behavior. This assumption stands in clear contradiction to the assumption of the mechanistic approaches which says that thoughts are not causal factors in behavior.

Cognitive theorists are primarily concerned with accounting for the choices that a person makes about what to do, since they consider most behavior to be under the person's voluntary control (see, for example, Vroom, 1964). Even William James (1890), who is generally considered to be a forerunner of behaviorism, claimed that once a behavior has occurred randomly or unintentionally it will be stored in memory, and a reenactment of that behavior can be set as a goal and voluntarily achieved. A cognitive viewpoint would extend this to assert that behavior can initially be engaged in voluntarily as a result of the processing of information which one has in his memory and in his cognitive representation of the environment.

Hunt, a one-time drive-reduction theorist stated, "In so far as freedom and rationality means actions and choices based on the organism's informational interaction with the environment, the newer evidence lends support to the claim that man is at least partially free to make decisions that are rational in the sense that they are based on the information available to him and on his ability to process it" (Hunt, 1965, p. 197).

A cognitive approach to motivation proposes that people make choices about what to do on the basis of their goals (or desired end states) and their assessment of whether various behavioral alternatives will lead them to these end states. This approach views humans as striving to satisfy their needs by setting goals and choosing behavior that they believe will allow them to achieve these goals.

If we look again at the guitar player (Harold) and ask why he is playing, we get still another answer. This time we must go back to the point at which he made the decision. Late this afternoon when he was in his office, feeling very hassled, his friend Allan called and asked if he'd like to get together for some guitar. At that time a number of alternatives may have been open to him for the evening: for example, to go back to the office to work on a case that needed to be completed shortly, to stay home and rest, to play the guitar with Allan, etc. At that point, based on his evaluation of the end state of each alternative, he thought that the alternative of playing the guitar was more desirable than the others. He may, for example, place positive value on the fraternal feelings of being with Allan, on the opportunity to practice the guitar, on the relaxation which he always experiences when he plays the guitar, and so forth. The combined value of the various aspects of this outcome is greater than the value of the outcome of the other alternative behaviors (e.g., returning to the office). Therefore, he chose to play the guitar.

From this example one can see that cognitive theorists are interested in how a person uses information from his environment and his memory to make decisions about what to do.

Although cognitive theory differs sharply from behaviorism in the assumption it makes about whether thoughts play a causal role in the determination of behavior, the two approaches agree that behavior is determined. Cognitive theorists would also say that if they had enough information about a person they could predict his behavior with certainty. It is determined that a person will select the behavioral alternative which he believes will have the most desirable outcome. Further, it is possible to predict how much a person will value certain outcomes, basing such predictions on his needs, past experiences, and other available information. So, for a cognitive psychologist, people choose, but their choices are determined.

A cognitive approach to motivation will be dealt with in substantial detail in Chapter 4, so it will not be discussed further now.

Humanistic Theories

Within the last two decades a new school of psychology—humanistic psychology—has been emerging. It is sometimes referred to as *third-force psychology* (the first two forces being psychoanalytic psychology and behaviorism). Its assumptions about people, its methods of investigation, and the questions that it asks are quite different from the other schools of psychology (see Buhler & Allen, 1972; Maslow, 1968). Humanistic psychology has its roots in existential philosophy (cf. Sartre, 1957), asserting first that man has free will. As I have said, this is only an assumption and is untestable, but it stands clearly in contradiction to all other schools of psychology. In other words, man is a free agent, who "defines himself" through making choices. These choices are not determined, as cognitive psychologists believe, so they are not fully predictable.

Humanistic theorists place great emphasis on personal experience (cf. Laing, 1967) claiming that the real meaning of behavior lies in the person's phenomenology. Laing proposed that a fully functioning person is one who is "in touch" with his own experience, but people have not been encouraged to do that. Rather, societies and parents make so many demands and do so much controlling, Laing contended, that people slowly lose touch with much of their own experience.

The primacy of experience follows from the assumption of free will. If one is able to make free choices, then these choices

will be based on his perceptions of himself and his environment.

Humanistic psychology is generally nonexperimental in the
traditional sense. Scientific data are seldom collected, and those
that are tend not to be rigorous. However, this makes sense in light
of humanistic psychology's assumptions about people (cf. Argyris,
1968). Since personal experience is primary, humanistic
psychologists tend not to be interested in careful measurement of
objective stimuli nor in assessment of internal states, which measurement they claim is not possible by using the techniques currently available. Humanistic psychology is to a large extent icono-
clastic, pointing out faults with theories and techniques of other
approaches. Its own theories tend at this point to be quite vague
and therefore are difficult to put into operation or test scientifically.
It seems to me that it is extremely important that this be done.
Humanism seems to have a great deal to add to psychology, yet
without more rigorous theory building and empirical validation, its
ideas will be ignored by the psychological community. There are a
few people who have begun to consider humanistic concepts and
who are using experimental methodology (e.g., Jourard, 1971; de
Charms, 1968), and I believe this is the beginning of an important
movement.

Objective vs. Subjective Reality

Not only do behaviorists claim that subjective states such as
feelings have no place in the analysis of behavior (e.g., Bindra,
1959), but they also claim that a subjective interpretation of a
stimulus has no place in the analysis of behavior (e.g., Skinner,
1953). The dominant influence of behaviorism has kept the
emphasis on the objective, external stimulus. This external
stimulus can generally be measured and recorded, and psychologists focus on this as the initiator of a response. This focus on
external, objective stimuli follows directly from the theories and
metatheories of behaviorism. Since a person's thoughts or perceptions do not cause behavior, one need not consider these in
understanding behavior.

For organismic theorists, however, the subjective experience is
more important. When a person perceives a stimulus, it is his

perception of the stimulus which is the information available to him for his use. It is important then according to organismic theorists, to consider the question of why a person's perception of a stimulus differs from the objective description of that stimulus (cf., Merleau-Ponty, 1963). It is also important to recognize that the stimulus as perceived by the person is the important stimulus to use in analyzing behavior, since the stimulus as perceived by the person is what he processes in his decision making. Imagine that a person is offered $50 for half a day of consulting with the Office of Education. If he mistakenly hears the offer as $15 per half day, he may very well respond with a "no," whereas he would have responded to an offer of $50 with a "yes." The stimulus was misperceived, and the resulting decision was different than it would otherwise have been. To develop an hypothesis that would account for the data of a person's responding to a stimulus of $50 without taking into account that he was in fact responding to $15 is misleading at best. The example is extreme, but the moral is clear. People perceive things differently, and it is the stimulus as it exists in their phenomenology to which they respond.

There is a plethora of studies that show that people perceive things differently. Psychophysics deals with the problem of how perceptions are influenced by various factors. More recently, person perception, an area of social psychology, deals with how people's perceptions differ when they are viewing persons rather than objects. One study by Dornbush, Hastorf, Richardson, Muzzy, and Vreeland (1965) demonstrated that when one person described two other persons there was greater overlap in descriptions than when two persons described one another. They interpreted this as emphasizing the importance of the perceiver's cognitive structure in perception.

Personal Knowledge

The stimulus as perceived by the person is one aspect of what is called personal knowledge (Polanyi, 1958). Each person has knowledge which is available only to himself and is derived from his own perceptions, emotions, behaviors, etc. This knowledge provides important information for a person to take into account in making decisions. For someone who acknowledges that internal states such as cognitions or affect have an effect on behavior, personal knowledge becomes very important (cf. de Charms, 1968). Yet, the use of personal knowledge in psychological theory raises many problems. An observer-scientist who wishes to use this information must have access to it. This can be done in at least three ways, though all of the ways are subject to error and bias: Bridgeman (1959) suggested the use of projection as a means of operationalyzing personal knowledge. Numerous other psychologists (e.g., Georgi, 1970; Malcolm, 1964) have suggested personal reports. Finally, one can hypothesize about personal knowledge and construct experiments very carefully in order to try to verify the hypotheses.

All of these methods are imprecise and subject to error. Yet to ignore this important information because it is difficult to collect is inappropriate, if not irresponsible.

About This Book

This is a book about human motivation. It presents a cognitive perspective and is concerned with accounting for the "whys" of voluntary behavior. It is assumed that most behaviors are voluntary, that people choose which behaviors to engage in, and that these choices are made because people believe that the chosen behaviors will lead them to desired end states.

Clearly, then, people's perceptions and cognitions will be foremost in our discussion of motivation. Since people make choices about what to do, their thoughts and perceptions are important causal factors in their behavior. It is being asserted that if a person perceives that he is engaging in a given behavior in order to make money, he will respond in accordance with his perceptions by engaging in that behavior only for money. Of course many behaviors are motivated by many factors. Therefore, a person who engages in a behavior in order to make money often has other motives for doing it, also. Hence, he would probably do the same thing (though to a lesser extent) without receiving money. At any rate, the person has available to himself an understanding of why he is doing something. This information may not necessarily be in his conscious thoughts, though it will still be operative, and it is accessible to his conscious thoughts.

A person's perceptions and thoughts are part of his personal knowledge. This information is available only to him and is information that he uses in making choices about his behavior. This knowledge can be influenced by external factors, and Chapters 5, 6, and 9 of this book will deal with the effects of external factors on internal states.

Since this book is about human motivation, it will concentrate primarily on findings from experimental studies with humans. At times it may be necessary to report research with animals to illustrate a point, though we can never be sure whether or not research with nonhumans is directly relevant to the study of humans. Since we will view motivation from a cognitive perspective, great emphasis will be placed on thought processes. Therefore, since animals do not have the same cognitive abilities as man, we will consider animal behavior to be only suggestive of what may be operative in humans. It may well be that the essence of human motivation is quite different from that of nonhumans. If so, the most important information about human motivation cannot be gained through studies with animals.

Finally, this book is primarily about a special category of human motivation—*intrinsic motivation*. Therefore, it does not attempt to survey the area of human motivation, but rather to survey the sub-area of intrinsic motivation. We begin in Chapter 2 by considering the available evidence on the existence of intrinsic motivation, and the various conceptualizations of intrinsic motivation.

2

Conceptualizations of Intrinsic Motivation

If one were to spend a short while observing a child, he would undoubtedly be delighted by the child's inquisitiveness. Children keep picking things up, smelling them, tasting them, feeling them, and asking, "What's this?" They seem to have an insatiable curiosity. Aristotle (980) recognized this when he stated, "All men by nature desire to know." He was, in essence, postulating an intrinsic motivation to learn.

Intrinsically motivated activities are ones for which there is no apparent reward except the activity itself. People seem to engage in the activities for their own sake and not because they lead to an extrinsic reward. The activities are ends in themselves rather than means to an end. This definition, which is the commonly accepted definition of intrinsic motivation, serves quite adequately as an operational definition of intrinsic motivation. One can observe that there is no apparent reward and that the person is deriving enjoyment from the activity.

However, the definition is not a very satisfactory one in a broader sense, since it does not help one to understand the psychological basis of intrinsic motivation. Berlyne (1971a), for example, pointed out that an activity cannot in any meaningful sense reinforce itself, but rather, what it can do is bring about certain internal consequences which the organism experiences as rewarding.

23

Therefore, a meaningful definition of intrinsic motivation will need to address itself to those internal consequences. This chapter does that; it deals with the psychological bases of intrinsic motivation by reviewing and contrasting various conceptualizations of intrinsic motivation. We will see that a precise definition of intrinsic motivation will depend on which conceptualization one chooses. Nonetheless, a common element seems to be that intrinsically motivated activities are related to internally rewarding consequences which are located in the central nervous system and have no appreciable biological effect on non-nervous-system tissues. On the other hand, activities which are motivated by extrinsic needs, such as hunger, do have primary effects on non-nervous-system tissues.

Many activities are intrinsically motivated. People spend large amounts of time solving puzzles, painting pictures, and engaging in other play activities for which there is no external reward. They are also intrinsically motivated to do challenging work which requires resourcefulness and creativity. The rewards for these activities are mediated within the individual. He engages in the activities not because they lead him to an external reward (like money, praise, food, etc.) but rather because they bring about certain kinds of internal states which he finds rewarding.

Only recently have psychologists directed much attention to the concept of intrinsic motivation. Koch (1956, 1961) was one of the first to make strong assertions that motivational theory needs to be revamped to give considerable importance to the notion of intrinsic motivation. He suggested that when a person engages in an intrinsically motivated activity he becomes fully absorbed in the activity and committed to it. Further, he can tolerate substantial fatigue and suppress primary drives such as hunger. According to Koch (1956) intrinsically motivated behavior is highly organized, energized, and motivated behavior; thus, it should be recognized by psychologists and incorporated into their theories.

Koch's paper (1956) was an important one in that it called attention to the need for giving considerable thought to the notion of intrinsic motivation, yet it did not deal with the possible psychological or physiological processes which are involved in intrinsic motivation.

Early History

Woodworth (1918, 1958) developed a behavior–primacy theory with which he accounted for intrinsically motivated behavior. He (1918) reported that behavior can provide its own drive in the following manner: There are general motives, such as curiosity, self-assertion, and constructiveness, which provide the energy for specific mechanisms or abilities to operate to satisfy themselves. The specific mechanisms derive from innate capacities—what Woodworth called "native equipment"—though, of course, they can be modified by learning. A person who dances particularly well may be motivated by general motives such as self-assertion and constructiveness, but the direction in which energy from these motives is directed would be due to good mechanisms for dancing.

Humans, Woodworth proposed, are active organisms. He stated "It may at least be said to be part of the native equipment to be active in a motor way, as well, indeed, as in the way of exploration." (Woodworth, 1918, p. 50). This tendency toward activity is clearly manifest when an activity is running by its own drive. Woodworth proposed that an activity can be initiated by an extrinsic motive but that "only when it is running by its own drive . . . can (it) run freely and effectively . . . " (Woodworth, 1918, p. 70).

This notion, that an activity, regardless of its initiating motive, can become intrinsically interesting, was given the name "functional autonomy" by Allport (1937).

Woodworth's early work placed great emphasis on instincts and derived in part from the writing of McDougall (1908). This is a much different framework from that taken by psychologists who have written about intrinsic motivation more recently. Further, Woodworth did not discuss the processes which are involved in intrinsic motivation, and, as we have said, it is not meaningful psychologically to say that an activity is run by its own drive.

Nonetheless, he did postulate intrinsic motivation and set the stage for later work in the area. His notion that an activity provides its own drive was an important initial contribution. Unfortunately, however, the strong emphasis on behaviorism which was beginning around the time of Woodworth's writing kept other psychologists from pursuing this important line of inquiry.

Drive-Theory Accounts

Drive Naming

In the thirty year period following Woodworth's early writing there was virtually no attention paid to the concept of intrinsic motivation *per se*. However, there were some animal studies which documented that exploration is a reinforcing activity. Dashiell (1925) and Nissen (1930) reported that rats will cross an electrified grid and endure shock in order to be able to explore novel stimuli in a maze. This showed not only that exploration is an intrinsically rewarding activity, but that the opportunity to explore also reinforces other responses.

In the late 1940s and early 1950s a great deal of work was reported which further documented that manipulation and exploration are important examples of intrinsically motivated behavior.

Berlyne (1950, 1955) demonstrated that rats are quick to explore novel spaces and objects and that they persist at this exploration so long as novel stimulation is available. Welker (1956a, 1956b) found similar results for chimpanzees. When the experimenter placed a novel object in the chimpanzees' presence, they readily explored it and once they had explored it and manipulated it, they appeared to lose interest. These experiments showed quite clearly that animals are motivated to explore and manipulate novel stimuli.

Montgomery (1952, 1953, 1954, 1955; Montgomery and Segall, 1955) also demonstrated that rats spontaneously explore novel places and that the opportunity to explore these places reinforces responses which afford that opportunity. He suggested that novel stimuli elicit not only an exploratory drive, but also a fear drive which may block exploratory behavior if that drive is of sufficient magnitude. Glanzer (1953, 1958) took a similar position.

Butler (1953, 1954, 1957, 1958; Butler and Harlow, 1957) has reported that visual exploration of novel stimuli is rewarding for monkeys and that the probability of such a response increases as the interval between successive opportunities to explore increases. These findings are quite compatible with those of Montgomery. Exploration was seen as an intrinsically rewarding activity which could be used to strengthen other responses. When an animal had been deprived of the opportunity to explore, exploration became even more rewarding. Butler accounted for his findings by positing a motive toward visual exploration of the environment while Montgomery suggested an "exploratory drive."

Myers and Miller (1954) and Zimbardo and Miller (1958) reported results supporting those of Montgomery and Butler, although these investigators suggested that animals explore novel stimuli in order to relieve a "boredom drive" which results from unchanging stimuli. This drive explanation focused on the boredom which results from insufficient stimulation (i.e., the lack of a stimulus), whereas Montgomery's drive explanation focused on the elicitation of an exploratory drive by a novel stimulus (i.e., the presence of a stimulus).

Isaac (1962) also suggested a boredom-drive explanation for curiosity and exploratory behaviors. The absence of stimulation or presence of unchanging stimuli increases boredom so that novel stimuli perceived through any sense modality become more reinforcing. Isaac (1962) reported an experiment which suggests that the absence of stimulation produces greater boredom than the presence of an unchanging stimulus to one of the sensory modalities. Therefore, monkeys who had been deprived of sound and light engaged in more behavior to turn on a light than those who had been deprived of light but were given an unchanging sound.

The importance of novel stimulation has also been documented in humans by the stimulus-deprivation studies (Bexton, Heron, & Scott, 1954; Heron, Doane, & Scott, 1956). These studies found that humans were generally unwilling to tolerate more than three or four days of unchanging stimuli even though they received substantial monetary payments for doing so.

Jones (1961) and Jones, Wilkinson, and Braden (1961) demonstrated a similar finding. Information deprivation was shown to have strong motivating properties.

The drive-naming approach to explaining intrinsically motivated behavior has also been used by Harlow in the realm of
manipulative behavior. Harlow and his associates (1950, 1953a,
1953b; Harlow, Harlow, & Meyer, 1950; Gately, 1950; Davis,
Settlage, & Harlow, 1950) have shown repeatedly that manipulating a complex mechanical puzzle made up of hasps, hooks, and
hinges is intrinsically rewarding and can be used to strengthen
various other responses. Harlow has posited a "manipulation
drive" to account for these findings, which is very similar to
Montgomery's notion of an exploratory drive.

Premack (1959, 1962, 1963) has also demonstrated the reinforcing potential of manipulatory responses with children and
monkeys. For example, in one experiment (Premack, 1962) the
opportunity to run in an activity wheel was used to strengthen
other responses in monkeys.

In sum, a plethora of data supports the notion that curiosity,
manipulation, and exploration are intrinsically motivated
behaviors. Organisms seem to need a certain amount of novel
stimulation to function effectively, and the opportunity for novel
stimulation (e.g., manipulating an object or exploring a new area)
has frequently been used to reinforce other responses. The most
common approach used to explain these phenomena during the
1950s was that of drive naming. Organisms were believed to have
an exploratory drive (Montgomery, 1954), a drive to avoid boredom (Myers & Miller, 1954), a manipulation drive (Harlow,
1953a), a sensory drive (Isaac, 1962), a drive for visual exploration
(Butler, 1953), or an instinct to master (Hendrick, 1942, 1943).

The drive-naming approach unfortunately has many short-
comings and has been criticized by many writers. For example,
Hunt (1965, 1971a) suggested that drive-naming was essentially a
return to the instinct naming of McDougall (1908), and that such
an approach may hinder the chances of a real understanding of
these phenomena.

White (1959) made a more detailed criticism of the drive-
naming approach. He began by saying that if exploration is to be
considered a drive, it must have the same functional properties as
the established drives such as hunger, thirst, and sex. According to
this traditional view: Drives involve a deficit or need in body tissues
outside the nervous system which (1) energizes behavior that

results in a consummatory response which reduces the need or deficit and (2) produces learning.

White then demonstrated that the exploratory "drive" does not fit this definition. It does not seem to be correlated with any non-nervous-system deficit, so no tissue need can provide the stimulus for behavior. White explained that even if one broadens the term *drive* to include a general drive in the reticular activating system which is responsive to sensory stimulation, it does not satisfy the condition of being a strong and persistent stimulus which initiates and sustains activities.

Furthermore, White noted that there is no consummatory response involved with exploration as there is with hunger and other primary drives. It is true, of course, that the exploration of a particular area can become satiated (Berlyne, 1950; Welker, 1956); however, this is not the same as a consummatory response.

Finally, the reinforcement provided by exploratory behavior does not seem to involve any need reduction. White used the work of Montgomery (1954) to show that animals often make choices which increase rather than decrease the exploratory drive. If the exploratory drive is instigated by a novel stimulus, as Montgomery and others suggest, then one would expect that animals should avoid novel stimuli, since the novel stimuli increase the drive instead of reducing it. Yet, just the opposite is true: animals seek out stimuli which would, by the drive account, increase the exploratory drive. Therefore, using a drive explanation, one must infer that animals are drive-inducers as well as drive-reducers. However, this inference would be unacceptable to most drive theories which assert that animals seek only to reduce drives.

Consider now the possibility that exploration is instigated by the boredom drive as suggested by Myers and Miller (1954) or Isaac (1962). If boredom causes exploration, then the reinforcement for exploratory behavior is the thing which returns the animal to a state of boredom. With eating, the end state is a full stomach and the reduction of hunger, whereas with exploration, the end state would be a return to inactivity and boredom. White stated, "It is distinctly implausible to connect reinforcement with the waning of an agreeable interest in the environment or with a general progress from zestful alertness to boredom," (1959, p. 302).

In sum, if one were to consider exploration, manipulation, etc. a primary drive, one would have to redefine drive in such a way as not to require tissue needs or deficits which (1) provide a persistent stimulus to initiate consummatory behavior, and (2) reinforce the behavior through the reduction of the drive.

It is clear, then, from the above analysis that drive naming as an approach to understanding intrinsic motivation is inadequate. There have been, however, attempts by other behaviorists to account for exploration, manipulation, and curiosity within a drive–theory framework. There are two possible approaches which White (1959) considered for doing this—secondary reinforcement and reduction of anxiety.

Secondary Reinforcement

A secondary reinforcement position (cf. Keller, 1971) would hold that, through the pairing of exploratory and manipulatory behaviors with primary drive reduction, those behaviors acquire reinforcing properties. For example, if an infant engaged in exploration at the same time he was being nursed, the exploration by itself would eventually become a reinforcer. To retain its reinforcing value, it is necessary that the behavior occur periodically in the presence of primary drive reduction. Without this occasional re-pairing, the secondary reinforcer will lose its ability to reinforce.

In the Butler (1953) experiment mentioned above monkeys learned discriminations by being reinforced with the opportunity to engage in visual exploration. Butler reported that these responses showed remarkable resistance to extinction—a fact which is difficult to reconcile with a secondary reinforcement position. White explained that since reinforcement of primary drives did not occur in the experimental situation, secondary reinforcement should not prevent extinction.

Both White (1959) and Berlyne (1966) argued that the acceptance of a secondary reinforcement explanation would require the assumption that exploration had often been paired with the reduction of primary needs such as hunger. This assumption is quite implausible since avid exploration occurs in neonates very shortly after birth, and it seems unreasonable to assume that this could have developed so quickly and strongly through the process of secondary reinforcement.

Anxiety Reduction

Finally, White explored the use of anxiety reduction as an explanation of exploration. To accept this explanation, one would have to accept that novel stimuli arouse anxiety and that the exploration of these reduces it. But, surely, if novelty induces anxiety, avoidance would be a more probable anxiety reducer than would exploration. Yet animals often seem eager to confront and explore the stimuli, which would, according to this approach, be anxiety producing.

In sum, White (1959) and Berlyne (1966) have argued quite convincingly that a drive explanation of exploratory and manipulative behaviors is suspect. I agree with their analysis. Drive naming is inadequate as an explanation of intrinsic motivation and also interferes with a fuller understanding of it. Furthermore, the evidence is indisputable that animals do not always behave in such a way as to reduce stimulation (i.e., drives). Frequently, in fact, they seek stimulation.

Fowler (1965, 1967), however, asserted that it is possible to account for intrinsically motivated behavior with drive theory, if drive theory is modified so as to include the concept of optimal arousal. As we will see in the next section of this chapter, organisms do seem to seek some level of optimal arousal. However, even if drive theory were modified to allow for the notion of optimal arousal, this alone would not be enough to account for intrinsically motivated behaviors with traditional drive theory, since there is no deficit in body tissues, nor persisting stimulus, nor consummatory response.

Optimal Stimulation

Much of the work related to intrinsic motivation has postulated that its basis is related to the organism's need for a moderate level of stimulation in order to function effectively. Some theorists have been concerned with the psychological level, positing a need for an optimum of psychological incongruity, whereas others have been concerned with the physiological level, positing a need for an optimum of physiological arousal in the central nervous system. We now consider theories and research which take this general approach.

Optimal Incongruity

The approach to conceptualizing intrinsic motivation which has received the most attention in the last two decades has discrepancy or incongruity as its central notion. Hunt (1963, 1965, 1971a, 1971b) has been the strongest spokesman for this point of view. Much of the work related to incongruity was not presented by the original authors within a framework of intrinsic motivation. However, Hunt has brought this work together within that framework.

The central issue for most of the work in this area is the extent to which people will approach or avoid incongruous (or dissonant or discrepant) inputs (or cognitions).

Some writers maintain that people are motivated to reduce all incongruity or dissonance between stimuli. Festinger's cognitive-dissonance theory (1957) asserted that two dissonant cognitions produce an aversive state which motivates people to behave in such a way as to reduce the dissonance and avoid situations which would produce further dissonance.

Festinger (1957) did not relate his theory to an "incongruity" interpretation of intrinsic motivation. However, doing so would lead to the following: Intrinsically motivated behaviors are behaviors which are motivated by the need to reduce dissonant cognitions. Festinger postulated that all dissonant cognitions produce discomfort and energize behavior to reduce the dissonance.

Hebb (1945, 1946a, 1946b; Hebb and Riesen, 1943) also seemed to imply that all incongruity is aversive. He (1946b) presented evidence that stimuli which were discrepant from the expectations of chimpanzees produced fear and avoidance behaviors. Fears caused by novel stimuli were spontaneous and did not result from pairing with other primary fear inducers. Rather, they appeared to result from the interruption of cerebral organization by incongruous stimuli. This, he asserted, can also account for fear induced by under-stimulation situations, such as children in dark rooms. Children typically develop cerebral organization from afferent inputs of visual stimulation during waking hours. Dark rooms are incongruous with the cerebral organization and therefore fear-arousing.

From Hebb's (1946b) paper one might infer that incongruity between input and cerebral organization is always aversive. This view would support Festinger's position. However, in later work Hebb (1949; Hebb and Thompson, 1954) suggested that in certain situations incongruity is pleasurable. Further, the proposition that all incongruity or dissonance is aversive is difficult to reconcile with the plethora of studies mentioned above which shows quite clearly that novel stimulation (i.e., incongruity) is rewarding and produces approach behaviors. This implies, of course, that Festinger's postulation that dissonance is always aversive is an overstatement. Although people sometimes behave so as to reduce and avoid dissonance or incongruity, it is clear that they also behave so as to induce and approach dissonance or incongruity.

In an attempt to account for the seemingly discrepant findings that people sometimes behave to reduce incongruity and other times behave to induce incongruity, Hunt (1965) presented a theory which centered around the notion of an optimal level of psychological incongruity. People, he asserted, are motivated to maintain an optimal level of incongruity. This notion, or a similar one, has also appeared in the work of McClelland, Atkinson, Clark, and Lowell (1953), Hebb (1955), Leuba (1955), Dember and Earl (1957), Fiske and Maddi (1961), and Berlyne (1967, 1969).

McClelland *et al.* (1953) were concerned with an optimal incongruity between some aspect of a perception and the adaptation level (cf. Helson, 1964) for that particular aspect. A person at any given time has developed an adaptation level, so that amount of the stimulus will cause a neutral response. Small deviations from that amount—either above or below—are desired and cause an affectively positive response. Large discrepancies, however, cause negative affect. Hence, people approach slightly discrepant situations but avoid highly discrepant ones. Haber (1958) presented evidence in support of this position from a study using human subjects who immersed their hands in water of varying temperatures above and below their adaptation level. Slightly discrepant temperatures were chosen, and highly discrepant ones were avoided.

The McClelland *et al.* theory of motivation is an affective-arousal theory. A discrepancy between perception and adaptation level, they claimed, causes a primary emotional response. Cues which have been paired with that affective state become capable of redintegrating that state, and the redintegration of an affective state is a motive.

McClelland *et al.* have not distinguished between intrinsic and extrinsic motivation. For them, *all* motives are learned through the pairing of cues with primary affective responses, and all behavior is motivated by the redintegration of these affective states. Cues which were associated with situations that involved mild incongruity would redintegrate positive affect and therefore motivate approach behavior. Cues which were associated with large discrepancies would redintegrate negative affect and would motivate avoidance behavior. One can see, then, that this theory has optimal incongruity or discrepancy as a central notion. However, the optimal discrepancy does not have to be present at the time that an activity is being intrinsically motivated. Rather, a cue need only redintegrate the affective state which was initially aroused by the discrepancy.

Using the conceptualization of McClelland *et al.*, one would say that a person is intrinsically motivated when some cue redintegrates an affective state, initially produced by the discrepancy between an input and an adaptation level, which leads the person to engage in a behavior for which there is not an extrinsic reward. Most of the work which has developed from McClelland's theory deals with achievement motivation (McClelland, 1961; Atkinson & Feather, 1966), which is within the category of intrinsic motivation (Horner, 1971). This will be discussed further in Chapters 3 and 4.

Dember and Earl (1957) have posited that the important incongruity or discrepancy in intrinsically-motivated behaviors is between a person's expectations and the properties of the stimulus. A person approaches a stimulus with certain expectations about some dimension of the stimulus, such as an expectation about water temperature, loudness of a noise, or brightness of a light. The stimulus has some value on that dimension, and the discrepancy between the expected level of the stimulus dimension and the actual level is of central importance to the theory.

In Dember and Earl's theory, "attention" is used to refer to all behavior which brings the organism into contact with the environment. There is also reference to the notion of "complexity", which is the discrepancy between a person's expectation about some stimulus dimension and the actual value. A stimulus has complexity value for a person based on the complexity values of each dimension. The theory also asserts that a person will give attention to stimuli which have optimal complexity. A *pacer* stimulus is a stimulus which has a complexity value at an optimal level above the person's abilities in regard to the various dimensions of the stimulus. An individual, Dember and Earl proposed, will direct his attention to (i.e., be intrinsically motivated to approach) pacer stimuli.

Walker (1964, 1973) has also postulated that organisms prefer optimal levels of psychological complexity. Essentially, he asserted that organisms behave so as to move toward the optimum of complexity. His theory is presented as a complete theory of motivation and, as such, subsumes hunger, thirst, pain, etc. within his basic postulate. Further, Walker (1973) interpreted learning and problem-solving behaviors using the postulate.

To the extent that expectations and adaptation level are the same thing, Dember and Earl's theory bears some similarity to that of McClelland *et al.* (1953). In essence, Dember and Earl hypothesized that the maintenance of an optimal level of incongruity between inputs and expectations is the psychological basis of intrinsic motivation, whereas McClelland *et al.* hypothesized that an optimal discrepancy between input and adaptation level is central to intrinsic motivation. One might assume that the expectations one holds about a stimulus dimension are based on his adaptation level for that dimension. Dember and Earl seemed to imply this when they said that the expectation about a stimulus property corresponds to traces left by previous exposure to that stimulus. Previous exposure, of course, determines adaptation level, so they were suggesting that expectation corresponds to adaptation level. This may, in part, be true. However, exposure is not the only determinant of expectations. Information in a person's memory, or obtained from the environment (e.g., from communication), can also affect his expectations. So, if a person is told to expect something other than what he experienced on last exposure, his expectations may differ from his adaptation level.

Consider the following example: A person goes for a swim in a small pool and adapts to the water temperature. When he gets out, the water temperature is changed drastically, and the person is told that the temperature has been lowered 15°F. He then goes back into the water. His adaptation level is approximately at the temperature of the water before the change (call it X°F) but his expectations are quite different; he expects a temperature of $(X-15)$°F. There is a discrepancy between stimulus and adaptation level, but no discrepancy between stimulus and expectation. Clearly, however, the person will experience arousal as a result of the discrepancy between adaptation and input which will motivate him to behave in some way (e.g., get out of the water, move quickly, shiver, etc.). This suggests, then, that the discrepancy between adaptation level and input is the critical discrepancy. However, the degree of arousal and motivation experienced by the swimmer will undoubtedly be less than it would have been had he expected X°F (His adaptation level) rather than $(X-15)$°F. This means that his expectations, apart from his adaptation level, are also important in determining his response. Clearly, then, his arousal and motivation will be a function of the discrepancy between input, on the one hand, and both adaptation level and expectation, on the other hand.

There is another important difference between Dember and Earl (1957) and McClelland *et al.* (1953). Dember and Earl's position asserts that intrinsically motivated behavior is caused by the need for an optimal discrepancy between input and expectation at the time the behavior is motivated. However, for McClelland *et al.*, the discrepancy need not exist at the time of the behavior.

Hunt (1963, 1965) incorporated these notions of optimal discrepancy into a general theory of intrinsic motivation. He regarded the human as an information-processing system and asserted that intrinsic motivation is inherent in information processing and action.

In outlining his theory of intrinsic motivation, Hunt (1965) enumerated and provided answers to several critical motivational questions.

The first question was the instigation question, "What initiates behavior?" Hunt answered the question within the framework of the feedback loop as conceptualized by Miller, Galanter, and Pribram (1960). Their model is called the TOTE unit, which stands for test, operate, test, exit. Within the TOTE unit there is a mechanism which compares the input to some standard such as an adaptation level, an expectation, etc. When there is an incongruity between the input stimulus and the standard of comparison, the organism will be motivated to behave, that is, it will in some way operate to reduce the incongruity. As it operates, there will be continual testing of the stimulus and standard. The operating will continue so long as the incongruity exists. However, when there is finally a congruity between the stimulus and standard, the operation will terminate (i.e., exit) and the organism will be freed of this process.

This operation of the TOTE unit may be processed either in the conscious or the nonconscious. For example, when someone pratices the violin, he listens to himself. The auditory input is compared with some standard in his memory, and if there is incongruity he goes back over the incongruous part (i.e. he operates) until he has matched the standard. At that point, he probably will go on to something else. This processing of information is done consciously—the person is quite aware of what he is doing.

However, at other times the processing is not conscious. Consider the case of hunger and eating. We know that there are many cues, both internal and external, that control a person's experience of hunger (e.g., Schacter, 1971a). Although it is not clear to what extent a person's blood-sugar level controls his hunger and eating, it is clear that blood-sugar level plays some part (see, e.g., Grossman, 1967, Chapter 6). We also know that the neural circuits which control hunger and satiation are centered in the ventral-medial and lateral hypothalamus. The processing then would proceed as follows: The blood-sugar level would be compared to a standard, namely, the optimal level of sugar concentration in the blood. If the present level is incongruous with the standard, the person's neural circuits are activated, he experiences hunger, and he initiates behavior to reduce the incongruity. The person is not aware of the TOTE processing operating in this case, but it seems to work in the same way as when the violinist perfects his music.

One can also see from these two examples that the standards can be either innate, as in the case of the optimal blood-sugar level, or acquired (at least in part) through informational interaction with one's environment, as in the case of the violinist.

The TOTE unit can provide the basis for the answer to the instigation question for either intrinsically or extrinsically motivated behavior. In fact, Hunt did not distinguish between the two in his discussion of the topic. The example of the onset of eating behavior given above was adapted from Hunt, and that would be extrinsically motivated behavior. So, for Hunt, intrinsically as well as extrinsically motivated behavior would be initiated by a discrepancy from some standard. This standard might be an adaptation level (Helson, 1964), an expectation, etc.

The next question Hunt dealt with was energization, "What is it that provides the energy for an organism to engage in an intrinsically motivated activity?"

The answer to this question also centered around the notion of incongruity. Hunt used this notion to answer the question in two general ways. The first was within the realm of drive theory, and the second, information processing theory.

First, the drive-reduction approach. Hunt pointed out that an incongruity between the situation and a person's expectations or plans involves either unfinished business or frustration, either of which is energy producing. The Zeigarnik effect is an example of how this would work. An abundance of evidence indicates that people are motivated to finish uncompleted tasks (Zeigarnik, 1927) and to remember uncompleted tasks more often than completed ones (Rickers-Ovsiankina, 1928). It seems reasonable, then, that incongruities which take the form of uncompleted tasks or plans would motivate the organism toward completion of these activities.

Hunt also suggested that incongruity causes frustration and that frustration can be motivating. When there is an incongruity between actions and plans, there is frustration because the plans are being interfered with. Since these plans are presumably intended to reduce some drive, the incongruity interferes with the drive reduction, thereby establishing the drive. Furthermore, frustration seems to energize some behaviors directly. Dollard, Doob, Miller, Mowrer, and Sears (1939), for example, have hypothesized that frustration energizes aggressive behavior.

By using a drive-theory approach to answer the energization question, Hunt was restricting the explanatory power of incongruity as a source of energy. Incongruity seems to energize only when it involves unfinished tasks or frustration. Surely, however, there are other forms of incongruity. The orienting reflex is one example of a response to an incongruity between a stimulus input and an adaptation level which does not necessarily involve an incomplete task or frustration.

When Hunt used an information-processing approach to answer the question, the answer had the advantage of being able to include all forms of incongruity. However, it had the disadvantage of being less precise in its formulation. In essence, Hunt postulated that incongruity between a stimulus and standard is, by itself, motivating. He cited the William James (1890) example of orienting to a clock only when its ticking ceases, and he pointed out that this incongruity produces energy which cannot easily be accounted for by drive theory.

Numerous other examples exist which indicate that any incongruity from an adaptation level can motivate a response. This supports the information-processing interpretation that when a stimulus is compared to a standard such as adaptation level, and there is a discrepancy, the organism will be aroused. Repeated encounters with this discrepancy will, of course, lead to such a change in adaptation that there will no longer be incongruity and, therefore, no arousal.

Another motivational question which Hunt considered was the direction-hedonic question. "Toward what, and away from what, will an organism move?

In answering this question, Hunt proposed the central hypothesis in this theoretical position: namely, that organisms need an optimal amount of incongruity and will seek out those situations which provide them with that optimum. When there is insufficient incongruity, they will approach situations which provide more (up to the optimum) and avoid situations which provide less. So also, if one is overstimulated by incongruity, he will approach situations with less and avoid situations with more of it.

The next motivational question that Hunt considered was the termination question. "What causes an organism to terminate an intrinsically motivated behavior such as manipulation or exploration?" The answer was based in the work on the orienting reflex (cf. Sokolov, 1960), and fitted neatly into Hunt's information processing approach to motivation. The essence of the answer is that organisms habituate to novel stimuli upon repeated presentation, so that the stimuli lose their incongruity. This notion is also central to Helson's adaptation level theory (1964). An organism's adaptation level changes in the direction of the stimulus which it encounters. Soon, the stimulus and adaptation level are the same and there is no discrepancy.

When a person explores, manipulates, or tries some new activity, he will work at it avidly for a while and gradually become bored. Leavitt (1962) has pointed out that a person, when encountering a novel or puzzling situation, programs the novelty in such a way that he understands it and becomes bored with it. For example, as soon as someone learns the algorithm to a puzzle, the puzzle is no longer intrinsically motivating. It provides no novelty or incongruity. Kagan (1972) made a similar point. Repeated exposure to a novel stimulus will eventually mean that the stimulus loses its intrinsically motivating properties. The incongruity is lost when the adaptation level becomes the same as the stimulus, or when the organism "understands" the stimulus.

In summation, then, there are two central notions in Hunt's theory. First, he asserts that organisms need an optimal amount of psychological incongruity. Second, he says that intrinsically motivated behavior is instigated when the organism experiences a discrepancy between an input and a standard such as an adaptation level or an expectation. This discrepancy provides energy for the behavior, and the behavior is terminated when the discrepancy has been eliminated.

These two notions, however, are not fully consistent with each other. It is undoubtedly true that behavior is often initiated by incongruity and terminated when there is congruity; that is precisely the central hypothesis of consistency theories such as cognitive-dissonance theory. However, this postulate does not allow for

Hunt's central notion of the organism's need for an optimal level of incongruity.

To be consistent, Hunt's theory must be modified slightly to say that intrinsically motivated behaviors will be initiated when there is a discrepancy between the existing amount of incongruity and the optimal level of incongruity. This way, if there is no incongruity in the person's phenomenology, behavior will be initiated because there will be a discrepancy between the amount of incongruity present and the optimal amount. In other words, I am suggesting that, to be consistent, the standard of comparison should not be an adaptation level or an expectation as Hunt suggested, but rather "an optimal amount of incongruity between an input and the standard" (e.g., an adaptation level or an expectation). This is shown graphically in Figure 1. The abscissa is incongruity between input and adaptation level. As presented by Hunt, the process is represented by Figure 2; however, that conceptualization does not incorporate the premise that humans are motivated to achieve optimal incongruity.

I have suggested, therefore, that to be consistent, Hunt would have to maintain that the standard of comparison is not an

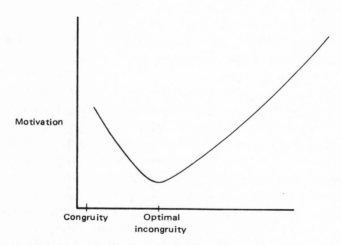

FIGURE 1. Proposed relationship between incongruity and motivation. Organisms are intrinsically motivated to seek an optimal level of incongruity between inputs and some standard (e.g., adaptation level).

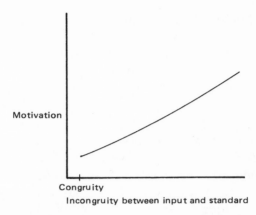

Congruity
Incongruity between input and standard

FIGURE 2. Relationship between incongruity and motivation as proposed by Hunt (1965, pp. 200–202).

adaptation level as he suggested, but, rather, an "optimal amount of incongruity."

However, even with this modification, the position would still be incomplete, since people are sometimes motivated to reduce all of the incongruity in a certain situation. People who are presented with puzzles frequently work at them until they are completely solved. Therefore, we see that people sometimes behave to reduce incongruity, i.e., they initiate behavior in response to an incongruity and terminate behavior when they have dispelled the incongruity. On the other hand, they sometimes behave in such a manner as to provide themselves with incongruity or stimulation.

This suggests that there are two mechanisms which can instigate intrinsically motivated behavior. The first was presented by Hunt, namely, that if the organism encounters a stimulus which is discrepant from some standard of comparison such as an adaptation level, he will behave in such a way as to reduce that discrepancy. The second process involves comparing the existing amount of incongruity to the optimal level, in such a way that, if there is a lack of incongruity in a person's environment, he will experience a discrepancy between the amount of incongruity present and an overriding standard which requires an optimal amount of incongruity, and thus will seek out an incongruous situation. In turn, then, he will proceed to reduce the incongruity.

In sum, I have suggested that using Hunt's general approach, one would have to postulate two mechanisms for instigating and energizing intrinsically motivated behavior. The first, which focuses on discrepancy between an input and an adaptation level or expectation, places central importance on the discrepant stimulus as the instigator of behavior. This process, if taken alone, implies that the organism is primarily responsive to stimuli rather than being active in the sense of seeking out stimulation. I have suggested, therefore, that a second process needs to be added to Hunt's theory, namely, that organisms will be active in seeking out optimal stimulation when they experience a discrepancy between the actual amount and the optimal amount. Then, of course, once they have encountered these situations, they will be likely to act to remove the incongruity, since the incongruity will initiate the first mechanism.

Another group of theories, which are to some extent related to these, centers around the need for optimal arousal. The difference is that the latter theories (e.g., Hebb, 1955; Leuba, 1955; Schlosberg, 1954) deal with the physiological rather than the psychological level. Arousal is a physiological concept referring to nonspecific cortical bombardment.

Optimal Arousal

Hebb (1955) postulated the need for an optimal level of arousal and stated, in essence, that functioning is most efficient when there is this optimal arousal. Since organisms have a need for optimal arousal, responses which lead the organism toward that optimum will be strengthened. If arousal is too low, a response that increases it will be strengthened; if it is too great, a response which decreases it will be strengthened (see Leuba, 1955, for more detail). For example, if a person is confronted with an angry bear, his arousal will probably be above the optimum for effective functioning. If it is not so high that he "freezes" he may be able to flee. The response of flight will lower his level of arousal and thereby be reinforced. On the other hand, if he were bored and safely behind a glass wall at the zoo, seeing the bear might raise his arousal toward the optimum, so the response of going to the bear cage would be reinforced.

It is important to note again that in Hebb's theory, optimal arousal is the key concept. This is different from optimal incongruity, which is central for McClelland *et al.* (1953), Dember and Earl (1957), and Hunt (1965). Yet Hebb provided the basis for a reconciliation when he briefly addressed himself to the question of intrinsic motivation (though he did not call it that). Looking at the psychological level, rather than the physiological level, he stated, "This taste for excitement *must* not be forgotten when we are dealing with human motivation. It appears that, up to a certain point, threat and puzzle have positive motivating value, beyond that point negative value" (Hebb, 1955, p. 250). In other words, optimal arousal may be achieved through optimal threat and puzzle, which involve an optimal incongruity between input and some standard such as adaptation level. Berlyne's work, which will be reviewed later, dealt in more detail with the relationship between the psychological and physiological levels.

Fiske and Maddi (1961) took a position similar to Hebb's. They suggested that there is a characteristic (i.e., optimal) level of arousal and that organisms seek to maintain this level. That optimal level, however, is not stationary, but rather, it varies with the stage of a person's sleep–wakefulness cycle. In other words, organisms do seek an optimal level of arousal. However, this optimum is a continuous variable and is a function of the organism's degree of wakefulness.

Discrepancies from the optimal level at any given time motivate the organism to engage in behavior which will restore the optimal stimulation. This stimulation can come from internal tissue needs, as well as from external stimuli. When a person is hungry, the hunger and the process of getting and ingesting food provides stimulation. Accordingly, when primary tissue needs for food, sex, etc., are satisfied, the organism will more likely need to seek out stimuli (either external, such as a puzzle, or internal, such as daydreaming) which increase his arousal. This suggests, then, that a person is most likely to engage in intrinsically motivated behaviors, such as exploration and manipulation, to increase his level of stimulation (up to the optimum for that stage of wakefulness) at times when his primary tissue needs are well satisfied.

Of course, if he is in a state of near-sleep, the optimal level of arousal will be quite low, so he will not be likely to seek out much stimulation. A soft pillow will probably suffice.

The optimal arousal theories have focused on physiological arousal. A complete theory would, of course, consider both physiological and psychological levels. It may be that optimal arousal is the physiological process which underlies the psychological need for optimal incongruity. There is not much evidence bearing on the relationship of the two processes, yet there is substantial evidence supporting each position, and the notion that the two processes may be linked is intuitively appealing.

Fiske and Maddi's notion that the optimal level varies with the sleep–wakefulness cycle seems to be an important addition to the theories. Whether one is considering incongruity of arousal, the organism's optimal level will undoubtedly be variable. The variation will also surely relate to sleep–wakefulness, though there may also be other factors that affect the optimum. This point seems to be one which deserves additional consideration.

Collation, Arousal Potential, and Arousal

Berlyne has undoubtedly written more about intrinsic motivation than any other author. His early work (e.g., 1950, 1955) concentrated on rewarding properties of drive reduction. He considered arousal (as did Hebb) to be a general drive state and concluded that behaviors which reduced this would be reinforced. Exploration, for example, could serve to reduce arousal, through familiarizing the organism with the novel stimulus. More recently, however, (1963, 1966, 1967, 1969) Berlyne has also recognized that increases in arousal can be rewarding.

In a recent paper, Berlyne (1971a) asserted that intrinsically motivated behaviors are ones which are aimed at establishing certain internal conditions that are rewarding for the organism. These conditions are bound up with the needs of the brain, and may be sought in order to avoid or reduce threats to the functioning of the brain. These threats to functioning, Berlyne pointed out, may be real time needs, such as a frightening stimulus (the growling bear). However, if there is no need for immediate attention to a stimulus, the organism will be involved in normal maintenance. This means that a person will behave so as to maintain an optimal level of stimulation, which is necessary for effective functioning.

Berlyne (1966) elaborated these points somewhat, by claiming that intrinsically motivated behaviors such as exploration can be explained physiologically with two sets of reasons. Both have to do with the needs of the brain and the fact that the human organism is primarily an information-processing system that uses information from the environment and its memory to make choices. Since there is always spontaneous activity in a peron's central nervous system, and since this activity can underlie many different responses, it is useful for the human to obtain information which will help him select adaptively from among the myriad of possible behaviors. The information which he needs to obtain may be about an immediate threat or about more leisurely decisions. Second, organisms are "designed to cope with environments that produce a certain rate of influx of stimulation, information, and challenge to its capacities...(hence) we can understand why organisms may seek out stimulation that taxes the nervous system to the right extent, when naturally occurring stimuli are either too easy or too difficult to assimilate" (Berlyne, 1966, p. 26).

In the course of normal information processing the organism must compare and contrast various stimuli from the environment or memory in order to note differences and similarities. It must also categorize these elements into a meaningful system for operating and storing. Berlyne referred to these processes as collation, and pointed out that things like novelty, incongruity, etc., all involve collation of stimuli from the environment and memory. One can see, then, that collation is central to intrinsic motivation. "Collative stimulus properties" increase a person's stimulation and are therefore intrinsically motivating so long as they are not greater than the optimal level of stimulation.

Collative stimulus properties hold what Berlyne (1960) has called *arousal potential.* Berlyne suggested that people approach stimuli which offer an optimum of arousal potential, thereby implying that people need an optimum of stimulation. If one is below the optimum, he can get this by encountering stimuli with collative properties. Hence, we find him searching out novel stimuli. If he is above the optimum, he can reduce the stimulus properties by withdrawing or exploring the arousing stimuli. This latter alternative involves a temporary increase in stimulation in order to bring about a reduction through exploration and understanding.

Hebb (1955), Leuba (1955), and Fiske and Maddi (1961) were concerned with an optimal level of arousal in the central nervous system. Berlyne, however, was concerned with an optimal level of arousal potential which is more akin to what Hunt (1965) and Dember and Earl (1957) have termed incongruity. Here the emphasis is on the stimuli and how they differ from a standard, an expectation, or an adaptation level, whereas for Hebb, Leuba and Fiske, and Maddi the motivation and behavior are initiated in the physiology of the central nervous system rather than in the psychological interpretation of the external stimuli.

Berlyne (1960) discussed the relation between arousal and arousal potential. At the optimum of arousal potential, arousal is at a minimum. When arousal potential is below optimum, arousal increases because there are insufficient collative-stimulus properties present and the organism experiences a boredom drive which can be reduced by encounters with more collative variables. Above

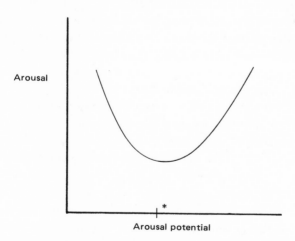

FIGURE 3. The relation between arousal potential and arousal according to Berlyne's (1960) position. The vertical marker (*) represents the optimal level of arousal potential. (After Hunt, 1965.)

the optimum, arousal also increases, thereby inducing generalized drive which can be reduced through escape from the overstimulation or through exploration of the stimulus. The relationship, then, between arousal potential and arousal approximates a U function with arousal potential on the abscissa and arousal on the ordinate. This relationship, derived from Berlyne (1960), has been depicted schematically by Hunt (1965, 1971a) and appears in Figure 3. This proposed relationship means that, at that time, Berlyne was within a drive-reduction framework. Since he equated arousal with generalized drive, he proposed that drive is reduced to a minimum by maintaining an optimal level of arousal potential.

More recently, however, Berlyne (1967, 1971b, 1973) developed a system to account for the findings that increases, as well as decreases, in arousal can be rewarding. He talked about the relationship between arousal potential and arousal increments. He pointed out (1973) that arousal or arousal level must be distinguished from arousal increments or decrements, (i.e., changes in arousal level). Berlyne's position was that there is a relationship between changes in arousal and hedonic value (i.e., preferences). Decrements in arousal have positive hedonic value (i.e., are preferred) if arousal is excessive. However, moderate increments in arousal also have positive hedonic value. A moderate level of arousal potential produces a moderate increment in arousal. This does not mean, Berlyne asserted, that an optimum of arousal (e.g., Hebb, 1955) is necessarily preferred. According to Berlyne (1971b, 1973) there are two separate mechanisms which must be distinguished. One mechanism seeks to reduce arousal; this mechanism is central to drive-reduction theories (e.g., Hull, 1943). The other mechanism (which is more related to intrinsic motivation) seeks moderate increments in arousal through encountering stimuli with moderate arousal potential. The optimal-level-of-arousal hypothesis (Hebb, 1955) asserts that low arousal motivates activity, yet Berlyne (1973) asserted that drowsiness is not necessarily uncomfortable, and that arousal below the "optimal" does not necessarily motivate behavior. Therefore, his two-mechanism theory more reasonably accounts for the data. Nonetheless, his theory, as yet, has not delineated when the two mechanisms might be expected to operate. For example, the mechanism which associates positive hedonic value with increments in arousal would also lead one to predict that an increment in arousal at a time of

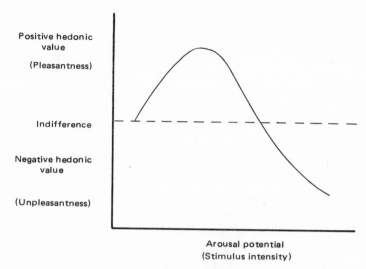

FIGURE 4. Berlyne's reinterpretation (1973) of Wundt's (1874) curve relating stimulus intensity to pleasantness. (After Berlyne, 1973.)

drowsiness would be pleasing. If it is not, it is important to deal with the issue of when increments in arousal—as produced by moderate arousal potential—have positive hedonic value and when they do not. It may be that Fiske and Maddi's notion of changes in optimal arousal as a function of one's sleep–wakefulness cycle, or other similar concepts, would be relevant here.

To clarify how his two-mechanism theory would operate, Berlyne (1973) reinterpreted Wundt's (1874) curve, relating stimulus intensity (roughly equivalent to arousal potential) to pleasantness (hedonic value). This appears in Figure 4. When there is low arousal potential (no change in arousal), the organism is indifferent. Hedonic value increases up to an optimum as arousal potential increases. After the optimum, hedonic value becomes less positive until once again there is a point of indifference. In this region between the optimum and the indifference, both onset of stimulation and termination of stimulation are rewarding, since both mechanisms will be operative. Beyond the point of indifference, the arousal potential is too great. The person experiences negative hedonic value; stimulation is punishing. Hence, the arousal-reduction mechanism is dominant. The mechanism which places value on moderate arousal increments will be essentially inoperative until arousal is reduced and arousal potential is at a more acceptable level. In this discussion, Berlyne does treat the onset of the two mechanisms, but it still does not make clear why, when someone is drowsy (i.e., at a very low level of arousal potential), he does not seek optimal arousal potential. Indeed, Berlyne's discussion implies that the person would seek this optimum.

In discussing the physiology of the two mechanisms, Berlyne draws on the work of Olds and Olds (1965) to note that there appear to be three hedonic systems in the brain. The first, a primary reward system, is located in the hypothalamus of the brain and can be inhibited by the second system, an aversion system located nearby in the midbrain. The primary reward system can be activated by collative stimulus properties, thus constituting the mechanism which finds moderate increases in arousal rewarding.

On the other hand, as I said, the aversion system can inhibit this primary reward system. When it does, it would be experienced typically as negatively hedonic. Therefore, if this aversion system were itself inhibited, it could not inhibit the primary reward system. Therefore, the inhibition of the aversion system would be rewarding. In fact, according to Berlyne, the third hedonic system located in the limbic system of the brain can inhibit the aversion system. The third system seems to be a de-arousal system. Hence, the second of Berlyne's motivating mechanisms works as follows: the de-arousal system is activated by the reduction of a drive such as fear, and this in turn inhibits the aversion system, causing more activity in the primary reward system. In other words, this rather roundabout mechanism involves drive reduction which ultimately allows for pleasurable arousal.

In sum, Berlyne's theory is the most comprehensive of any of the "optimal" theories. He discussed how organisms behave to reduce arousal, but also to approach stimuli with an optimum of arousal potential. In so doing he has focused on the psychological level, but has also paid considerable attention to the physiological processes which underlie the behavior. For him, intrinsically motivated behaviors (1) do not produce biologically important effects on tissues other than the nervous system and the special senses and (2) depend on collative stimulus properties.

The Reduction of Uncertainty

Another approach to explaining intrinsically motivated behavior involves uncertainty reduction. Kagan (1972) has asserted that this is the goal of one class of human motives. For him, a goal is a cognitive representation of future events which will make one feel better, and a motive is the cognitive representation of the desired end state. Kagan believes that resolving uncertainty is one of the important classes of motives, and that it can explain a considerable amount of behavior.

Uncertainty "is characterized, in part, by incompatibility between [two or more] cognitive structures, between cognitive structures and experience, or between cognitive structures and behavior" [Kagan, 1972, p. 54]. This notion is similar to Festinger's theory of cognitive dissonance (1957), which asserted that organisms are motivated to reduce dissonance, since dissonance is experienced as a disphoric state. Incompatibility between two cognitions is precisely what Festinger meant by cognitive dissonance. Further, incompatibility between a cognition and behavior is also frequently considered within the realm of cognitive dissonance. For example, a person who believes in one thing and behaves in a way that is discordant with the belief will hold two dissonant cognitions; the first is the knowledge of his belief and the second is the knowledge of his discordant behavior. This form of incompatibility has been the basis of many studies on attitude change. If a person has an attitude which is dissonant with his behavior, he can reduce that dissonance in several ways, the most likely being to change the attitude or change the behavior. Work on counter attitudinal advocacy has shown that, if a person is asked to argue in favor of a position other than that in which he believes, he will experience dissonance and will reduce this by changing his attitude in the direction of the position which he advocated. Aronson (1966) and Zimbardo (1969) have reported substantial support for this notion.

A third source of uncertainty which Kagan considered was incompatibility between a cognition and an experience. This is quite clearly related to the incongruity or discrepancy which we have considered already. McClelland *et al.* (1953) asserted that a motive is the redintegration of an affectively toned association which generally arises out of a discrepancy between an experience and a cognition–in particular, the awareness of an adaptation level. Dember and Earl (1957) also accounted for intrinsically motivated behavior in terms of incompatibility between an expectation and an input, and Hunt (1965) considered the incompatibility between a cognition (or standard) and an experience. Kagan pointed out that Hunt considered only this incompatibility and ignored the other sources of uncertainty. While this may be so, Hunt's information processing theory could easily incorporate the other two sources of uncertainty previously mentioned. Indeed, a behavior provides an input into the information processing system (i.e., the central nervous system) which is compared to a cognition (i.e., a standard). So, also, a cognition can be compared to another cognition within Hunt's basic framework.

We have seen, therefore, that the reduction of uncertainty as considered thus far bears considerable similarity to the notion of incongruity. The important difference, however, is that Kagan and Festinger proposed that organisms are motivated to reduce all uncertainty or dissonance, whereas others, such as Hunt, proposed that organisms need some optimal amount of incompatibility (i.e., uncertainty) which is greater than zero. The evidence previously reviewed seems to support this latter position quite clearly. While organisms often behave to reduce uncertainty, dissonance, or incongruity, they also behave to induce uncertainty, dissonance, or incongruity.

A final source of uncertainty which Kagan considered was one's ability to predict future events. This goal is particularly salient when there is a possibility that the event may be unpleasant or painful, because this type of uncertainty is likely to be anxiety provoking and distressful.

When a person experiences uncertainty as a child, Kagan said, he may develop one of many different strategies for dealing with it. He can, for example, use the strategy of sticking close to his parents, in which case he will develop a dependency motive, or he can seek praise and reassurance, in which case he will develop a motive for recognition or approval. He can also choose to bully a weaker child and develop a motive for dominance, or he can learn to withdraw because the people whom he has approached for help in dealing with his uncertainty have, somehow, failed him. Any of the strategies which he employs will lead to the development of specific motives; all, however, are fundamentally motivated by the intrinsic need to reduce uncertainty.

The first three sources of uncertainty considered by Kagan stem from an incongruity. Hence, the need to reduce this uncertainty is the same as the need to reduce incongruity. The final source of uncertainty is in future events. People want to be able to predict the future, so they engage in some behaviors, not to reduce incongruity, but rather to gather information which will allow them to predict the future more accurately. While this class of behaviors may seem to be the same as the class of behaviors intended to provided optimal incongruity, it is not. Kagan (1972) stated that this kind of uncertainty is especially concerned with "potentially unpleasant events like punishment, physical harm, failure or rejection" (p. 55). According to this conceptualization, the person gathers information to prevent the onset of unpleasant events. Therefore, Kagan's position is that the need to reduce uncertainty motivates behaviors which reduce incongruity and forestall future discomfort. It does not, however, take account of behaviors which are aimed at producing congruity or providing stimulation, so it can explain only a subset of intrinsically motivated behaviors.

In the realm of information gathering (i.e., curiosity, exploration, etc.) as in the more general realm of all intrinsically motivated behaviors, the need to reduce uncertainty is too narrow to be useful as an integrating concept. A two-mechanism theory such as Berlyne's theory, or such as the modification which I suggested for Hunt's theory, would be more useful.

Berlyne (1971a) elaborated two kinds of exploration. *Specific exploration* refers to behaviors which are responses to a person's experience of uncertainty. It does not, therefore, include exploration which is aimed at providing stimulation, or which derives from a person's desire to know. Such kinds of behaviors are examples of what Berlyne referred to as *diversive* exploration. When a person experiences too little stimulation he seeks out novelty, that is, he explores, manipulates, etc. Thus, exploratory behavior which appears to be for its own sake and is not a response to an incongruity is motivated by the need for moderate incongruity.

Berlyne called this diversive exploration in contrast to specific exploration which is aimed at reducing incongruity. In sum, if a person experiences uncertainty he engages in specific exploration to reduce this uncertainty. However, if there is no uncertainty, he engages in diversive exploration to achieve the needed stimulation.

Lanzetta and his associates (e.g., Lanzetta, 1963, 1971) have done a considerable amount of research on the motivating properties of uncertainty. Their investigations were concerned primarily with response uncertainty and choice behaviors. Their research has shown that search behavior is motivated by response uncertainty and that this search behavior will be a monotonically-increasing function of the amount of uncertainty. Further, people will choose alternatives that they believe will be most instrumental in reducing uncertainty.

The research of Driscoll and Lanzetta (1964) and Hawkins and Lanzetta (1965) also supports Kagan's (1972) notion that the need to reduce uncertainty is not a tension or deprivation need by showing no relation between uncertainty (induced experimentally) and arousal.

To summarize, people engage in many behaviors which seem to be motivated by a need to reduce uncertainty. However, all uncertainty is not aversive; in fact, organisms sometimes seek uncertainty. Further, the need to reduce uncertainty does not provide a general theory of intrinsic motivation. As such, it can be subsumed by an optimal stimulation theory, such as Berlyne's. It can also be subsumed by another general approach, the need for competence and self-determination.

Competence and Self-Determination

The focus of this approach to understanding intrinsic motivation is on the need and capacity of organisms to deal effectively with their environment. Woodworth's behavior-primacy theory (1918, 1958), for example, holds that one's behavior is generally aimed at producing an effect on his environment. This behavior is ongoing and basic, so that behavior directed at satisfying deprivation needs, such as hunger, has to break into this flow of activity. Woodworth, then, viewed a human as a more complete organism which is in continual interaction with his surroundings and himself. He acts on his environment and attends to his own internal biological needs.

White's (1959) concept of competence is within the same general camp. It rejects drive-reduction theory and attaches considerable importance to a person's interaction with his environment. Competence refers to one's ability or capacity to deal effectively with his surroundings. This concept encompasses such things as exploration, manipulation, attention, perception, thought, and communication, since all these activities are necessary for acting effectively on one's environment. However, the concept is a motivational one; that is, White posited a *competence motivation* or *effectance motivation*, which is what directs exploration, manipulation, attention, etc. The behaviors that lead to effective manipulating, for example, are selective, persistent, and directed. They are not random; they are motivated by the intrinsic need to deal effectively with the environment.

White, like Berlyne, asserted that the energy for intrinsically motivated behavior comes from the central nervous system, rather than from tissue needs. External stimuli influence the direction of intrinsically motivated behavior, yet they play very little part in energizing it.

Effectance motivation is persistent in that it is always available to occupy "the spare waking time between episodes of homeostatic crisis" (White, 1959, p. 321). That is, effectance motivation is not intense and immediate in the sense that thirst, fear, etc. are, but rather it is an ongoing process which is periodically interrupted by tissue needs (though, of course, there are also times when a hungry, cold, or pained person will stick to an intrinsically motivated activity in spite of his tissue needs).

Effectance motivation causes behaviors which allow a person to have feelings of efficacy. Therefore, he is intrinsically motivated by effectance motivation to engage in behaviors which allow him to feel competence or efficacy.

White pointed out that in young children, effectance motivation may be quite undifferentiated, whereas with additional experience they become differentiated into more specific motives for mastery, cognizance or achievement. These specific motives would be learned through experiences which emphasize different aspects of effective functioning *vis-a-vis* the environment, yet effectance motivation is the source of these later differentiated motives.

This concept of differentiation of motives through experience parallels Kagan's (1972) formulation, and will be dealt with in considerable detail in Chapter 3.

Angyal (1941) preceded White in attaching considerable importance to the notion of competence in dealing with one's environment. An organism increases autonomy through acquisition of competency in dealing with its environment. Angyal suggested that humans have a tendency toward self-determination, which is a notion very similar to that of effectance motivation, since someone who is self-determining will feel efficacy. In other words, for Angyal the tendency toward self-determination would seem to be the essence of intrinsic motivation.

Kagan (1972) proposed that humans have a motive for mastery which has its origins in their desire to achieve standards, predict the future, and define their selves. Kagan equated this motive with White's effectance motivation. However, Kagan actually defined the motive for mastery much more narrowly than White has defined effectance motivation. White's concept seems to be sufficiently broad to encompass not only behavior energized by Kagan's motive for mastery but also the behavior energized by his motive to reduce uncertainty.

The notions of competence and self-determination also appear in the work of de Charms (1968). He stated, "Man's primary motivational propensity is to be effective in producing changes in his environment. Man strives to be a causal agent, to be the primary locus of causation for, or the origin of, his behavior; he strives for personal causation" (de Charms, 1968, p. 269). For de Charms, then, intrinsically motivated behaviors result from a desire to feel personal causation. He pointed out that personal causation is not the motive of all behavior. Rather, proposing a notion similar to that of Kagan and White, he asserted that this general motive differentiates into specific motives as a result of experiences with one's environment. Indeed, according to de Charms, the desire to be in control of one's fate is a contributing factor in all motives.

In further discussing the notion of intrinsic motivation, de Charms used Heider's (1958) concept of perceived locus of causality. De Charms (1968) stated, "Whenever a person experiences himself to be the locus of causality for his own behavior...he will consider himself to be intrinsically motivated. Conversely, when a person perceives the locus of causality for his behavior to be external to himself... he will consider himself to be extrinsically motivated" (p. 328).

Deci (e.g., 1972a; Deci, Cascio, & Krusell, 1973) has also asserted that people engage in many behaviors in order to feel a sense of competence and self-determination. He has done a considerable amount of research (see Chapter 5) which is readily interpretable by utilizing this conceptualization of intrinsic motivation. As such, it gives credence to this formulation.

One's need to feel competent and self-determining will motivate two general classes of behavior: The first includes behaviors which seek out situations which provide a reasonable challenge to the person. If he is bored, he will seek an opportunity to use his creativity and resourcefulness. If he is overchallenged, and therefore frightened, he will seek a different situation which will provide a challenge which he can handle. In short, this motivational mechanism leads people to situations which provide challenges which make optimum use of their abilities. One can see, therefore, that this bears similarity to the mechanism which I said earlier would have to be added to Hunt's optimal incongruity theory to make his theory consistent.

The second class of behaviors motivated by the need for competence and self-determination includes behaviors which are intended to conquer challenging situations. In other words, people are motivated to "reduce uncertainty" or "reduce dissonance" or "reduce incongruity" when they encounter it or create it. Hence, reducing uncertainty or dissonance is one class of intrinsic motivation. I am suggesting, therefore, that the need for feeling competent and self-determining motivates two kinds of behavior: behavior which "seeks" optimal challenge and behavior which "conquers" challenge.

The work of humanistic psychologists, most notably Goldstein (1939) and Maslow (1943, 1954), has developed and emphasized the concept of self-actualization. This is a motivational concept, in that Maslow asserted that man is motivated to actualize his unique potential, that is, to become all that he is capable of. This bears some similarity to the notion of effectance motivation, yet there are differences. Maslow has posited a hierarchical nature to needs, such that self-actualization is the salient need only after all other needs have been satisfied. This presumably would happen relatively late in life, if at all. Effectance motivation, however, is always present and motivates behavior from the time of birth. The positions seem most easily reconciled by assuming that self-actualization is a specific motive, like achievement, etc., which

TABLE I. *A Summary of Various Conceptualizations of Intrinsic Motivation along with the Primary Proponents of Each Approach*

Approach	Proponent
Drive naming	
Exploratory drive	Montgomery, 1954
Avoid boredom	Myers & Miller, 1954
Manipulation drive	Harlow, 1953a
Sensory drive	Isaac, 1962
Visual exploration	Butler, 1953
Optimal incongruity (Psychological processes)	
Optimal incongruity	Hunt, 1955; Dember & Earl, 1957
Optimal arousal potential	Berlyne, 1971a
Discrepancy from adaptation level	McClelland, *et al.,* 1953
Optimal arousal (Physiological processes)	Hebb, 1955; Leuba, 1955; Fiske & Maddi, 1961
Uncertainty reduction	
Resolve uncertainty	Kagan, 1972
Dissonance reduction	Festinger, 1957
Uncertainty reduction	Lanzetta, 1971
Competence and self-determination	
Effectance	White, 1959
Self-determination	Angyal, 1941
Personal causation	de Charms, 1968
Competence and self-determination	Deci *et al.,* 1973

develops from the basic undifferentiated effectance motivation. This point is developed more extensively in Chapter 3.

In sum, this approach suggests that intrinsically motivated behaviors are behaviors aimed at bringing about certain internal rewarding consequences that are independent of non-nervous-system tissue needs; specifically, they are intended to bring about the feeling of competence and self-determination.

Table I summarizes the various approaches discussed in this chapter.

Concluding Comments

The evidence is quite clear. People as well as lower animals engage in a substantial amount of intrinsically motivated behavior, and theories of motivation need to be able to account for "rewards that do not reduce tissue needs" (Eisenberger, 1972).

Theories will have to account for the fact that behavior is motivated by desires both to *reduce* stimulation and to *induce* stimulation. These facts seem to be quite easily handled by three approaches to understanding intrinsic motivation: (1) optimal arousal theories (e.g., Hebb, 1955; Leuba, 1955); (2) optimal incongruity theories (e.g., Hunt, 1965; Dember and Earl, 1957; Berlyne, 1973); and (3) competence and self-determination theories (e.g., White, 1959; de Charms, 1968; and Deci, 1972).

The reduction-of-uncertainty approaches (Kagan, 1972; Lanzetta, 1971), however, failed to consider that many behaviors are intended to induce stimulation or uncertainty. Therefore, although the postulate of a need to reduce uncertainty has been useful in accounting for a considerable amount of research data, it is less useful than other approaches for integrating the work on intrinsic motivation.

Similarly, as we saw earlier, drive naming has been judged inadequate as a means of understanding intrinsic motivation, so optimal incongruity, optimal arousal, and competence theories are the approaches which seem to hold the greatest potential.

Optimal arousal theories, one will recall, focus on the physiology of the central nervous system, whereas the other two approaches are primarily psychological. A complete understanding of intrinsic motivation will include both levels. It is clear that arousal is central to the physiology of intrinsic motivation. Berlyne has stated that optimal arousal, *per se*, cannot account for intrinsically motivated behavior. However, both increases and decreases in arousal are involved. Berlyne's discussion of the Olds and Olds work on hedonic systems seems in some ways to be useful as a modification of the optimal arousal notion. However, it will be necessary to determine when arousal increases are rewarding and when arousal decreases are rewarding. Although the optimal arousal concept seems to do this, it is clear, as Fiske and Maddi pointed out, that the optimum is changeable. Clearly, there is need for additional work on this general question.

The optimal-incongruity and competence approaches are both psychological theories. Whether one chooses to focus on the psychological or physiological level is really a matter of preference. Both are important and necessary, both have heuristic value, and both have a considerable amount of existing theory and research. Further, Tolman (1959) has stated, "While not denying that in one sense physiology 'explains' psychology...I assert that in another equally important sense ... psychological phenomena control (explain) neurophysiological ones" (p. 96).

Choosing between optimal incongruity theories, on the one hand, and competence theories, on the other, is also, to a large degree, a matter of preference. The two theories are certainly talking about the same phenomena and are somewhat related. There is, however, an important difference. The end state for optimal incongruity theories is that organisms achieve this optimum, whereas for competence theories the end state is positive affect, *viz.*, feelings of competence and self-determination. Having positive affect as the end state is intuitively appealing in that it is clearly an internally rewarding condition. An optimal level of incongruity is, intuitively, less clearly a rewarding state, and therefore seems to have less heuristic value.

Further, we pointed out in discussing Hunt's theory that the postulate of a need for optimal incongruity is inadequate, since there seem to be two mechanisms which initiate and energize intrinsically motivated behavior. One seeks to reduce incongruity and the other seeks out optimal incongruity. In this regard, my extension of Hunt's position bears close similarity to Berlyne's (1971b) recent formulation.

Using a competence and self-determination approach would also involve the two mechanisms which we discussed in expanding Hunt's position. Here, however, we consider the concept of challenge, rather than incongruity. I am suggesting that a person will feel competent and self-determining when he is able to deal with challenging situations. (This is roughly equivalent to saying that he will need to reduce incongruity or dissonance when he encounters it). However, organisms need to be challenged, so if there is no challenge (or stimulation) they will seek it. Further, if they encounter a situation which is too challenging (or too stimulating) they may leave it for another situation which offers a challenge which is more reasonable for them. (This is roughly equivalent to saying that organisms need to encounter some optimal incongruity.)

I am asserting that to feel competent and self-determining (or in White's words to feel effective in interacting with the environment) one will not only deal effectively with situations which he encounters, but he will seek out situations in order to be able to deal with them effectively.

Intrinsic Motivation Defined

Intrinsically motivated behaviors are behaviors which a person engages in to feel competent and self-determining. The primary effects, therefore, are in the tissues of the central nervous system rather than in non-nervous-system tissues. Intrinsically motivated behaviors will be of two general kinds. When there is no stimulation people will *seek* it. A person who gets no stimulation will not feel competent and self-determining; he will probably feel "blah." So he seeks out the opportunity to behave in ways which allow him to feel competent and self-determining. He will seek out challenge. The other general kind of intrinsically motivated behavior involves *conquering* challenges or reducing incongruity. Only when a person is able to reduce incongruity (or reduce dissonance, etc.) and only when a person is able to conquer the challenges which he encounters or creates will he feel competent and self-determining. He will feel satisfied when he is able to seek out pleasurable stimulation and deal effectively with overstimulation. In short, people seem to be engaged in the general process of seeking and conquering challenges which are optimal for them.

Summary

In this chapter we have considered various approaches to the study of intrinsic motivation. The evidence seems indisputable that intrinsic motivation exists and that it involves the needs of the central nervous system.

Early work focused on drive theory accounts, particularly drive naming. This approach is clearly inadequate as it does not help us understand the basis of intrinsic motivation. Similarly, secondary reinforcement is unable to account for the findings.

Another approach has focused on the reduction of uncertainty or dissonance. While it is clear that much behavior is motivated by a desire to reduce uncertainty, it also is clear that much behavior is intended to increase uncertainty.

An approach which considers both reduction and induction of uncertainty is the optimal incongruity approach. The basic postulate of this is that people are motivated to maintain an optimal level of psychological incongruity. A related approach focuses at the physiological, rather than psychological, level and posits that organisms need an optimal amount of arousal (i.e., nonspecific cortical bombardment).

Finally, we considered the conceptualization of intrinsic motivation which asserts that organisms have a general need for feelings of competence and self-determination. This need may differentiate into specific needs as a result of one's interaction with his environment (see Chapter 3). This "competence and self-determination" approach provides the basis for the remainder of the book. It asserts that intrinsically motivated behavior is behavior which is motivated by one's need for feeling competent and self-determining. This relates to needs of the central nervous system and has no appreciable effect on non-nervous-system tissues. Further, there are two general classes of behavior which are intrinsically motivated. The first involves seeking out situations which provide the person with challenge. This challenge will be one with which he has the ability to deal. If there is too little challenge (i.e., if he is bored), or if there is too much challenge, he will seek a situation which provides a challenge which he can handle. The second class of behaviors which are intrinsically motivated are ones which involve conquering challenges which he encounters or creates. This includes behaviors which are generally said to involve dissonance reduction, reduction of uncertainty, or reduction of incongruity.

3

Intrinsic Motivation and Development

Intrinsic motivation is based in the human need to be competent and self-determining in relation to the environment. We now look at how this develops and evolves. In so doing we will consider both how intrinsic motivation affects development and how intrinsic motivation develops.

Intrinsic motivation is innate. All humans are born with the basic and undifferentiated need for feeling competent and self-determining. Humans are active organisms in continual interaction with their environment, and the basic intrinsic need provides much of the motivation for this interaction.

Intrinsic motivation manifests itself in different kinds of behaviors for newborns than it does for slightly older children. Hunt (1971b) has outlined three developmental stages of intrinsic motivation which begin at birth, 4 months, and 9 months, respectively. The third stage in Hunt's outline represents the beginning of intrinsic motivation as we generally think of it. At this point (about 9 months) the child begins to seek out novelty and stimulation. He seeks out challenge, and both finding the challenge and conquering it leave him feeling competent and self-determining.

As the child interacts with his environment, the basic undifferentiated need for competence and self-determination begins to differentiate into specific motives. Therefore, adults may be high-need achievers, or self-actualizers, or intellectuals. These needs (for achievement, for actualization, for cognizance, etc.) are all specific intrinsic motives which develop out of the basic intrinsic need as a result of the person's interaction with his environment.

In this chapter we will review work which relates to the way intrinsic motivation evolves and differentiates. We will see that the process of differentiation is ongoing and continues to some extent into one's adult life so that the strength of a particular motive, while reasonably stable, does change over time.

Since most psychologists who have written about intrinsic motivation and development have worked within a Piagetian framework, I will begin with a very brief review of Piaget's position. This will involve considering the work of Piaget, Mischel, and Elkind and relating that to the present conceptualization of intrinsic motivation. Following that we will turn to the development and differentiation of intrinsic motivation.

The Intrinsic Motivation of Development

Piaget has not written extensively about motivation, yet his basic view of motivation is implicit throughout his writings. Using a biological model, Piaget has developed a theory and approach to child development which outlines stages of development of cognitive structures. Growth in cognitive structures occurs through the processes of assimilating and accommodating to the environment.

Assimilation is a process whereby the organism incorporates aspects of the environment into its preexisting cognitive structures. This may involve modifying one's perceptions of the environment so that they fit with his existing cognitive structures. A person's perception of a stimulus is generally not an exact replica of the objective stimulus; rather, his cognitive structure influences his perception and interpretation of the environment.

Accommodation is a process whereby the organism adapts its own cognitive structure to fit the environment. Inputs of new information to the central nervous system generally involve some changes in that system. These changes are accommodations. For example, going for a drive in a new area might involve studying a map to learn the layout of the area. This would involve accommodating to the environment. A new cognitive structure would be developed to handle the new information.

Development involves continual assimilation and accommodation. Piaget's work describes this development in cognitive structures, which are called schemata. Implicit in his work is the notion that a child is intrinsically motivated to develop schemata through these two processes.

When an organism encounters an informational input from the environment, some schema will be activated. If the input is highly discrepant from existing schemata the input will most likely be ignored, since the child's cognitive structures are not equipped to handle it. If there is no discrepancy between the input and some schema, the input is said to be completely assimilable. When inputs are completely assimilable, children generally lose interest in them. On the other hand, if an input is moderately discrepant from some schema a process of assimilation will begin. Since moderately discrepant inputs are not completely assimilable, the child will have to accommodate somewhat to the input. In other words, his cognitive structures will develop through his interactions with moderately discrepant inputs.

According to Piaget, organisms are intrinsically motivated to encounter activities which involve some assimilation and accommodation. A moderately discrepant input can be handled by an existing schema, but it necessitates some adaptation of the organism. It is challenging. Piaget's findings indicate that a situation is intrinsically interesting to a child only when there is a moderate discrepancy from existing structures. Overly discrepant inputs are not assimilable; nondiscrepant inputs are completely assimilable and therefore are not intrinsically interesting.

In Chapter 2 I stated that organisms are intrinsically motivated to seek situations which provide a challenge that is optimal for their abilities. They then set about conquering that challenge. Piaget would say that organisms seek situations which are assimilable but not completely so (i.e., which provide some challenge) and then accommodate to and assimilate those situations (i.e., conquer the challenge).

Mischel (1971) has reviewed and expanded Piaget's (1952, 1954, 1959, 1967) view of motivation. He stressed the inextricable interrelation between cognition and affect. Cognition provides the structure for affective states, and affect provides the energy for cognitive functioning. For Piaget affect subsumes intrinsic motivation in that affectivity gives psychological value to activities and provides energy for the activities.

Affect and hence intrinsic motivation depend on the cognitive structures available to the child at that stage of development. This view, which has been elaborated by Hunt (1971b), will be considered later in the chapter. We will look first at the way affect (intrinsic motivation) influences cognitive development.

In Piaget's theory, the child is continually involved in assimilation and accommodation as a result of his awareness of disequilibrium. Disequilibrium is essentially an awareness of a discrepancy between an input and a cognitive structure, which activates the assimilation schema and returns the organism to equilibrium. The assimilation schema involves both assimilation and accommodation. Hence, we get from Piaget the notion that organisms are in a continual process of adapting cognitive structures and that this is activated by an awareness of a discrepancy. Activities, then, are motivated by the organism's natural tendency to develop cognitive functioning. For example, Piaget (1959) made the point that learning is simply an aspect of assimilation. Hence, we need not consider the question of the motivation of learning as a separate activity. We need only recognize that the assimilation schema is intrinsically motivated and that learning results from the operation of that schema. Piaget did not deny that learning or other activities can be extrinsically motivated; he simply suggested that they are motivated by an intrinsic motive for the assimilation schema, even in the absence of extrinsic rewards.

The overriding motivational principle in Piaget's theory seems to be that a human organism is by nature motivated toward the development of increasingly accurate and complex cognitive structures, which manifest themselves in terms of rational thought processes and consistent structures. This is accomplished through the intrinsic motivation of the assimilation schema.

According to the conceptualization that the basis of intrinsically motivated behavior is the need for feeling competent and self-determining in interactions with the environment, it follows directly that humans would be continually involved in a process of development of cognitive structures, since more complex and rational structures are both indicators and tools for one's feeling competent and self-determining. By this I mean that rational processes allow one to function more effectively in interacting with the environment, and they also indicate that one has been functioning effectively.

Mischel (1971) discussed in detail the motivating properties of inconsistency within Piaget's framework, suggesting that directed thinking implies a move toward consistency. This point, however, needs some additional consideration. In Chapter 2 we reviewed evidence which indicated clearly that organisms seek inconsistency as well as consistency. If consistency were the desired end state, a person would avoid rather than approach novel situations, and be content in situations of sensory deprivation.

Instead, organisms seek inconsistent situations to conquer. The move toward consistency is an indication that the person is competent and self-determining, yet the achievement of consistency is only one aspect of the general picture of motivation. When a person achieves consistency he will seek new situations where there is inconsistency, which he can then assimilate and accommodate to. Piaget's work does imply this, though it is necessary to make one point more clear. The emphasis on discrepancy between input and cognitive structure, which then activates the assimilation schema and motivates the organism to achieve consistency, overplays the importance of the stimulus and the need for consistency, for it seems to imply that an organism would be unmotivated when there was consistency until an inconsistent stimulus appeared.

My position is that the organism, in striving to feel competent and self-determining, is involved in a continual process of seek and conquer. He seeks inconsistency and then the inconsistency motivates conquer behavior to reduce the inconsistency. Piaget's findings substantiate this notion, and, indeed, his theory implies this, though in addressing the motivation question *per se*, he and Mischel seem to have overemphasized the conquer part and underemphasized the seek part. Mischel (1971) in interpreting Piaget's work, stressed that organisms need to make sense out of the novel. While I agree with this, I would also stress the organism's need to find a novel situation so he can make sense out of it.

Cognitive Growth Cycles

Elkind (1971) has suggested that cognitive development is characterized by growth cycles. These cycles accompany the development of each cognitive ability and its associated behaviors.

Cognitive growth cycles have several phases, beginning with the child's seeking stimulus inputs which provide the *nutriments* for further growth. Elkind pointed out that this seeking is not elicited by the presence of a stimulus; it occurs even in the absence of initiating stimuli. Children can nourish their cognitive growth through a wide variety of stimulus inputs, and in so doing, Elkind posited, they are probably developing long-term preferences. This seeking of stimulus nutriment often involves repetitive behaviors. As we will see when we review Hunt's work, repetitive behaviors are the primary goal of children's behavior when they are between 4 and 9 months old. Then, after they develop interest in the novel, beginning around the age of 9 months, they will still engage in repetitive behaviors to facilitate development of schemata.

Growth cycles also involve *gating* and *storage*. The child must gate out some of the onslaught of stimuli in order to attend to stimulus nutriments. Further, the child will store certain stimuli in memory which he recalls and attends to at later points when there are fewer stimulus inputs impinging on him.

Finally, Elkind has contended that growth cycles involve *intellectual play*. Play has a function of demonstrating mastery. The child who has acquired a new cognitive ability will use that repeatedly, since it allows him to feel competence and self-determination. Of course, he will eventually tire of that activity and no longer be intrinsically motivated to continue, and hence that growth cycle will be complete.

Elkind has proposed that these characteristic cycles of development are intrinsically motivated by what he calls *intrinsic growth forces*. Once the cycle has been completed and the schema is fully assimilated, the behaviors are no longer intrinsically motivated and are engaged in only if motivated by extrinsic factors. This is, of course, quite consistent with Piaget's hypothesis that humans are intrinsically motivated to engage in activities which are assimilable but not completely so. In other words, there must be some growth involved for an activity to be intrinsically motivated.

This hypothesis is also consistent with the assertion that activities are intrinsically motivated by a need to feel competent and self-determining in relation to the environment. With the vast array of stimuli in the environment people will not feel competent for long if they stick to fully assimilated activities. They must move on. They must seek new situations to conquer.

Elkind has essentially elaborated the seek-and-conquer process into four specific stages. He said that organisms seek nutriment; that is, they seek challenge. Then they work with the challenge through repetitions, gating, storing, and playing; in other words they conquer the challenge in these characteristic ways.

Elkind has raised an issue of the difference between form and content of thought. Form of thought is what Piagetians refer to as cognitive structures. These are what develop through cognitive growth cycles. Elkind pointed out that Gestalt psychologists—as well as Kant who proposed the distinction between form and content—believed that form was innate. Piaget, however, found that form, as well as content, develops as a result of a child's interaction with the environment, and the notion of growth cycles is Elkind's account of this development.

Content, Elkind reported, involves the use of fully formed structures (i.e., form) in dealing with a particular situation. Learning can be thought of as the acquisition of content, and occurs primarily as a result of extrinsic motivation.

This distinction seems to me to be misleading. Piaget suggested that learning occurs during assimilation of new inputs. The two are inextricable. Since the assimilation schema is intrinsically motivated, then, according to this view, learning would be, at least in part, intrinsically motivated. The view that intrinsic motivation involves one's need for feeling competent and self-determining implies that learning of content *can* (though need not) be intrinsically motivated.

Elkind went on, in line with Flavel and Wohlwill (1969), to suggest that "competence" (i.e., development) should be distinguished from performance. Whereas the former has to do with the development of structures (which is, clearly, intrinsically motivated), the latter has to do with the utilization of fully formed structures and therefore will generally require extrinsic

motivation. I am in general agreement with this point. Performance, if it involves an activity which is fully assimilated, will not be
intrinsically motivated. Only if it is used in a new situation—which
therefore means that it is not fully assimilated—will it be intrinsically motivated. Hence, to sustain performance of a fully assimilated activity, extrinsic rewards will be necessary. People will not
feel competent and self-determining if they continue to do fully
assimilated activities; they must move on to new situations.

Having now briefly considered the way intrinsic motivation
influences development, we turn to the way intrinsic motivation
develops.

The Development of Intrinsic Motivation

Early Development of Intrinsic Motivation

Hunt (1965, 1971b), in outlining the apparent epigenesis of
intrinsic motivation, pointed up the importance of cognitive structures in intrinsic motivation. Hunt suggested that there are three
major stages in the developmental sequence which the child passes
through during the sensory motor period (i.e., from birth to the
age of 2).

During the first stage, which lasts until he is about 3–5 months
old, the child is responsive to changes in sensory inputs and to
patterns of inputs. This latter point relates to the orienting
response (e.g., Sokolov, 1960, 1963) mentioned in Chapter 2.
When a stimulus input is different than an adaptation level
(Helson, 1964), the person responds with an orienting reflex. For
example, if a constant buzz in the environment ceases, it causes a
response. The person's adaptation level reflects the buzz; so, when
it ceases, there is a difference between input and adaptation level
which causes a response. Continued exposure to the new input
leads to a gradual change in adaptation level and a gradual decline
in the magnitude of the orienting response until the adaptation
level matches the input and there is no response.

Hunt stated that the earliest form of intrinsic motivation is this
responsiveness to changes in inputs and patterns of inputs. This

responding to changing stimuli, Hunt has contended, seems to play an important part in psychological development. Responding to changes in inputs keeps the child alert and facilitates rapid development. Over time the form of the intrinsic motivation changes as the child's cognitive capacities expand.

At the second stage, ranging perhaps from the age of 4 to 9 months, the child is concerned with maintaining certain stimulus inputs. Not only is the child capable of responding to inputs, he now seems intrinsically motivated to maintain, or create, positively affective stimulus inputs. For example, Hunt suggested that when an infant in this stage is being dandled on someone's knee and the motion stops, the infant not only has an orienting reflex, he then engages in behaviors which are apparently intended to restore the dandling.

At this stage, the child is capable of engaging in behavior which is not only responsive but is more like intentional behavior. Until the age of 4 or 5 months, a child does not have the cognitive structures necessary for even rudimentary intentional behavior.

Hunt reported that these behaviors seem to have *maintenance of stimulus inputs* as their goal. They are intentional in that there is apparently some anticipation of future states, though the behaviors themselves are of a trial and error sort in that they don't demonstrate a real understanding of the causal relationship between acts and effects or of the way to achieve certain effects.

The second stage, then, is one in which a child is intrinsically motivated to prolong pleasurable stimulus inputs. The process of recognition is involved in this stage, and children respond positively (e.g., with smiles) to their recognition of these inputs and negatively to their failure to regain the pleasurable inputs.

This period of being intrinsically motivated to prolong certain stimulus inputs serves an important function for the assimilation of new material. By repeated babbling or kicking, the child begins to develop an understanding of self-control. For example, he learns that he can produce certain visual stimuli by kicking his foot as he looks at it, or that he can produce certain auditory stimuli by babbling. This is the period when the child gains an understanding of coordination of his sensory and motor modalities. This period also characterizes the beginning of an understanding of how actions are separate from perceptions. Hence we observe children beginning to grasp objects which apparently appear attractive. This grasping is intentional (i.e., goal directed) in that the child shows persistence. If one action fails to achieve the goal, the child may engage in others.

The third stage in the development of intrinsic motivation is characterized by the child's interest in novelty. For Hunt, this is the beginning of the child's need to experience optimal incongruity which we discussed in detail in Chapter 2. The child's primary interest changes from the familiar to the novel. Hunt has postulated, following the work of Hebb (1949), that familiar behaviors become semiautonomous schemata, which operate more rapidly than the inputs, leaving the child dissatisfied. Hence, the child begins to seek out novel stimuli (which do not have corresponding semiautonomous nervous-system processes) so that the stimulus inputs will precede the central-nervous-system processes.

A second reason why children gain interest in the novel as their cognitive capacities develop is, according to Hunt, that they develop a generalized learning set which has as an implicit goal that things should be recognizable.

This interest in the novel is, of course, the basis of adaptive behavior. No longer is the child responding to inputs and seeking continuation of the familiar; he is now beginning to act on the environment in new ways. The child begins to recognize and understand more aspects of the environment, which is essential for his feeling competent and self-determining in relation to the vast surroundings.

Differentiation of Intrinsic Motives

As the child continues to interact with the environment, his intrinsic motivation continues to evolve by differentiating into what are often referred to as intrinsic motives or social motives. This differentiation hypothesis is not new. White (1959) made the assertion clearly, and a similar proposition has been made by Kagan (1972). Further, it is compatible with Elkind's suggestion that preferences for stimulus inputs develop out of experiences with various inputs during the nutriment-seeking phase of a cognitive growth cycle. While, at first, the child is relatively indifferent among various stimulus nutrients, his preferences develop out of his experiences. Further, the differentiation hypothesis relates to Hunt's (1971b) suggestion that individual differences in curiosity are influenced by an individual's attitudes and beliefs. Since attitudes and beliefs are learned, he was suggesting that the curiosity is affected in part by learning processes. Curiosity is integrally related to the motivation for competence and self-determination, and what Hunt was suggesting is essentially that one's general curiosity becomes channeled toward certain kinds of things.

White (1959, 1960) said that it is useful to think of effectance motivation as undifferentiated in infants and young children. However, these young children are having experiences which are beginning the process of differentiation. Through life experiences of interacting with the environment, White asserted, specific differentiated motives such as cognizance, mastery, and achievement develop. He added that these later motives are complex in that they have developmental antecedents in things other than effectance motivation. For example, they may be influenced by things like anxiety, extrinsic rewards, or unconscious processes. Yet, although they are complex, they have roots in effectance motivation and have to do with the person's need for feelings of competence and self-determination.

Kagan (1972) has posited that one of the basic motives in humans is the motive to reduce uncertainty. As we saw in Chapter 2, substantial evidence indicates that, although humans do behave as though seeking to reduce uncertainty, they also behave in a manner intended to induce uncertainty in some situations. Therefore, the need to reduce uncertainty is not the same thing as the need for feeling competent and self-determining. Instead, it is a subset of intrinsic motivation. Nonetheless, it is relevant to consider Kagan's discussion of the way the motive to reduce uncertainty becomes differentiated, since his argument can be applied just as easily to the differentiation of the competence and self-determination motivation.

Kagan proposed that when a child experiences uncertainty he sets up a motive to resolve it, and if he is unable to do so, he will be left with feelings of anxiety, fear, shame, guilt, etc. The way a child chooses to resolve this uncertainty depends on what strategies he has learned. Kagan gave several examples. The child who has learned that a close relationship with parents helps to resolve uncertainty will develop a dependency motive. Many parents are quick to resolve a child's uncertainty; thus, the dependency motive develops in many children, and we therefore find that many people turn to others when there is uncertainty present.

This interpretation is loosely supported by the work of Schacter (1959), Darley and Aronson (1966), Zimbardo and Formica (1963), and numerous others who have shown that first-borns, when faced with anxiety-provoking situations, tend to be more affiliative. If one can assume that first- or only-borns receive more attention from parents, especially when there is uncertainty, then these results seem compatible with Kagan's hypothesis.

There are some people who withdraw from others when there is uncertainty, and this, Kagan proposed, is because others were not helpful to them in resolving uncertainty when it occurred in the past.

Kagan further suggested that other children may learn to seek praise in situations of high uncertainty–hence, the motive for recognition or approval. Another might seek comfort in dominance over others. Dominance implies less uncertainty for the child, since, if others are not dominant over him, he will not be subject to the demands of others (i.e., to one form of uncertainty). These strategies, as well as others that lead to motives for autonomy, achievement, sexuality, etc., are ways that a child learns to handle uncertainty. The motives are referred to by Kagan as secondary motives, and although he said that the reasons for the great variety in secondary motives is not clear, he suggested that it probably relates to environmental factors in society. This, as we will see below, was found to be true for the development of the achievement motive (McClelland, 1961).

Kagan reported an example of observations of a Botswana culture where the uncertainty around the availability of meat makes a food motive salient. Of course there are alternative interpretations of this anecdote (e.g., in terms of Maslow's need hierarchy, which will be discussed later in this chapter); however, there does seem to be merit in Kagan's derivation.

The example of uncertainty affecting the food motive leads us to an important point, namely, that these various differentiated motives, which we are suggesting differentiate out of a need for competence and self-determination are also affected by other factors, such as primary drives. Eating behavior or a food motive might be affected by uncertainty, or by thwarted love needs, or by a host of other things, but it is clearly also affected by the primary hunger drive. Similarly, other motives which derive from the basic undifferentiated intrinsic motivation can be affected by other primary motives. However, although this muddies the waters somewhat, it does not detract appreciably from the differentiation hypothesis.

Having discussed the differentiation hypothesis in general, let us look now at the specific case of achievement motivation. I am suggesting that this is a specific intrinsic motive which differentiates out of the basic intrinsic motivation. There has been a fair amount of attention paid to the development of the achievement motive. Although the theoretical basis of that work is different than mine, the work, nonetheless, can be readily interpreted as support for the differentiation hypothesis.

Achievement Motivation

In the last two decades there has been an enormous amount of research on achievement motivation. The concept developed out of the affective arousal theory of McClelland *et al.* (1953), which was described in Chapters 1 and 2, and is concerned with behaviors which are related to the tendency to strive for success against some standard of excellence.

McClelland's theory postulates that all motives are learned through the pairing of cues and affective experiences. Achievement motivation is learned when cues related to competing with a standard of excellence become associated with positive affect. The achievement motive is an intrinsic motive; the reward is in the achievement. As de Charms (1968) pointed out, however, achievement generally is accompanied by extrinsic rewards, and, indeed, need for achievement is measured by a projective technique which may score people high in need for achievement when the stories they tell in response to a cue picture on a thematic apperception test (TAT) are loaded with references to extrinsic rewards. In spite of this potential difficulty in measurement, the concept is clearly an intrinsic one in its formulation.

It is my contention that need for achievement is a specific motive which differentiates out of the basic need for feelings of competence and self-determination. The data which we will review below do show that environmental factors affect the development of achievement motivation. They do not, however, allow for a test of the affective-arousal interpretation of McClelland (1961) *vs.* the differentiation hypothesis. They are presented as being consistent with my view, though they cannot substantiate it *vis-a-vis* McClelland's view.

Child Rearing. McClelland (1961) has asserted that the most important determinant of achievement motivation is found in child-rearing practices. This assertion derived out of both theoretical and empirical considerations. Proceeding from the Freudian notion that the unconscious is greatly influenced by parent–child interactions during the first few years of psychosexual development, McClelland concluded that achievement motivation (which is assessed by analyzing fantasies) must be strongly influenced by parent–child relations.

Further, empirical studies have supported the notion that, the child's need for achievement is influenced by the rearing process. For example, Winterbottom (1958) has demonstrated a relationship between need for achievement in 8- to 10-year-old boys and the attitudes of their mothers. Rosen (1959) found the same results in samples of children from various ethnic backgrounds. McClelland and Friedman (1952) reported a relationship in various Indian tribes between need for achievement and the childhood training for independence. Child, Storm, and Veroff (1958) discovered a relationship between mothers' reports of achievement-related training and the need for achievement displayed by their sons in three foreign countries.

McClelland (1958) observed differences between the level of achievement motivation in children as young as 5 years old, and Moss and Kagan (1961) found a correlation between the achievement scores of 6-year-olds and the achievement scores of the same people as adults.

The evidence, then, is quite clear that the achievement motive begins to differentiate during childhood, that the motive of adults is correlated with the motive which they displayed as 6-year-olds, and that parental attitudes and behaviors affect the development of the achievement motive. Let us now look more carefully at some of the data related to the last point, since an understanding of the antecedents of achievement motivation has an important bearing on our differentiation hypothesis.

Rosen and D'Andrade (1959) observed parent–child interactions in their own homes. They used 20 boys (aged 9–11) whose achievement scores had been in the upper fourth of the distribution, and 20 boys whose scores were in the lower fourth. The task was for each child to build a tower with one hand out of various oddly-shaped blocks while blindfolded. (Other tasks were also used and produced essentially the same results.) The parents were present and were allowed to help by speaking to their sons. Further, parents were told that the average-sized tower for all children tested was eight blocks, and they were asked to estimate how well their sons would do.

The results indicated that parents of sons with high needs for achievement had higher expectations for their sons than had parents of low achievers. This supports the hypothesis that parental expectations about achievement and independence influence a child's achievement motivation. Further, the investigators reported that parents of high achievers tended to be more warm and supportive of their sons. Finally, mothers of the high achievers tended to be not only more warm and loving, but also more dominant and "pushy" than mothers of low achievers. The fathers of high achievers, however, tended to be less dominant than fathers of low achievers. These results of dominance behavior have been interpreted as indicating that authoritarian, dominating fathers tend to have obedient, dependent sons who are non-achievement-oriented. The dominance behavior of mothers is said not to matter, since sons are more likely to look to their fathers for their conception of the male role, than to their mothers. These results seem to me to be somewhat ambiguous and the interpretation is questionable. For example, if one believes that a boy looks to his father as a role model, as McClelland suggests, then it would be just as reasonable for a child to imitate his father's dominance as to become dependent and obedient.

However, although there are some ambiguities about the effects of dominance behavior of mothers and fathers on development of achievement motivation, there is a fairly consistent body of data which indicates that parental expectations about achievement and independence, and mother's warmth and supportiveness, are important determinants of achievement motivation.

There are other relevant data as well which relate religious, cultural, and class information to achievement motivation. McClelland's contention is that these relationships, which will be presented below, are a result of the fact that religion and other such factors influence the parents' attitudes, behaviors and motives, and that they in turn influence development of motives in children. In other words, McClelland's view is that child-rearing practices are the primary determinants of achievement motivation and that other factors work through this mechanism.

Studies have tended to show that traditional Protestantism, probably because of its emphasis on the work ethic, self-reliance, and independence, correlates with more achievement-oriented behaviors and is more favorable to economic growth than other religions.

Social class and social mobility also have been shown to be somewhat related to achievement orientation. These studies, which are certainly not clear-cut and definitive, have been reviewed by Berkowitz (1964), who interpreted them, as McClelland (1961) did, to support the notion that parental expectations, warmth, and the stressing of independence influence achievement motivation.

Virtually all of the research on achievement motivation has been done with boys and men, and the findings have not held up for girls and women (see Stein and Bailey, 1973, for an exhaustive review). Horner (1968, 1970, 1972) has introduced the concept of fear of success to account for these sex differences. Horner found that women often have a motive to avoid success, and that this seems to develop from the conflict they experience between a desire to succeed and a fear that success is inconsistent with appropriate feminine behaviors. In response to verbal TAT success cues of women (e.g., Mary finds herself at the top of her law school class), college women wrote stories which indicated that they were afraid that performance would interfere with a woman's chances of marriage and happiness. In short, a woman could not be a "successful achiever" and also be "happy." Horner's work will not be discussed in detail here since it is not, in itself, fully germane to our consideration. However, the findings do suggest that environmental factors such as "appropriate role behaviors for women" do influence the way intrinsic motivation differentiates into the motive structure of adults.

There is a further point of interest: Horner's (1972) data indicate that from 1964 to 1970 the motive to avoid success increased substantially. Whereas in 1964 there was only a 9% occurrence of fear of success in male college students and 66% in females, in 1971 there was 47% in males and 88% in females. While this seems somewhat difficult to explain, a recent study by Krusell (1973) helps to shed light on this problem and indirectly on the differentiation hypothesis.

Krusell found 42% of the male college students and 51% of the female college students demonstrating high fear of success. This suggests that the motive to avoid success in undergraduate males has risen substantially over the last decade, whereas for females it has declined. The reasons for this are speculative, but Krusell's analysis of stories revealed very interesting results. The scoring method for fear of success is outlined in Horner (1970). People write stories in response to TAT verbal cues. If the stories show negative consequences, anticipation of negative consequences, or negative affect associated with success or movement away from success, conflict about denial, or bizarre responses, they are scored for fear of success on an all-or-none basis. Krusell's analysis indicated substantial differences in the stories of females *vs.* males who scored high in fear of success. Females' stories indicated negative consequences associated with success in the realm of "feminine behavior." They feared that success blocked dating, marriage, happy family life, etc. Males, on the other hand, wrote stories which were bizarre or "flip," suggesting that it was not "cool" to be too successful. They referred to "grinds" or "cutthroats" (the pejorative colloquialisms for students who study hard and value high grades) and made fun of materialism, suburbs, cars, and parents.

These data suggest that in the last decade there may have been changes in values among students at the large and more prestigious American· universities (see also Alper, 1974). With the new consciousness of women's roles, female college students seem somewhat less fearful of success. With emphasis shifting away from materialism, males seem to scoff at success. If, indeed, this interpretation is correct, it indicates that motives which differentiate out of the basic need for competence and self-determination as a result of environmental factors continue to be modified throughout one's life as the environmental influences change.

This postulate has received some support from the work of McClelland and his associates, who have demonstrated that people's achievement behavior can be influenced by achievement motivation training courses (McClelland, 1965; Kolb, 1965; Lasker, 1966). Kolb showed that achievement motivation training courses improved participants' grades if they were middle-class boys. Lasker's data showed that training programs have affected the achievement behavior of small businessmen in India.

These data, as well as those of Krusell, are merely suggestive and open to many interpretations. However, they do suggest that intrinsic motives may change as a result of environmental factors.

One set of studies reported by Miller (1971) provides indirect evidence for this position. Miller suggested that, with the growth of cognitive abilities, children will develop expectancies based on interaction with the environment which affect their intrinsic motivation for learning and, hence, their cognitive growth. Miller suggested further that these expectancies about learning can be modified and thereby affect the child's view of himself and his potential for learning.

We have reviewed data which provide support for the differentiation hypothesis in relation to achievement motivation. The need for self-actualization can also be considered an intrinsic motive which develops out of the basic need for competence and self-determination. Although Maslow (1954, 1970) did not present it in that way, it seems reasonable to reinterpret his work in regard to the differentiation hypothesis.

Hierarchy of Needs

Maslow has categorized human needs into five sets and has hypothesized that they are arranged in a hierarchical fashion.

The most basic and prepotent human needs are physiological. These include all of the primary drives, and seem to be governed by homeostasis. The most prepotent need is for oxygen, and if that need is not satisfied it becomes the focus of attention for the person. Yet, the need is usually satisfied, so it seldom serves as a motivator. The second set of needs is for safety. When physiological needs are reasonably well satisfied, safety needs begin to emerge as the prepotent motivators. The third set is love needs, the fourth, needs for esteem, and finally, the fifth set and top of the hierarchy is the need for self-actualization. Self-actualization means that one is becoming all that he is capable of becoming; he is utilizing his potentials fully (Goldstein, 1939; Maslow, 1943).

This brief review of the need hierarchy raises several key issues. First is the question of what a need is: Maslow's (1955) answer reflects his primary interest in psychotherapy. A need is something which when satisfied prevents illness, when unsatisfied causes sickness, when restored cures illness, is prefered by the deprived person, and is inactive in the healthy person.

Maslow, therefore, viewed physiological needs in the same way as higher-order needs such as love or esteem. When oxygen or food is absent, the organism becomes sick. When love or esteem is absent, the organism also becomes sick, said Maslow (though this would seem to be so only after it has emerged as the predominant need).

Maslow asserted that satisfied needs do not motivate. Hence, a person proceeds through the hierarchy in a more or less serial fashion, satisfying one set of needs and then having another set become prominent.

Maslow proposed that one progresses through the stages in a fairly slow fashion; in other words, one might be at one level for many years before progressing to the next. And, indeed, many people never reach the self-actualization stage. Maslow has said, however, that people are often working to satisfy more than one set at any one time. That is, as the physiological needs tend toward satisfaction, safety needs emerge and people become motivated by safety considerations as well as by physiological ones. Further, there would seem to be both long- and short-run aspects to the theory. While it may take years to progress from being primarily at one level to being primarily at another, one can also change from one to another level from minute to minute. For example, if one is primarily at the level of love needs, he will at any time be motivated by safety needs if danger is imminent. So too, will he be motivated by physiological needs on a regular basis. He becomes hungry and is motivated to get food if it is absent, and so on.

While there is something esthetically pleasing about the thoroughness, and at the same time parsimony, of Maslow's theory, there are some difficulties. Smith (1972, 1973) has discussed these difficulties cogently.

The first difficulty, though Smith did not mention this, seems to me to be the fact that the hierarchy implies that infants are motivated almost entirely by physiological needs. Yet, surely, a child is motivated by safety- and love-needs in a very prominent way. Harlow's (1953b) work with monkeys makes it clear that babies have very strong love needs which, if not satisfied, impair development. Love needs, the third level on the hierarchy, are important from the time of birth and do not emerge only after physiological and safety needs have been more or less fully satisfied.

A second difficulty is that there is, in the hierarchy, no consideration of the basic, intrinsic need for competence and self-determination. The evidence presented in Chapter 2, as well as the work of Piaget and others, makes it clear that this need is present from birth. Smith (1969) made a similar point by suggesting that people whose lower-order needs are not satisfied are still concerned with behavior to promote self-determination. Maslow (1955) has recognized this problem by asserting that in addition to the hierarchy of needs there is an overriding *growth-motivation*. Growth needs are related to creativity, human potentialities, talents, etc. Maslow asserted that these growth needs take one through the lower needs to self-actualization needs.

This point bears some similarity to the differentiation hypothesis. Out of basic growth needs (i.e., needs for competence and self-determination) develop the need for self-actualization. For Maslow, all persons have the need for self-actualization, though, apparently, many never develop to that stage. Hence, Maslow's theory suggests that growth needs lead naturally into self-actualization as soon as the lower-order needs are sufficiently satisfied. I am suggesting, however, that the need for self-actualization differentiates out of the basic intrinsic need for competence and self-determination just as the need for achievement, or the need for cognizance, or any other adult intrinsic need does.

This does not contradict Maslow's notion that everyone has the potential for self-actualization. It simply says that this need will be operative for some persons and not for others because of the developmental processes which lead to differentiation of intrinsic motivation. Similarly, all persons have potential for being strongly motivated by the need for achievement, though some are not primarily motivated by this need because of the way that intrinsic motivation differentiates for them.

Maslow makes very clear that his theory is a value laden theory. We need to look more carefully at the concept of self-actualization before considering this more fully.

Maslow (1970) defined self-actualization as the full development of one's potentials or capabilities. He then described the characteristics of a person who is self-actualizing. The person would have clear perceptions, be self-accepting, be spontaneous and natural, have an orientation toward problem solving, require a certain amount of privacy and detachment, be autonomous, continue to appreciate the basic qualities of life, have a deep affection and sympathy for all humans, carry on deeper and more meaningful love relationships, have peak experiences (i.e., mystical or transpersonal experiences), understand "humanness" and "nonhumanness," and so on.

What all this means is that Maslow has defined humans in a particular way. Since all humans are capable of self-actualization, and since self-actualizers (the most healthy of people) have certain characteristics, then Maslow has defined humanness. Further, he has stated quite clearly that it is better to be self-actualized than not to be self-actualized, and that psychologists should be concerned with helping humans toward self-actualization. Smith pointed out that people such as Van Gogh, though he had fully (or nearly) developed his potentials for painting, could not be considered a self-actualizer according to Maslow's theory, since he lacked many of the attributes.

Herein we see the problem of sameness *vs.* differentness of humans. In some ways two self-actualizers would be the same; they would possess such qualities as those listed above. In other ways they would be different; one might be a musician and one a surgeon. Hence, as Smith pointed out, one would be a self-actualizer only if he lived up to Maslow's values, that is, if he had all the same characteristics which Maslow says characterize human-ness.

Smith (1973) suggested that self-actualization tends to be a concept for the affluent. Only when one's lower needs are satisfied will self-actualization take over. It is largely in the affluence of modern America and upper levels of other countries that we observe people who seem concerned with self-actualization, who frequent growth centers and talk of mystical experiences. In earlier years of less affluence high value was placed on achievement. The societal values, however, have changed somewhat; self-actualization is "in" and achievement is "out." This is not meant in a pejorative way, nor does it deny that all persons have the potential for self-actualization; it merely suggests that environmental factors have much to do with the way intrinsic motivation develops to influence adult behavior.

Motives and Values

Maslow made clear that he considered self-actualizing to be the highest and best state of humanness. To raise the question of whether it is better to be motivated primarily by achievement motivation or by actualization motivation raises the criterion problem: What does one mean by "better"? This takes us into the realm of values and assumptions which we discussed in Chapter 1. If the answer to the question is, "It is better to be in the state which is most human," one has gained little in terms of scientific specificity. What is most human? The answer seems to come down to one of two things: "that which matches our assumption of what human beings are" or "that which we like better because of our own values." Maslow (e.g., 1955) has been quite explicit about both of these and is to be commended for that. Perhaps it is true that the "highest" form of humanness is the state of self-actualization. However, the evidence on that is not clear-cut; only one's values and experiences can really be clear-cut on this issue.

Berkowitz (1964) clearly places high value on achievement. He, in fact, presents prescriptions for how to raise a child, the essence of which seems to be, raise the child (boy child) to be an achiever. Hence, Maslow and Berkowitz seem to be differing on what is best. The two probably have different criteria based on different values.

The Search for Meaning

Maddi (1970) has presented a broad theoretical view of human functioning which is relevant to our discussion of intrinsic motivation and to the differentiation hypothesis. It is also related to Maslow's theory.

Maddi's central hypothesis is that humans by nature search for meaning, and that this is the fundamental question in the psychology of motivation. This proposition bears considerable similarity to the work of White (1959) and de Charms (1968), who have asserted that humans seek to be effective in dealing with their environments and that this is the central concern for motivation. This similarity will be even more apparent as we review Maddi's theory.

Maddi drew a distinction between a person's core personality and his peripheral personalities. The *core personality* is common to all people. It is what might be called "human nature." It is innate and represents a group of characteristics and tendencies. Key among these characteristics is the need for meaning. Humans, said Maddi, have three sets of needs: biological, social, and psychological. Biological needs motivate behavior whose only goal is to satisfy these needs which relate to survival. One must eat, breathe, eliminate, etc., to survive.

Social needs include the needs for communication and human contact. While these are not directly related to survival, Maddi has contended that the absence of satisfaction of these needs leads to frustration and suffering.

Psychological needs are what Maddi called *needs of the mind.* Humans need to "symbolize," "imagine," and "judge." This definition bears a close relationship to Berlyne's (1971a) suggestion that intrinsic motivation relates to needs of the brain. Psychological needs often interact with biological and social needs; for example, dining in a fine restaurant undoubtedly relates to the need for food (a biological need), the need for human interaction (a social need), and the need for esthetic surroundings (the psychological need to judge). If eating were only motivated by the hunger drive, one would as soon eat a hamburger at home, alone. This point relates to White's suggestion that most adult motives and behaviors have their roots in effectance motivation but are affected by other kinds of motivation, such as primary drives.

Whereas the core personality is common to all humans, *peripheral personalities* are different for each person. One's peripheral personality is a complex mix of core personality and environmental factors. This postulate is essentially the same thing as our differentiation hypothesis. Maddi stated his proposition more globally in terms of personality, yet he was, in fact, concerned in large part with motivation. Translating his proposition into motivational terms (which would be a subset of his proposition), we may state that the core motivational propensity is the search for meaning and that the peripheral motives are derived from this basic propensity as a function of one's encounters with the environment during development. This is, in fact, our hypothesis, though we speak of the need for competence and self-determination, rather than the search for meaning. In discussing developmental considerations, Maddi talked of ideal and nonideal development, thus reflecting his interest in the ideal *vs.* nonideal personality. Hence, we look first at the two classes of personality (or more accurately, at the two ends of a continuum of personality).

Maddi has termed the non-ideal personality *conformism.* This personality would demonstrate minimal imagination, symbolization, and judgment in living (the psychological needs). Instead, these needs would be suppressed, since they are associated with anxiety for the person who responds by defending against them. This person would tend to have high needs for approval and conformity.

The ideal personality is, according to Maddi, individualism. These people are frequently motivated by psychological needs and these needs will be actively influencing the way the biological and social needs get satisfied. These people would overall perceive themselves to be competent and self-determining, though they would sometimes have doubts about themselves. Maddi emphasized that these doubts are an integral part of individualism, for to be active and changing implies some unsureness and doubt.

Development

The ideal development (i.e., one that leads to individualism) is one which encourages expression of all three sets of needs (biological, social and psychological). The child, said Maddi, will need to receive unconditional positive regard (Rogers, 1961), that is, the child should be respected as an individual and appreciated as a person, irrespective of his specific behaviors. Further, the child must be with adults who value psychological needs (symbolization, imagination, and judgment) and receive support when he displays behavior related to these needs. Encouraging him when he expresses doubts about himself is also important. The child also needs to be supported for expressing biological and social behaviors which are satisfying, though not necessarily conforming. If a child grows up in this setting he will be self-reliant and individualistic, suggested Maddi. If not, he will be more conforming.

Reinterpreting Maddi's proposal we see that humans have an innate intrinsic motivation (psychological needs related to meaning) which differentiates into specific motives as a result of experience. When supported and encouraged, the basic need seems to differentiate into motives for self-fulfillment, self-reliance, independence, and achievement. If the child is not supported, it differentiates more into needs for approval, acceptance, conformity, and so on.

Considering this latter category more carefully, we see that the focus is outside of the person. Causality is more external than internal. These motives seem to be extrinsic in nature. In other words, certain environmental factors seem to leave an intrinsically motivated person less intrinsically motivated and more extrinsically motivated. This topic will be considered in great detail in Chapter 5.

Implicit in Maddi's theory are some interesting metatheoretical issues. Maddi is concerned with healthy and unhealthy personalities, and his view of a healthy personality is quite apparent: It is one which is individualistic. As such, his theory is not only a description of behavior; it implies judgments and prescriptions.

Individualistic is the best way to be, one can infer; it is the criterion for psychological health. Maddi also begins with the set of humanistic assumptions which we discussed in Chapter 1. He accepts that humans by nature seem to be good; that is, if a person develops as an individualist and does not necessarily live according to norms and conventions, said Maddi, he will not act like a "monster." His judgment will be developed and he will act "human."

Locus of Control

There has been continual reference in this book to the concept of locus of causality (Heider, 1958). In Chapters 5 and 10 we will discuss in detail the relationship between an internal locus of causality and an external locus of causality. When a person is intrinsically motivated, the locus of causality for that behavior is internal, whereas when the person is extrinsically motivated, the locus of causality is external. A related concept, and one which is sometimes confused with locus of causality is "locus of control" (Rotter, 1966).

Deriving from his work on social learning theory (Rotter, 1954) is Rotter's suggestion that people differ in the extent to which they believe that rewards are contingent on their own behaviors or attributes. Some people perceive that rewards or other reinforcing events follow from their behaviors or attributes; these people are called *internal controls.* The term refers to the fact that, since they believe in a relationship between their behavior and rewards, they perceive that they can have some impact on their environment. If they act, changes will occur in the environment. Other people believe that rewards are determined primarily by luck or fate and have no particular relationship to their behaviors or attributes; they are termed *external controls,* since they do not perceive that they can have an impact on their environment.

The relationship of locus of control to intrinsic motivation is a bit confusing. Rotter's theory focuses largely on extrinsic rewards, i.e., on one's perceiving that he is able to obtain rewards if he attempts to get them. However, Rotter's theory also relates to one's believing that he is competent and self-determining. Therefore, we can see that someone who is an internal control may be motivated either intrinsically or extrinsically. Hence, the *locus of causality* may be either internal or external for someone who is high on internal *locus of control*. External-locus-of-control people tend not to be motivated for either intrinsic or extrinsic rewards, since they do not believe that the environment will respond to them or that rewards will follow their behavior.

We can therefore view Rotter's concept of internal locus of control as being a necessary condition for intrinsic motivation. An internal-control person is one who would tend to be intrinsically motivated in many situations. He believes that he can affect his environment, and he will therefore do many things for the feelings of competence and self-determination which follow from being an effective causal agent. An external control person is one who would seldom be intrinsically motivated. He believes that he cannot affect his environment, so he will not often engage in behaviors in order to try to feel competent and self-determining.

Rotter views external control, at least in part, as a defensive response to failure. As we will see in Chapter 5, failure and negative feedback decrease people's intrinsic motivation. Therefore, it makes sense that repeated failures and negative feedback would lead a person to believe that he is not competent and self-determining and therefore would lead to his becoming an external control person. Herein lies the relationship between Rotter's concept and the differentiation hypothesis. In essence, Rotter's work suggests that negative encounters with the environment tend to make people less intrinsically motivated. That is, their intrinsic motives (whether achievement, cognizance, etc.) will become weakened. Rotter (1966) has presented some data which suggest (though don't really test) the notion that internals tend to be more achievement-oriented than externals. One would expect that people who meet repeated failures would become low achievers and externals even if they had initially been high achievers and internal controls. In short, interactions with the environment affect the way intrinsic motivation develops and changes.

Summary

In this chapter we have discussed the intrinsic motivation of development and also the development of intrinsic motivation.

First, we considered Piaget's work, noting that the assimilation schema is intrinsically motivated in children. They seek events which are assimilable but not completely so, and they then proceed to accommodate to, and assimilate, the events. We reviewed Elkind's work which outlined more clearly the processes involved in seeking out challenge and then conquering that challenge.

Children are born with a basic undifferentiated intrinsic motivation, the need for being competent and self-determining in relation to their environment. The form of this motivation is dependent on their cognitive capacities (Hunt, 1971b), yet it is present through the various stages of development. As a result of interactions with the environment the basic undifferentiated intrinsic motivation becomes differentiated into specific intrinsic motives such as achievement, self-actualization, etc. The work of White and Kagan was discussed in relation to the differentiation hypothesis, and the work of McClelland, Maddi, and Maslow was reviewed in relation to the development of specific intrinsic motives. Finally, it was suggested that intrinsic motive structures continue to change throughout life as a result of interactions with the environment. In this regard, we considered Rotter's work on locus of control.

4

The Intrinsic Motivation of Behavior

Although intrinsic motivation has begun to gain recognition as an important aspect of human motivation, and theories of intrinsic motivation have been developed, very little work has been done to incorporate the concept of intrinsic motivation into a broader theory of motivation. This chapter will use a cognitive perspective to present the basic outline of a general theory of motivation which incorporates intrinsic motivation.

The importance of cognitive processes in motivation is now widely recognized. Weiner (1972) said that in the last two decades the strong grip of mechanistic theories has begun to weaken, and now many psychologists recognize that cognitive processes affect behavior and are beginning to study how this happens.

A cognitive approach to motivation is concerned primarily with choice behavior (cf. Taylor, D. W., 1960). It assumes that people make choices about what to do by processing information which they receive from the environment or memory. I am asserting, further, that they also use information which might be called "personal knowledge." That is, people's attitudes, feelings, and other internal states also provide information which they use in their decision making. This notion will be considered in much greater detail later in this chapter.

In making choices about what to do, people work with a cognitive representation of the environment. This cognitive representation includes stimuli which come from each of the sources

93

mentioned above—environment, memory, and internal states. By operating on this representation, people choose behaviors to engage in which they believe will lead them to a desired end state or goal. These goals, as Kagan (1972) stated, are also cognitive representations. They are, in essence, cognitive expectations about future states.

The cognitive approach, then, in its more recent formulations (e.g., Baldwin, 1969; Weiner, 1972) considers a sequence of events beginning with stimulus inputs and ending with the termination of a behavior. This approach has developed out of the pioneering work of Tolman (1932, 1959) and Lewin (1936, 1938, 1951), who first recognized the importance of cognitions as causal factors in behavior.

Tolman was concerned primarily with learning phenomena, whereas Lewin was more concerned with social behavior. Yet the essence of their motivational systems was similar. The basic elements of their systems can be summarized quite simply. (See Figure 5.) They begin with an energy source. Tolman has referred to it as *drive stimulation,* by which he meant internal conditions that might loosely be termed *needs.* Lewin spoke of tensions as the energy source, and in so doing was defining this factor somewhat more broadly than Tolman. For example, as Heider (1960) reported, a tension can be set up in a person when someone asks him to perform a task. Later in the chapter we will consider the question of what factors are involved in establishing energy sources for behavior.

Tolman and Lewin agreed that these energy sources lead to the establishment of goals. Tolman spoke of drive stimulations as having value-giving properties, that is, they set up both positive and negative goals. Lewin also used the term *goals* and introduced the notion of valence to refer to the psychological value of a particular end state.

FIGURE 5. The basic elements of a cognitive model of motivation.

When one has established goals, one will engage in behaviors which lead to the goals and subsequently decrease the drive stimulations or reduce the tension. The direction of the behavior, according to Tolman, will be toward a *positive terminal stimulus* (i.e., toward a positive goal) and, according to Lewin, will be toward regions in one's "life space" which have positive valence. The basic meaning of the two formulations is the same: a person behaves so as to approach goals which will decrease drive stimulation or tension.

It must be pointed out that the notion that drive stimulations or tensions will be reduced is not the same as the notion of "drive reduction." This is so, of course, because of the difference in meaning between *drive* on the one hand, and *drive stimulations* or *tensions,* on the other. The meaning of *drive* was discussed in some detail in Chapter 2, and one can see from that that the traditional meaning of *drive* is more narrow than that of *drive stimulations* or *tensions.* The most critical difference is that drives involve deficits in non-nervous-system tissues, whereas tensions need not.

It may be less confusing to use the term *need* to refer to the energy source. In so doing, we would define it broadly enough to include more than the primary drives. For example, Maslow (1943) has spoken of needs for esteem and self-actualization. These needs could certainly be the basis of tension. Lewin did not, however, consider the "energy source" in much detail. Similarly, he did not consider the way a person perceives and encodes stimuli.

Weiner has proposed that a cognitive model would involve (1) antecedent stimuli, (2) mediating cognitive events, and (3) behavior. The cognitive aspects of Lewin's theory are primarily in the link between the last two of these, namely, perceived path to a positively valient goal. The question of needs would be included in the antecedent-stimuli aspect of the model. Hence, a more complete cognitive theory would focus on the early parts of the sequence, as well as the later parts.

Let us review the basic ideas of a cognitive theory of motivation. This approach asserts that humans process information and make choices about what behaviors to engage in. Implicit in this is the assumption that cognitions are causal determinants of behavior—an assumption which contradicts behavioral theories (see Chapter 1). Further, people will choose behaviors which they expect will lead them to desired end states. A complete cognitive theory of motivation will consider antecedent stimuli, mediating cognitive events, and behavior. Expectancy theories of motivation, which began with the work of Lewin and Tolmon and have since been expanded by Atkinson (1964) and Vroom (1964) focus primarily on expectations about the achievement of goals. These deal with later elements in the sequence of events just mentioned, to the exclusion of earlier elements. In this chapter we will present a general cognitive theory of motivation which—in line with expectancy theories—views behavior as goal directed. It will, however, also pay greater attention to earlier elements in the sequence, and in so doing, will provide a means for integrating the construct of intrinsic motivation into this approach.

A Cognitive View of Behavior

The first element in a cognitive model of behavior must be stimulus inputs to the central information processing system. These stimuli come from one of three possible sources or combinations of the sources: the external environment, memory, and internal sources.

The second element in the cognitive model is the energy source, or the motive. We might, for example, call it the "awareness of potential satisfaction." Using a cognitive model of motivation, we define a motive as a cognitive representation of a desired future state. Therefore, the energy for behavior will come from the awareness that there is potential satisfaction for the organism. This awareness has nothing to do with whether or not the environment will allow satisfaction. It is simply an awareness of a particular state which the organism has the potential to achieve and which is more satisfying than its current state. Traditionally, in experimental psychology, the "energy" for behavior has been derived from basic drives such as hunger, thirst, and sex, or secondary drives which develop out of pairing with primary drives. I am suggesting that other needs, such as social needs for self-esteem or achievement, are also operative and that these needs are not secondary drives. Further, affective states are integrally involved in motivational processes and also play a part in energizing behavior. Emotions can serve to organize either approach or avoidance behaviors. Negative affect, such as fear, can motivate behavior which leads to reduction of the fear. Positive affect, such as pleasure derived from a stimulus input (say, the sight of an esthetically pleasing painting) can lead to behavior which increases that affect (e.g., viewing more paintings to enhance the pleasure).

The common thread running through these processes (primary drive, secondary drives, social needs, emotions) is that they act as cues which provide information to the central information processing system to the effect that satisfaction can be experienced. Hunger pangs suggest that satisfaction can be achieved. Fear suggests that satisfaction can be achieved, and so on. Therefore, the second element of the cognitive model will be called "awareness of potential satisfaction."

It is important to note that this is a more precise statement than one might first think. For example, if one has no stimulus inputs related to food (e.g., low blood sugar level, a picture of a hot fudge sundae) he will have no "awareness of potential satisfaction" in regard to eating behaviors. The awareness develops directly out of the experience of stimulus inputs to the central processor. The awareness is not just an abstract which is always present; it is an awareness to which the person is attending as a result of processing stimulus inputs.

The third element in the cognitive model is the establishing of a goal. The person chooses a goal from among the set of alternatives which he feels to be open to him. The question of establishing goals is of primary importance in the expectancy theories of motivation (e.g., Tolman, 1959; Lewin, 1951; Atkinson, 1964; Vroom, 1964). Since this will be considered later, suffice it to say that a person selects a goal by considering his awareness of potential satisfaction and his expectations about achieving that satisfaction.

The fourth element in the model is the goal-directed behavior. Once a person has chosen a goal, he will behave in a manner intended to achieve that goal.

Finally, the fifth element is reward and satisfaction. Achieving the goal will (if the person's expectations were accurate) provide him with rewards (extrinsic, intrinsic, or affective) and lead to satisfaction.

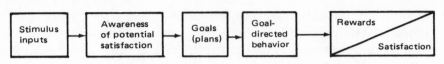

FIGURE 6. A cognitive approach to behavior.

This model is represented graphically in Figure 6, and each element will now be considered in turn.

Stimulus Inputs

As was mentioned above, stimulus inputs can come from external stimuli, memory, or internal states. External stimuli are conditions which exist in the environment. They are conditions, such as time of day (which is an ongoing, regular condition), the occurrence of an earthquake (which is totally unexpected), or the passing of a bake shop in one's way to an appointment (a predictable, though not planned, occurrence). If the external stimulus is a planned occurrence, then that is the goal of a previous chain of events which could similarly be analyzed using the current model. For example, when one is at an ice cream parlor, the menu, the smells, etc. are the external stimuli. These stimuli exist for the person because he planned to be there, that is, earlier decision making and goal-directed behavior led him to the external stimuli which currently exist for him.

Stimulus inputs can also come from memory. Some external stimulus can lead a person to recall some event, which then serves as a stimulus input to the present chain of events. For example, to use the guitar playing example from Chapter 1, when Allan asked Harold to play guitar, Harold may have recalled past situations where he played guitar with Allan and those memories may have provided information useful in making a decision about whether to play this time.

Information from memory may also come into conscious awareness in a less systematic way. In a situation relatively free from external stimulation, a person may remember past situations which serve as stimulus inputs to the current sequence of events. For example, as one sits waiting for the train, his mind begins to wander and the information which comes to him may be an input to a sequence of goal-directed behavior.

Finally, the inputs may come from internal factors such as blood sugar level, glandular secretions, or affective responses.

Awareness of Potential Satisfaction

The second element of the model asserts that the organism's awareness of how it could be satisfied will provide the energy for setting goals and engaging in behavior. In other words, motives provide energy for the behavior, and these motives are defined as cognitive representations (i.e., awareness) of desired end states (i.e., potential satisfaction).

People are in constant interaction with their internal and external environments. Information is continually being received by the central processor, and these inputs make the person aware of potential satisfaction. This awareness of potential satisfaction comes from the information, which in other motivational systems, has been labeled *drives, intrinsic motivation,* and *affective states.* I am suggesting that tissue deficits, glandular secretions, external stimuli, etc., are all pieces of information which lead the organism to an awareness of potential satisfaction. The question of how the information is processed is an important and intriguing one. In the current model it is represented by the arrow between inputs and awareness of potential satisfaction. There has been some work by Schacter and his associates (1971a, b) on the way the informational inputs are processed. Their work has shown that both internal and external stimulus inputs are used by individuals to arrive at an awareness of "hunger" or of certain affect. Additional work should continue to help clarify this question.

Let us now consider the three processes—drives, intrinsic motives, and affect—which underlie the awareness of potential satisfaction.

Drives

The importance of primary drives in the motivation of behavior is clear. Hunger and thirst, for example, can provide energy for behavior. When an organism is "hungry," it is aware that it could be satisfied, so it may engage in a variety of behaviors to satisfy its hunger. The specifics of how drives work to motivate behavior has generated much debate. Mechanistic theories assert that associations exist between internal stimuli and responses. The cognitive view, however, is that internal stimuli, such as low blood sugar or gastric motility, provide the organism with information about its current state and about how it could be more satisfied. Although this information may in turn lead the organism to take some action, there are no inflexible links between the stimuli and the responses. Rather, people use the information to choose to engage in behaviors which they expect will lead them to satisfaction.

Intrinsic Motivation

Intrinsically motivated behavior is behavior which is motivated by a person's need for feeling competent and self-determining in dealing with his environment. This is a basic motivational propensity which is continually present and will be the primary motivator of behavior unless some other factor interrupts the process. Therefore, at any given time a person's intrinsic needs are potentially operative to motivate goal-directed behavior. In this sense, they operate as primary drives do. A person's intrinsic need for feelings of competence and self-determination makes him aware of potential satisfaction, which, in turn, provides the energy for him to set goals (i.e., to decide what to do) and to behave in such a way as to try to achieve these goals.

At any time some stimulus inputs which have generally been called *primary drives* can break into the goal-directed, intrinsically motivated behavior. Whether or not they do depends on their salience in relation to the awareness of potential satisfaction which motivated the ongoing activity. If the ongoing activity is very rewarding, the salience of the primary drive will need to be very high. Witness the example of people who refuse to eat when they are actively engaged in interesting tasks.

The postulate that a person's need for feelings of competence and self-determination can provide the energy for goal-directed behavior raises the important point of "What is the reward?" As was stated in Chapter 2, an activity cannot in any meaningful sense be its own reward. In line with Berlyne (1971a) I suggested that the reward is the internal state which is brought about by the behavior. Therefore, the reward is the feeling of competence and self-determination. Irwin (1971) has also asserted that states of the organism may be treated as objects of preference, thereby supporting the notion that people may choose to behave in ways which they believe will lead to certain affective states. This implies, then, that intrinsically motivated behavior operates in the same general goal-directed way as extrinsically motivated behavior.

When a person becomes aware of potential satisfaction, he makes a decision about engaging in goal-directed behavior which he expects to result in the attainment of a goal, the experience of a reward, and satisfaction. This is so whether the satisfaction comes from a reduction of hunger or from a feeling of competence and self-determination. There are, however, at least two important differences between behaviors motivated by intrinsic needs and ones motivated by primary drives.

The rewards for behavior motivated by primary drives are extrinsic—*e.g.*, food, water, etc., which replace deficits in non-nervous system tissues. For intrinsic needs the reward is the feeling of competence and self-determination which has its primary effect in the nervous system tissues. The other important difference has to do with the relation of the reward to the need. When a primary drive, such as hunger, motivates eating behavior, the goal will be attained, the behavior will be rewarded and the need will be temporarily reduced. With intrinsically motivated behavior, however, the goal will be attained and the behavior will be rewarded, but the need will not be reduced. Rather, the need is ever-present, so it will remain, and other goals will be set, unless the process is interrupted by a drive or an emotion.

I have suggested that affective states play a role both as energizers of behavior and as rewards for goal-directed behavior.

Let us now turn to a more careful consideration of the role of affect in motivational processes.

Affect

The role of emotions in human behavior has received much attention but little consensus. Young (1961), while asserting that affective processes are clearly motivational in nature, defined emotions as seriously disturbed affective processes. He did say that emotions are only one kind of affective process (some others being sensory feelings, moods, affect, interests, aversions and so on), yet a key word in the definitions of both emotion and affect is "disruption." Leeper (1948) staunchly criticized the early writings of Young (1943) and others who considered emotions to be disorganized responses.

Leeper, who does not distinguish between emotion and affect, asserted that emotions are organized responses of various intensities. For the less intense emotions, such as affection or esthetic pleasure, there is no sign of disorganization, and in very intense emotions of strong fear or anger there will be disruption of ongoing behavior, but it will be replaced by a dominating organization. By this he seems to mean some learned response or set of responses. Emotional responses whether mild or intense are seen to operate as motives. They energize, direct, and sustain behavior.

Arnold (1960) also viewed emotion as an organized motivational process. She took a more total view of emotional processes by considering perception, appraisal, emotion, expression, and behavior. Emotion is defined as an approach or avoidance tendency toward the stimulus input (which was perceived and appraised).

Antecedents and Consequences

The views of Leeper and Arnold are very important. Emotions do function as motives. Yet it is important, for a fuller understanding, to recognize that emotions are both antecedents and consequences of behaviors. In the cognitive model suggested above, an energizing element precedes behavior and a rewarding element succeeds behavior. Emotions are related to both elements of the model. If a person experiences positive affect as a result of a stimulus input, this provides information that greater positive affect and hence, greater satisfaction, can be achieved in this realm. For example, if Shirley passes a store window and sees some furniture which makes her feel excited or happy, she may become aware that more satisfaction is probably available in the store. That awareness can provide the energy for the behavior of entering the store. Similarly if Jayjay becomes anxious when she begins freeway driving, she would be aware that the anxiety could be reduced, perhaps by practicing or by giving up driving on freeways.

The antecedent emotion is information which establishes awareness of potential satisfaction. The more intense the emotion, the greater the awareness and the greater the expected satisfaction, so the more likely it is that that awareness will energize the behavior.

Affect will also follow from behavior. When a person achieves a goal, he experiences positive affect, which may be the reward, or at least part of the reward, for the activity. Hence, a person will engage in many behaviors with the aim of having positively affective experiences.

I have, in essence, taken a hedonistic position—humans are sometimes motivated by the expectation of positive, or the avoidance of negative, affect; though I am not suggesting that affect is the only motivation. Rather, the awareness of potential satisfaction which provides energy for behavior may have its roots in drives (and the expectation of satisfying the drives), in the intrinsic need for feelings of competence and self-determination (and the expectation of achieving these feelings), or in antecedent affect (and the expectation of achieving more positive, or less negative, affect).

People can, within this framework, be engaged in behaviors which they expect will lead (over the short run) to unpleasant feelings. For example, one may choose to explore a dark room when he knows that he will be in near-panic because of his fear of darkness. The reason for doing this is that he is intrinsically motivated toward feeling competent and self-determining. Going into a dark room, while aversive in its immediate sense, is aimed at helping him to overcome the fear and, thereby, to feel more competent and self-determining. Engaging in the behavior results from a choice made by the person that the behavior will eventually lead him to a desired end state which is very satisfying. The goal is exploring a dark room. The reward (and hence, satisfaction) is the feeling of competence and self-determination which results from having done that.

Affective Arousal

The assertion that emotions are both antecedents and consequences of behavior and that they often motivate behavior bears some relation to affective arousal theories (e.g., McClelland *et al.*, 1953), yet this position is much different than that of McClelland *et al.* McClelland (1965) posited that motives are affectively toned associative networks which determine behavior. Cues redintegrate affective experiences which motivate behavior.

My alternative interpretation is that stimulus inputs (i.e., cues) produce affect, which reminds the person of a past affective experience and leads him to expect future satisfaction. The affect is information which the person considers in making his choices about what behaviors to engage in. The redintegration of the affective state does not determine the behavior through associations, as McClelland said, but rather, it provides the person with information which may or may not lead to some behavior, depending on his evaluation of the various behavioral alternatives.

The second point of disagreement with affective arousal theories is that, although affect is a motivational process, it is not the only motivational process, as affective arousal theories assert.

Relation of emotion to other motives: A person's intrinsic motivation is ongoing as a motivator of behavior. Behavior motivated by primary drives may break into this ongoing sequence of behaviors. Further, behavior motivated by emotions may break into either ongoing, intrinsically motivated behavior, or behavior motivated by primary drives.

Simon (1967) submitted that emotions work like interrupt mechanisms to break into behavior and substitute new goals for the ones being pursued. He emphasized that he meant "interrupt" rather than "disrupt," thereby agreeing with the notion that emotional behavior is usually organized, motivated behavior which is adaptive for the organism.

Simon pointed out that a person will respond to real time needs in an ever-changing and unpredictable environment. An unpredicted event, such as an occurrence in which a car pulls out in front of one, represents a real time need, which interrupts the goal-directed behavior that is in progress at the time, whether the behavior is intrinsically motivated or motivated by a primary drive.

However, not all emotions call for interruption in the way that real time needs do. Behavior motivated by less intense emotions, such as esthetic pleasure, may simply be deferred to a later time when other needs are less salient.

In sum, we have seen that three kinds of processes may underlie the awareness of potential satisfaction which energizes behavior: (1) drives, (2) intrinsic needs for feelings of competence and self-determination, and (3) affective responses to stimulus inputs. Further, intrinsically motivated behavior will be ongoing in a person's interaction with the environment. It will be interrupted when a primary drive becomes sufficiently salient. Finally, affective processes may interrupt either intrinsically motivated behavior or behavior motivated by primary drives if the affective processes are real time needs. They will be queued up if they are not sufficiently salient to interrupt.

Peak (1955) has discussed a similar framework for viewing the energization question; however, she spoke of disparity between two processes as the basis of motivation. The two processes must be similar enough to be two parts of a person's cognitive structure, but they must be disparate enough to motivate behavior. These processes, she said, may be either affective or nonaffective, which is also true of the current conceptualization. My interpretation of her postulate is that awareness of potential satisfaction would result from a disparity between a stimulus input and some other element, such as an adaptation level, an expectation of an affective state, etc., though I have not focused on the notion of disparity. Nonetheless, the present conceptualization is quite compatible with that of Peak (1955), since awarenesses of potential satisfaction implies a disparity between the present state of the organism and some potential state.

At any given time a person has some set of potential energizers, i.e., awareness of potential satisfaction, and these awarenesses provide the basis for the establishment of goals. The person then chooses a behavior which he expects will lead him to the end state which is preferred. However, at any time that he is pursuing the most preferred goal, the situation may change in such a way that some other awareness interrupts the process and leads the person to engage in some other behavior whose goal becomes more preferred at that moment.

Goal Selection

The third element in the cognitive model involves the person's evaluation of the various alternative behaviors open to him, on the basis of his expectations of the end states to which the behaviors would lead. For example, if Ann experiences hunger, she is aware of the potential satisfaction from reduction of that hunger. She could set a number of possible goals whose accomplishment would, to some extent, reduce hunger. She could prepare and eat a meal, she could eat something sweet, she could drink something, etc. Each of these goals requires some goal-directed behavior or set of behaviors. It is the person's task at Stage Three of the cognitive model to evaluate these end states and select the one which is most valent.

The second element of the model "awareness of potential satisfaction" is independent of goals and behaviors. In the hunger example, the awareness is that "hunger could be reduced" not that "eating would reduce hunger." However, although the awareness is independent of behaviors and end states, the awareness is what provides the basis for evaluation of the end states. The most preferred end state will be the one which gives the greatest satisfaction at the least cost, i.e., which is most valent.

At the beginning of this chapter we saw that Tolman spoke of positive and negative goals and that Lewin spoke of goals having valence. Their work provided the basis for subsequent models which dealt in more detail with the evaluation of end states. We will now review two of these models which are frequently referred to as instrumentality or expectancy theories. They have been used in predicting achievement oriented behavior (Atkinson, 1964; Atkinson & Feather, 1966) and in predicting behavior in organizational or industrial settings, (e.g., Georgopoulos, Mahoney, & Jones,

1957; Vroom, 1964; Porter & Lawler, 1968; Galbraith & Cummings, 1967).

Atkinson's Model

Atkinson (1957, 1964) has specified a mathematical relationship between what he considers to be the various determinants of achievement behavior. We saw in Chapter 3 that achievement motivation is a special case of intrinsic motivation, that is, achievement motivation differentiates out of the basic motivational propensity of needing to feel competent and self-determining in relation to the environment. Hence, with Atkinson's model one can make precise predictions about certain kinds of intrinsically motivated behaviors. My aim in this chapter is to present a framework for incorporating both intrinsically and extrinsically motivated behaviors into a cognitive theory. Doing so will have the advantage of being more inclusive than Atkinson's theory but will have the disadvantage of being less precise.

Atkinson's theory asserts that the tendency to approach (or avoid) an achievement-related situation is the resultant tendency to approach success and to avoid failure.

One's tendency to approach success is a function of the motive for success, the probability of success, and the incentive value of success.

The motive for success (M_s) is simply one's need for achievement, that is, one's need to match some standard of excellence. This is a relatively stable personality characteristic which, according to McClelland (1965), develops from the association of achievement cues to positive affect. It is generally assessed by scoring story responses to the Thematic Apperception Test (Murray, 1943) for achievement imagery (see Appendix I of Atkinson, 1958 for details of scoring procedures).

Hence, in Atkinson's theory, the value of M_s is a constant within a person and across situations. It will be manifest when the situation allows the person to feel responsible for the outcome (i.e., when it is personally caused rather than environmentally caused), when there is feedback of results, and when there is some risk of failing.

Probability of success (P_s) is one's expectancy of achieving the goal. As Atkinson (1964) pointed out, this concept derives from Tolman's notion of "expectancy of goal." A person's expectation about reaching a goal through a given behavior will be based on his experience in similar situations in the past. This is represented by a subjective probability of success and takes on values from 0 to 1.00, representing certainty of not succeeding, on the one hand, and certainty of succeeding, on the other. One's estimation of the probability of success is determined from whatever information is available to him. As we said above, Atkinson asserted that it is based on past experiences. This follows closely from Tolman's belief that expectancy of goal is determined by the number of previously rewarded trials which a rat has had in maze learning. It also relates closely to McClelland's theory that the development of associations between cues and affect is critical in motivation and that these associations develop through past experience. However, in putting into operation the concept of probability of success for experimental purposes, Atkinson and others have done this in a variety of ways, most notably by presenting the probability of success to the subjects.

Incentive value of success (I_s) relates to the pride a person will feel in achieving the goal. This value depends on the difficulty of the goal. The accomplishment of a difficult goal has greater incentive value than the accomplishment of an easy goal. In fact, Atkinson has proposed that incentive value of success is equal to one minus the probability of success ($I_s = 1 - P_s$). This shows quite clearly the importance of "achievement" *per se,* in Atkinson's theory. For Lewin, Vroom, and others the *valence of a goal* is a general term referring to the psychological value of a goal. This may be unrelated, or related in a small way, to the difficulty of the goal in their theories, whereas for Atkinson the valence of the goal is a function of the probability of success.

Combining the elements of the tendency to approach success (T_s) yields:

$$T_s = M_s \times P_s \times I_s$$

It should be noted, since I_s is equal to $(1 - P_s)$, that T_s will be greatest when $P_s = .5$ since $(.5)^2$ is greater than $P_s(1 - P_s)$ when P_s takes on any other value between 0 and 1. So a person will have a strong tendency to approach moderately risky situations, and this tendency will be particularly pronounced in people with high motives for success. These predictions have received support from an earlier study of risk-taking behavior in children (McClelland, 1958).

The second major component in Atkinson's theory of the resultant tendency toward achieving is one's fear of failure, or tendency to avoid failure (T_{af}). Like the tendency to approach success, the tendency to avoid failure is determined by three factors combined in a multiplicative way. They are: motive to avoid failure, expectancy about failure, and the incentive value of failure.

The motive to avoid failure (M_{af}) is also a relatively stable personality factor. It relates to one's desire to avoid negatively affective situations, such as failure situations, which cause shame, and is generally measured by tests of anxiety. The probability of failure (P_f) is one's expectations about failure and is equal to $(1 - P_s)$. In other words, it is assumed that the probability of success and the probability of failure sum to 1.0.

Finally, the incentive value of failure (I_f) reflects the value a person places on avoiding failure in achieving the particular goal being sought. It is a negative value, since it is assumed to be aversive. The emotions of shame and embarrassment accompany failure, and it is assumed that the easier the task (i.e., the lower P_f) the greater the shame and the greater the incentive to avoid failure. Hence, with easy tasks the incentive value of failure will be strongly negative. This all implies that incentive value of failure (I_f) = $-(1 - P_f)$.

The tendency to avoid failure (T_{af}) then becomes: $T_{af} = M_{af} \times P_f \times I_f$ and will be a negative number. In other words, the tendency to avoid failure represents the person's tendency *not* to perform the activity, so that he can avoid failing at it.

The resultant tendency to approach or avoid an achievement situation (T_a) is equal to the tendency to approach success plus the tendency to avoid failure (the latter being a negative number):

$$T_a = (M_s \times P_s \times I_s) + (M_{af} \times P_f \times I_f)$$

If T_s is greater than $-T_{af}$, the person will approach the situation (i.e., engage in the behavior), but if $-T_{af}$ is greater than T_s he will avoid the situation.

It can be shown, through algebraic manipulations that the resultant tendency to approach or avoid is equivalent to

$$T_a = (M_s - M_{af})(P_s \times (1 - P_s))$$

In other words, a person's tendency to achieve depends on the two independent personality factors of motive to succeed and motive to avoid failure, on the one hand, and the more immediate and unstable factor of probability of success, on the other hand. Probability of success, of course, relates to both a person's ability and the difficulty of the task, so Atkinson's model has considered factors related to the person and to the environment, which is one of Lewin's basic postulates.

Atkinson's model, while based on the general motivational notions of Lewin and Tolman, is specific to achievement situations. The components of the model are stable achievement-related motives and less stable achievement-related incentives. In other words, his model predicts achievement behavior based on achievement motivational concepts. Hence, the focus of the model is to predict behavior on the basis of one kind of intrinsic motivation. All of the emphasis is on the intrinsic satisfaction of achieving. Since achievement motivation is a special case of the intrinsic motive for feelings of competence and self-determination, I am proposing that a cognitive model can be developed which would be broader than Atkinson's and therefore would incorporate intrinsically motivated behaviors which are not achievement oriented.

Furthermore, it is important to recognize that many behaviors are motivated at least in part by extrinsic rewards. A cognitive model of motivation would need to include extrinsic, as well as intrinsic motivation to be complete. Feather (1961) pointed out that even in achievement situations there are extrinsic rewards for behaviors and that an account of the tendency to approach or avoid an achievement situation must include the tendency to do a task for extrinsic reasons (T_{ext}). Hence, Atkinson's final formulation included that as follows:

$$T_a = T_s + T_{af} + T_{ext}$$

The extrinsic component of the model has received virtually no attention, yet it does set a precedent for the development of a model which is concerned with both intrinsic and extrinsic motivation.

Vroom's Model

Vroom's model, developed within the realm of industrial motivation, focuses primarily on the extrinsic aspects of motivation.

Vroom (1964) was concerned with force toward action (i.e., the motivation to do a particular act) and began with the assumption that any act could lead to a variety of outcomes. The force toward some action (F_i) is determined by the valence of each of these outcomes (V_j) and the expectancy that the action will lead to each of the outcomes (E_{ij}). The expectancy notion is, like Atkinson's, a subjective probability ranging from 0 to 1. The specific proposition is that the force toward the ith action is a function of the algebraic sum of the valence of each outcome (V_j) multiplied by the expectancy that action i will lead to outcome j:

$$F_i = f\left[\sum_{j=1}^{n} E_{ij} \times V_j \right]$$

The expectation is simply a probability estimation; however, the determination of valence is somewhat complicated, and it is here that we observe the great importance placed on extrinsic motivation.

Valence of an outcome (V_j) is determined by (1) the valence (V_k) of all other outcomes (call them second order outcomes) which outcome j might help one achieve, and (2) the instrumentality of outcome j for achieving each second-order outcome k. Specifically, the model asserts that the valence of outcome j is a function of the algebraic sum of the valence of each outcome k multiplied by the instrumentality of outcome j for achieving each outcome k:

$$V_j = f\left[\sum_{k=1}^{n} V_k \times I_{jk} \right]$$

The instrumentality can take on values between -1 and $+1$. It represents a person's belief about whether or not one outcome will help him attain some other outcome. In other words, Vroom has asserted that outcomes have valence only in relation to other outcomes to which they lead a person. An outcome's valence depends on the consequences of that outcome.

The formal statement of Vroom's model is somewhat complex, so let us consider an example: Suppose we are interested in assessing one's motivation (i.e., force toward action) for applying for a job in the psychology department of Campus X of the University of California. We must begin by enumerating all of the possible outcomes that could follow from this behavior. It could lead to (1) his getting that job, (2) his getting a free trip to California for an interview, (3) his meeting several noted psychologists who work there, (4) his hearing about other available jobs, (5) his spending some time and money on the application procedure, (6) etc.

Once these are enumerated, he must assign valence to each of the outcomes, and he will do that in accordance with the consequences of the outcomes. Take as an illustration the first-order outcome of getting a free trip to California. What are the potential consequences of this outcome? Perhaps they are (1) missing the opportunity to participate in a symposium, (2) having a chance to visit with friends in California, (3) getting a few days away from Wisconsin snow to enjoy California sunshine, (4) avoiding an unpleasant meeting which will be held while he's away, (5) etc. Now, each of these second-order outcomes has a valence, and there is also an instrumentality that the first-order outcome of getting a trip to California will lead to the second-order outcomes. For example, it may not be a certainty that he'd get to visit friends, since they may be out of town or his own trip may have to be too short; maybe the instrumentality is .8. This would be multiplied by the valence of the second-order outcome of seeing his friends, and so on for the other second-order outcomes. After all the second-order outcomes have been assigned valence and the instrumentalities have been determined, it is possible to determine the valence of the first-order outcomes. For example, it's now possible to determine the valence of "getting a free trip to California for an interview." The person will then proceed in a similar fashion to determine the valence of the other first order outcomes, such as getting the job, meeting famous psychologists, etc.

Finally, when the valences of all first-order outcomes have been determined, we can determine the motivation to make the application. To do this we need to determine the subjective probabilities that making application will lead to each outcome. For example, the probability of getting the job may be .08, of getting an interview trip, .19, etc. Then, the contribution of the outcome "getting the job" to the force toward applying is the product of the valence of getting the job and the probability of getting the job. When each of these has been computed, the summation is a numerical representation of the motivation to perform the activity.

There are a number of points which might be raised about this model. First, there is no mention of the intrinsic value of the attainment of first-order outcomes. Galbraith and Cummings (1967) have suggested that Vroom's model can be modified to include the notion of intrinsic rewards. They suggested that the valence of first-level outcomes is determined by the function proposed by Vroom, plus a function of the valence of the intrinsic rewards. This notion (like the addition of the extrinsic component to the Atkinson model) has received relatively little attention, yet this, too, suggests that it is important to include both intrinsic and extrinsic outcomes in a cognitive model of motivation.

A second point about the Vroom model is that there is no discussion of how second-order outcomes take on valence. It is possible that a first-order outcome in one situation may be a second-order outcome in another situation, so when it's a first-order outcome the valence is computed in the complex way mentioned above, but when it's a second-order, apparently one is supposed to know its valence. The other possibility (aside from knowing the valence) is that second-order outcomes take on valence in the same manner that first order outcomes do. But if this were so, we would have an infinite regression of valences and instrumentalities, leaving one with confusion. This problem is a conceptual one. However, in applying the model, it may not be such a problem as it seems. In studies using the Vroom model, the valence of second-order outcomes is generally assessed by self-report scales. While it may be that these second-order valences are due in large part to their own instrumentality for attaining still other outcomes, apparently people have some sense of the valences of the second-order outcomes and are able to report them.

Comparison of Expectancy Models

The commonality in the theories of Atkinson and Vroom is the assertion that behavior is, in large part, determined by a multiplicative relation between one's expectation about attaining a goal and the valence of that goal. This commonality points out quite clearly that both theories derive from the earlier work of Tolman who posited that one's expectancy of a goal and demand for a goal mediate between stimuli and responses. Further, this commonality can be seen in the work of Lewin who asserted that behavior is affected by the valence of a goal and the person's knowledge about the path to that goal. Lewin's concept of "potency" really refers to one's expectancy of achieving success.

There are, however, substantial differences between the theories. First, as we have seen, Atkinson's model includes an individual difference component, while Vroom's model does not. For Vroom, one's achievement motive, and other stable factors, are not considered directly, though they may, in some unknown way, be reflected in one's assignment of valence to outcomes so that they would not need to be considered as a separate variable. If so, this needs to be addressed directly.

A second difference is in the incentive value and valence notions. For Atkinson, the value of attaining a goal has to do with goal attainment *per se,* whereas for Vroom it has to do with the consequences of attaining the goal. This points up the main conceptual difference between the two theories, which was already mentioned; Atkinson focused on one kind of intrinsic motivation (achievement motivation) while Vroom focused on extrinsic motivation. However, alterations have been suggested that would permit both models to consider intrinsic and extrinsic motivation.

A final difference is that Atkinson has posited a relationship between expectancy and incentive value (*viz.,* $I = 1 - P$), whereas Vroom has not addressed this issue. One is left to assume that Vroom considers them independent. If so, this highlights a differential prediction made by the two theories.

Imagine a situation where a person is striving for some goal. Atkinson's model predicts clearly that motivation would be at a maximum when the goal was of moderate difficulty. The probability of success of a moderately difficult task is about .5, and the formula for predicting motivation, using Atkinson's model, shows motivation to be at a maximum when probability of success is .5. In Vroom's model, however, motivation (i.e., force toward action) is an inverse function of difficulty. As the probability of success increases, motivation increases. Therefore, using Vroom's model, the prediction would be that motivation would be maximum when the goal was easiest (assuming constant valence).

It is interesting, also, at this point to consider the work of Locke (1968), for his prediction in the situation just mentioned would be that motivation would be at a maximum when the goals were most difficult. Locke's theory places primary importance on goal setting and asserts that goals are the most critical factor in motivation. Further, his studies show that there is a positive relationship between difficulty of goal and motivation.

Each of these theories has a reasonable amount of support from the experimental literature. It is not our purpose here to review that literature. Rather, we shall consider some similarities and differences between the theories and then discuss the possibility of reconciling the positions. While it is true that one could design a critical experiment, the evidence suggests that each theory has merit, since each has received empirical support. Hence, it seems more reasonable to try either to reconcile the theories or to discover the circumstances in which each might be most predictive.

Considering first the work of Locke and Atkinson, we see that for Atkinson the incentive value of a goal is a direct function of goal difficulty, though, of course, motivation has a curvilinear relationship to goal difficulty, since motivation is a function of difficulty (stated as the probability of success) times (1-probability of success). For Locke, motivation is a direct function of goal difficulty. To investigate this question, one must take great pains to differentiate these concepts. In becoming operational, the constructs often lose precision and since goal, incentive value, and motivation are such closely related constructs, it is sometimes not clear which construct is being considered.

In one study Atkinson (1958) found a curvilinear relation between probability of winning and performance (which presumably reflects T_a). This finding is consistent with his model, and on the face of it, inconsistent with Locke's. However, there was no assessment of goals so again it is difficult to use that study as a test of the two models. Further, there was no operational assessment of incentive value, though the extraneous variable of monetary incentives was introduced. Then, as Locke pointed out, McClelland (1961) was unable to replicate the Atkinson finding and, in fact, found results which support Locke's position. It would seem that the issue is still open.

To contrast the three models it is important to make the intrinsic-extrinsic distinction more clear. Intrinsically motivated behavior is behavior which is motivated by a need for feelings of competence and self-determination. One way that this is manifest is in achievement situations, though it is operative in many other ways. When behavior is intrinsically motivated, people seek out challenging situations; conquering them leads to feelings of competence and self-determination. Yet if a person attempts too difficult a task he is likely to experience failure and frustration which (as we will see in Chapter 5) causes decrements in both intrinsic motivation and performance. This is similar to Piaget's notion (1952) that children seek situations which are assimilable but not completely so; that is, that they seek challenging situations. But too challenging a situation will not be assimilable and so, will tend to be avoided. This also relates to the Yerkes–Dodson (1908) finding that there is an "inverted U" relationship between motivation and performance.

Since performance, motivation, incentive, and goal are so closely related, it is not possible to sort them out in most studies. For example, the Atkinson (1958) study used performance as the dependent measure. Yet Atkinson's later model is posited in terms of "Tendency to approach or avoid," which is a motivational, rather than a performance, construct. Given the Yerkes–Dodson assertion about the "inverted U" relationship between performance and motivation, and the Atkinson assertion about the "inverted U" relationship between difficulty and motivation, it is difficult to tell which assertion received support from the Atkinson (1958) study. Hence, the issue, needs careful study.

I suspect that intrinsic motivation will be directly related to challenge or task difficulty up to some point beyond which it will drop off. This is close to Atkinson's prediction, though I am making no specific mathematic formulation. It may indeed be that the optimal challenge is more difficult than 50%, in which case the answer lies somewhere between Atkinson and Locke. Further, as Locke pointed out, a person will be motivated only if he accepts some goal. Hence, if a task is too difficult, he may very well not accept it as "his goal." So, there may be a direct relationship between intrinsic motivation and difficulty of *accepted goal,* and the apparent curvilinear relationship may be due to the fact that the performer never really accepted the very difficult goals.

All of this discussion would seem to contradict the derivation from the Vroom model which predicts a negative relationship between difficulty and motivation. However, this is not the case. We have been considering intrinsically motivated behavior where "the challenge" plays an important part. Vroom, however, was considering extrinsically motivated situations. It makes perfectly good sense that if a person were doing something for an extrinsic reward and saw two paths open, an easy path and a difficult path, he'd take the easy path, as Vroom suggests. Were a person intrinsically motivated, he would be likely to choose a difficult path, since that has potential for greatest intrinsic reward (i.e., feelings of competence and self-determination), but if he were extrinsically motivated, he would take the easier path because that increases his chance of getting a desired external reward.

In sum, one's extrinsic motivation seems to increase as the desired reward becomes easier to achieve. However, his intrinsic motivation increases as the goal difficulty increases, up to some optimal level. The problem in real life situations is that both kinds of motivations are operative. So, the findings become very complex.

Goals, Outcomes, and Rewards

In this discussion of various theories I have used several different words which may cause confusion. Let us now clarify the meaning of these words in relation to the present cognitive framework for studying motivated behavior.

People engage in goal-directed behavior which they expect will be followed by some reward. By *goal* I mean the completion of some behavior or set of behaviors. A reward is not the same thing as a goal. Goals lead to rewards. A reward, on the other hand, can be an extrinsic reward, such as money or praise, or it can be an internal affective state. In the former case, satisfaction follows the reward; in the latter case, it is more difficult to separate reward and satisfaction. In fact, I will consider them synonymous in the case of affective rewards. Included in the category of affective rewards are intrinsic rewards, since intrinsic rewards are feelings of competence and self-determination. The distinction between goals and rewards highlights the point made in Chapter 2 that intrinsically motivated activities cannot be their own rewards. A person can perform an activity or accomplish a goal, but that is not the reward; the reward is the internal condition brought about by the attainment of the goal (i.e., the satisfaction).

The term *goal* as I have used it, relates closely to the notion of first-order outcomes in the Vroom sense, though Vroom spoke of one behavior's leading to several outcomes. These various first-order outcomes are aspects of the goal, and any goal may have several aspects. These aspects may be subgoals—that is, milestones in a chain of behaviors—or they may occur simultaneously upon the completion of the behaviors.

Simon (1967) has said that a goal need not be a unitary thing. He used the example of a man's dressing in a dinner jacket for a roast beef dinner. The goal, suggested Simon, could as easily be to dine in a dinner jacket as to satisfy hunger. I agree with Simon and would say the goal is the completion of this composite of behaviors which has many aspects (dining in formal wear, eating, etc.). In so doing a person can be satisfying many needs. Translating this last sentence into our language yields that a person will have awareness of many potential satisfactions and that he will choose a goal which may allow him to achieve many of these satisfactions. There will be many aspects to the goal (i.e., first-order outcomes), and these will lead to many rewards/satisfactions.

Atkinson's use of the term *goal* is similar to mine. Someone motivated to achieve will be striving to accomplish some behavior or set of behaviors. This goal may have many aspects though Atkinson's basic model considers achievement only. When expanded to include extrinsic tendencies, it comes very close to our scheme.

Irwin (1971) referred to outcomes as states which follow behaviors. Outcomes could be internal states. Therefore, he used

TABLE II. *The Relation of Our Terms (Goal, Reward, and Satisfaction) to the Terms of Other Authors*

Author	Goal	Reward	Satisfaction
Vroom (1964)	First-order outcomes (A goal is a composite of first-order outcomes)	Second-order outcomes	
Simon (1967)	Goal(s)		
Atkinson (1964)	Goal		
Irwin (1971)		Outcomes	Outcomes

the term to refer either to rewards or satisfaction. Finally, Vroom's use of second-order outcomes closely relates to my use of the term extrinsic rewards. He used second-order outcomes to refer to external consequences of first-order outcomes (i.e., goals). I would say that extrinsic rewards are the external consequences of goals. See Table II.

In this section of the chapter we have considered research and theory related to goal selection. We turn now to the fourth aspect of the cognitive framework—goal-directed behavior.

Goal-Directed Behavior

This aspect of the model is a direct corollary of a basic assumption of cognitive theories of motivation, namely, that people behave in ways which they expect will lead them to desired goals.

Irwin (1971) has proposed that an organism will select the behavior which it expects will lead to a desired outcome. His use of outcomes is roughly equivalent to our use of rewards, so this means that organisms behave in ways that they expect to lead to rewards.

I assert that organisms engage in behaviors which lead to the most valent goals. Since goals take on valence in accordance with the rewards—either affective or extrinsic—which accrue from the attainment of the goal, this assertion is very similar to Irwin's.

For Atkinson, people would behave in accord with the highest tendency to approach. In other words, behavior is a direct function of (T_a). Similarly, Vroom predicts that people will engage in the behaviors which have the greatest force toward action.

People, then, behave so as to achieve desired goals. However, this raises the question of how goal directed behavior will be terminated.

There are several conditions which can lead to the termination of goal-directed behavior. The first has already been discussed. Awarenesses of potential satisfaction resulting from primary drives can interrupt intrinsically motivated behavior, and awareness resulting from real time emotional needs can interrupt either of the first two. In other words, at any given time goals can take on different valences in accordance with changes in the person's awareness of potential satisfaction. For example, after several hours of not eating while working on a puzzle, a person will become aware of potential satisfaction from reducing his hunger. This will lead to a reevaluation of the valences of the puzzle solving *vs.* the eating goals and may lead to a shift in behaviors.

The second involves goal attainment. As a person behaves, he is aware of his goal and is continually comparing his current state to the goal. Miller, Galanter, and Pribram (1960) have dealt with this in detail in their TOTE unit. This mechanism, which was discussed in Chapter 2, compares inputs to standards (I am proposing that these standards are goals). If there is congruity, the behavior terminates; if not, the organism operates.

Simon (1967) has enumerated three other termination mechanisms. *Satisficing* refers to terminating when a goal has been achieved well enough. This, however, it seems, has to do primarily with goal selection. In other words, in house hunting, a person can either search for the "perfect" house regardless of how long it takes, or he can take the first house he finds which meets a minimum set of requirements. This is a goal-setting strategy and relates to a person's assignment of valence to outcomes based on his own potential satisfaction: e.g., he may be very satisfied by getting the chore over with, quickly.

The other two mechanisms for termination which Simon discussed are closely related—"impatience" and "discouragement." When a person becomes impatient, he may select the best alternative thus far, and terminate. If he has tried and failed, he may give up in discouragement. This simply means that an affect is experienced which in turn motivates new behavior that causes termination of the previous goal-directed behavior. An emotional state resulting from failing to achieve the goal fully (as represented either by impatience or discouragement) may interrupt the goal-directed behavior, resulting in termination.

Rewards and Satisfaction

I have already mentioned several points related to the final elements in the cognitive model—rewards and satisfaction. I asserted that people seek goals which they expect to bring rewards. The rewards may be (1) extrinsic rewards which relate to drives, (2) intrinsic rewards which relate to the need for feelings of competence and self-determination, (3) changes in affect which are relatively positive by comparison with the affect which initiated the behavior.

Conceptually, satisfaction follows the reward. When a person is rewarded for achieving a goal, he will feel satisfied. In fact, in the case of intrinsic or affective rewards, it is difficult to separate out the positive affect which is the reward from the feelings of satisfaction. Still, we can think of the satisfaction as following the feeling which is the reward. The satisfaction is the final step in the sequence, and will lead to termination of the sequence. The termination is of that particular goal-directed sequence which was initiated by an awareness of potential satisfaction.

There are, however, feedback mechanisms in the model. The satisfaction will be feedback to the "awareness of potential satisfaction" element. If the two do not match, the person may begin another sequence, by setting a new goal. For example, if a person is "hungry," his goal-directed sequence will be energized by his awareness of potential satisfaction of the hunger drive. The goal might be to have a pastrami sandwich and a glass of milk. However, the achievement of the goal may not produce the satisfaction which was expected, so a new sequence may begin leading him to a piece of banana cream pie. If the satisfaction matches the expectation, then that particular awareness will no longer serve as an energizer.

In other words, the achievement of a goal will terminate a goal-directed sequence of behavior, but only an achievement of expected satisfaction will dismiss the awareness that energized the sequence. I am suggesting therefore that a second kind of TOTE mechanism is operative. The first one, which is a subroutine, compares the behavior to the goal and exits when the goal has been achieved. The TOTE mechanism now being discussed compares the satisfaction to the potential satisfaction and exits when the two match. Of course, one will remember that the process may be interrupted at any time if some other awareness of potential satisfaction becomes sufficiently salient.

It is interesting to note the difference between intrinsic and extrinsic motivation in this regard. If an extrinsically motivated activity leads to the expected satisfaction of a primary drive, that will mean the drive will not be operative for some period of time. Since primary drives operate largely in a cyclical fashion related to homeostasis, the achievement of the goal, and hence the satisfaction, means that the need will be in equilibrium for some period following the satisfaction. With intrinsically motivated behavior this is often not the case. A person is in continual interaction with the environment and has a continual need for feelings of competence and self-determination; hence, when satisfaction is achieved a new awareness will arise which can energize a new sequence if a basic drive or an affective experience is not more salient at that time.

There are other feedback mechanisms as well. In Chapters 5 and 6 we will consider research which shows that extrinsic rewards may affect a person's intrinsic motivation. That is, there is feedback

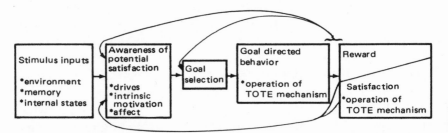

FIGURE 7. Schematic representation of a cognitive model of motivated behavior.

from the behavior—reward linkage which affects the person's later goal selection and awareness of potential satisfaction. For example, we will see in Chapter 5 that when someone is paid for doing an intrinsically motivated activity, he may lose intrinsic motivation for that activity. This means that at a later point the activity will no longer be one which he selects as a goal for satisfying his intrinsic needs for feelings of competence and self-determination.

Model Summary

In summarizing the cognitive framework (Figure 7) I will consider the important motivational questions of instigation, energizing, directing, and terminating behavior.

The model begins with stimulus inputs which may come from the environment, memory or internal sources such as blood sugar level, feelings, etc.

These stimulus inputs set up in the person an "awareness of potential satisfaction" which instigates and energizes a goal-directed sequence. The awareness may be that the person could (a) satisfy a drive, (b) satisfy the intrinsic need for feelings of competence and self-determination (or any of the specific motives that develop out of this basic motivational propensity), or (c) increase his positive (or decrease his negative) affect.

These awarenesses cause the person to establish goals which he expects will lead to the rewards, and hence the satisfaction, which he became aware of in the previous step.

The goals lead to goal-directed behavior. This means of course that the goals provide the direction for the behavior, and the behavior is terminated when the goal is achieved.

Behavior may be followed by rewards (extrinsic, intrinsic, or affective) which lead to satisfaction. If the satisfaction matches the person's awareness of potential satisfaction, which initiated the sequence, the awareness will be dismissed. If not, the awareness may lead to the establishment of a new sequence of goal-directed behavior.

A sequence may be interrupted at any time that the person's awareness of potential satisfaction changes. Specifically, I have asserted that intrinsically motivated behavior is ongoing and continuous unless interrupted. It will frequently be interrupted by awareness deriving out of primary drives. Further behavior motivated both by intrinsic needs and primary drives will be interrupted by real time emotional responses such as fear of a stone which the person sees coming at him.

There are feedback loops in the model. Satisfaction is feedback to the awareness step of the model. This can either dismiss that awareness as an energizer if the two match, or it can lead to the establishment of a new goal. Also, the link between behavior of rewards will provide feedback which can affect one's intrinsic motivation and his establishment of goals which were energized by one's intrinsic need for feelings of competence and self-determination.

Operationalization

The outline of motivated behavior which has been sketched in this chapter is a broad conceptual framework intended to provide a means for incorporating intrinsically, extrinsically, and affectively motivated behaviors into one system.

It is not, however, a theory in that it has not been operationalized or stated as a testable proposition (Nagel, 1961). Rather, I have presented a general outline and used existing work to explicate the various elements of the outline. In order to have predictive or explanatory power, the outline will need to be operationalized with measures, precise postulates, limiting conditions, and so on. It is not my purpose here to do that. Such operationalization will require a substantial amount of rigorous research. I have offered the outline as a starting point for such efforts.

Summary

This chapter has presented a general framework for the understanding of human motivation. It asserted that people choose behaviors which they believe will lead them to desired goals.

Energy for the behavior comes from "an awareness of potential satisfaction" which develops out of stimulus inputs to the central nervous system from the environment, memory, or internal states.

When a person achieves his goal, rewards follow which in turn provide satisfaction. If that satisfaction matches the original awareness, the sequences are terminated. If not, new goals will be established to provide the satisfaction.

Intrinsically motivated behaviors are ones which a person engages in to provide himself with a sense of competence and self-determination. These behaviors are ongoing in the person's interaction with his environment. However, they may be interrupted by extrinsically or affectively motivated behavior.

Extrinsically motivated behaviors are related to basic drives which generally operate in a cyclical fashion to interrupt the ongoing intrinsically motivated behavior.

Affectively motivated behavior is initiated when a person is aware that he could have a more positive or less negative feeling than he has at that time. He then chooses to behave in a way which he expects to produce relatively more positive affect. Affectively motivated behavior may be a response to real time needs which impinge on the person from the environment, or it may consist of less urgent desires for esthetically pleasing experiences. Real time needs will interrupt either intrinsically or extrinsically motivated behaviors.

We also considered how choices of behaviors might be made, and in this regard we reviewed specific models by Atkinson and Vroom.

Finally, I pointed out that the chapter presented a general outline of motivation, rather than a specific theory. The latter will require a substantial amount of empirical work.

II

EXTRINSIC REWARDS AND INTRINSIC MOTIVATION

5

Cognitive Evaluation Theory: Effects of Extrinsic Rewards on Intrinsic Motivation

If a person who is intrinsically motivated to do something begins to receive an extrinsic reward for it, what will happen to his intrinsic motivation? When Nancy entered school and began to receive A's and gold stars for doing well on tests, what happened to her intrinsic motivation for learning? Did the grades and stars make her more intrinsically motivated to learn, did they make her less intrinsically motivated, or did they have no effect on her? When Lou's mother told her she'd be punished if she didn't practice the piano regularly, what happened to her intrinsic motivation to play the piano? Was it increased, decreased, or unchanged?

Woodworth (1918) and Allport (1937) have posited that many activities regardless of their initiating motive can become intrinsically interesting. So, for example, if Louise began to wash floors because she was paid for it, she might develop an intrinsic interest in that activity. Allport called this phenomenon "functional autonomy." This does not speak directly to the question of whether the introduction of extrinsic rewards will affect a person when he is engaging in an activity which he already experiences as intrinsically interesting. However, it is a short extrapolation from their assertion to the hypothesis that external rewards will enhance a person's intrinsic motivation, even for an activity which is already intrinsically motivated. Some support for this hypothesis is provided by a study from the Harlow primate laboratory. Davis, Settlage, and Harlow (1950) had monkeys solve an intrinsically interesting puzzle apparatus for no extrinsic reward. Then during a second period they introduced an incentive—they put a raisin inside the apparatus every ten minutes. Finally, the raisins were withheld. The investigators reported that, when the food was given to monkeys for working on the puzzle apparatus, there was an initial disruption, but then performance was better after the disruption than it had been during or before food was introduced. That is, except for an initial disruption of performance, monkeys solved the puzzle more quickly and with less error after food was withheld than they had before it was introduced.

Although this study seems to support the hypothesis that rewards enhance intrinsic motivation, these results seem to be more reasonably interpreted in terms of resistance to extinction. Often in conditioning studies with animals there is a period following removal of reinforcements in which there is increased responding. This does not represent an increase in intrinsic motivation but simply an increased effort to get the reward—i.e. a resistance to extinction. However, since monkeys do not have the same cognitive abilities as man, motivational processes are different for monkeys than for humans. Humans would be less susceptible to the phenomenon of resistance to extinction, since, once they have understood that rewards will not follow their behaviors, they will not continue to emit the behaviors. Monkeys, however, do not seem to have the same ability to understand about contingencies and make choices about what behaviors to engage in. In sum, then, the Davis *et al.* results seem to be best interpreted in terms of resistance to extinction, though the phenomenon would not occur for humans in the same situation.

Behavioral learning theorists would also predict that the introduction and subsequent removal of extrinsic rewards would increase persistence and performance on an activity. They would not, of course, speak of it as the enhancement of intrinsic motivation, but nonetheless, the behavioral consequences would be the same. There are two mechanisms which behaviorists would use to account for their prediction: resistance to extinction and secondary reinforcement (cf. Keller, 1969). Secondary reinforcement, which was considered in Chapter 2, is simply a process whereby the continued pairing of an activity with a reward strengthens the reinforcing properties of the activity. Aronfreed (1968) summarized many studies which demonstrated that behaviors persist after intermittent rewards have been removed. This, he suggested, supports the notion that internal control of behavior develops through reinforcement of that behavior. In sum, there is some theoretical justification for predicting that extrinsic rewards will enhance intrinsic motivation; however, there is very little experimental evidence for this prediction, and all of that evidence has been obtained from studies with animals. These findings seem to be more reasonably accounted for by resistance to extinction.

Another hypothesis which has been suggested is that extrinsic rewards will decrease intrinsic motivation. De Charms (1968) suggested that external rewards cause a person to lose his feeling of personal causality and make him a "pawn" to the rewards. This would, of course, leave him less intrinsically motivated. Festinger (1967) proposed that external rewards affect a person's concept of why he is working and lead him to believe that he is working for the rewards. Both theorists cite the work of Harlow as support for their assertions. These studies employed the same puzzle apparatus as the Davis *et al.* study, and monkeys solved the puzzles for no rewards (i.e., they were intrinsically motivated). Harlow, Harlow, and Meyer (1950) reported that when a raisin was placed inside the puzzle apparatus of four monkeys, there was a disruption effect, that is, the four monkeys made more errors in opening the puzzles to get at the food than a control group which got no food. Gately (1950) observed four monkeys using the same apparatus for periods of 5 minutes each and reported that, when a raisin was placed inside the puzzle, they responded more in the first minute of the 5-minute period than in the last minute.

These studies do seem to support the hypothesis that extrinsic rewards decrease intrinsic motivation. However, the results are equivocal. Since the observation periods were only 5 minutes, the phenomenon which they reported may have been a disruption effect which would last only a short time. Indeed, the Davis *et al.* study (1950) from the same laboratory lends support to this speculation. Hence, although the Harlow *et al.* and Gately studies showed a short-term interruption in performance following the introduction of an extrinsic reward, this does not really provide support for the proposition that extrinsic rewards decrease intrinsic motivation of humans.

Recently a number of investigators have recognized that although there have been various hypotheses about the effects of extrinsic rewards on intrinsic motivation, there is very little empirical evidence, and the evidence which does exist is quite equivocal. Consequently, there have been a number of studies conducted which have investigated various aspects of this question.

The first studies reported in the literature (Deci, 1971) supported the hypothesis that if monetary rewards are given to subjects for doing an intrinsically motivated activity, and if the rewards are made contingent on their performance, their intrinsic motivation for the activity will decrease.

In the first experiment, subjects participated in three 1-hour sessions of puzzle solving. The puzzle used in this experiment, as well as in several others to be reported in this chapter, was a kind of mechanical, spatial-relations puzzle called Soma. The puzzle consisted of seven pieces; each piece was shaped differently and looked as though it were made up of either three or four one-inch cubes. These seven pieces could be arranged into millions of configurations, only a few of which were used in the experiments. The configurations which were used were drawn on a paper, and subjects were asked to use the puzzle pieces to produce the configuration shown in the drawings. One of the configurations which was used is shown in Figure 8. Pilot testing substantiated that the puzzle was intrinsically motivating—at least for college students.

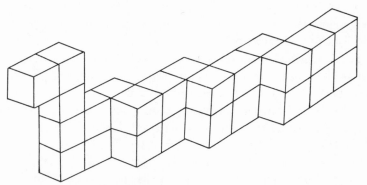

FIGURE 8. Sample puzzle configuration.

During each session, both the experimental and the control subjects were given four puzzle configurations to solve and allowed 13 minutes for each. If a subject were unable to solve any of them within the time allowed, he was stopped and shown the solution so that he would know that they were possible, and so that the Zeigarnik (1927) effect would not influence his later performance. The only difference between the experimental and control subjects was that the experimentals were paid $1 for each puzzle they solved during the second session. This, then, constituted the experimental manipulation: experimentals were paid contingently for engaging in an intrinsically motivated activity, whereas controls performed the same activity for no pay.

In each of the three sessions, the experimenter left the room for a period of just over 8 minutes between the second and third puzzles. He told the subject that, since this was an experiment in problem solving, he was going to the computer to feed in the data from the first two puzzles to determine what were the most appropriate puzzles for the remainder of the session, in order to study the concepts of interest. The subject was told that he could do anything he wanted, but he was asked to remain in the room. In fact, the experimenter merely went outside the room and observed the subject through a one-way window for eight minutes. The subject was alone in the room with more puzzles, as well as recent magazines and other distractions. It was reasoned that if he spent time working on the puzzles when he was alone and when there were other things to do, he must be intrinsically motivated. Hence, the amount of time out of this 8-minute "free-choice" period which the subject spent working on the puzzles was used as the measure of his intrinsic motivation for that activity. This measure is quite consistent with the operational definition of intrinsic motivation presented in Chapter 2, which states that a person is intrinsically motivated toward an activity if he engages in it for no apparent external reward.

It should be noted, of course, that for the experimental group during session II, this measure reflected not only intrinsic motivation but also the effects of the external reward, because the subjects would be extrinsically motivated to practice with puzzles in this session in order to improve their chances of earning the $2 in the second part of the session. Therefore, this measure was believed to reflect both intrinsic and extrinsic motivation during session II for the experimentals, but only intrinsic motivation during the first and third sessions for the experimentals and during all sessions for the controls.

Comparisons were then made for the change in the amount of intrinsic motivation displayed by the experimentals from the first to the third sessions, relative to the controls. The results indicated that those persons who had received money in the second session showed less intrinsic motivation in the third session than they had in the first, whereas there was not a decrease in the intrinsic motivation of the controls from the first to the third sessions. In other words, the experience of solving intrinsically motivated puzzles for money had decreased the intrinsic motivation for that activity.

There were two possible weaknesses in the experiment just described. First, the experimenter was in the room during the puzzle-solving sessions, which introduced the possibility of experimenter bias (Rosenthal, 1966). Second, since the experimental subjects received payments during the second session and not the third, the decreased intrinsic motivation may have been due to something like an emotional reaction toward the experimenter for withdrawing rewards. This seems unlikely since subjects did not expect to be paid during the third session and no one expressed any emotional upset; moreover, another study was done which corrected these two weaknesses and still replicated the findings (Deci, 1972a).

This replication was a laboratory experiment which employed a one-session, after-only design. The paradigm for this study was essentially the same as that used in several other experiments to be presented in this chapter. Therefore, the general paradigm will be presented first, and then the specific manipulation for the present experiment will be discussed.

General One-Session Paradigm

Each person participated for a 1-hour session during which he spent much of his time working with the Soma puzzle described earlier.

The first experimenter met each subject in a waiting room and escorted him to the experimental room where he was seated at a table. The experimenter then left through a door at the back of the experimental room so that he would be outside the room observing through a one-way window. The subject knew, of course, that the experimenter was observing him, and he communicated with the experimenter through an intercom.

On the table in front of the subject were the seven puzzle pieces, each with a number on it so that the experimenter could refer to it over the intercom. To the left of the subject was a stack with either three or four configurations that he would be asked to reproduce. To his right were three other configurations. The top one of the three was a sample; the other two will be discussed below. On another table to the subject's right were the microphone, speaker, an ashtray, and recent issues of several magazines (e.g., *New Yorker* and *Time*).

When the experimenter got to his position behind the one-way window, he read the instructions to the subject. The subject was told that it was an experiment to study certain problem-solving concepts, and that he would be asked to solve some puzzle problems. After the instructions were read, the experimenter told the subject to look at the sample to his right. He was told how the puzzle could be solved and was allowed about a minute to manipulate the pieces and reproduce the solution. The subject then worked on the puzzle configurations in turn.

During the session the subject was asked to reproduce the configurations which had been drawn on paper for him. The time to complete each configuration was measured with a stopwatch, and if a subject were unable to reproduce a configuration within 10 minutes, he was stopped and then he assembled it as the experimenter explained how. This let him know that all the configurations were possible.

In each experiment, the subjects in the control group were asked to reproduce puzzle configurations. They received no rewards and no feedback about their performance. The experimental subjects in each study also were asked to reproduce puzzle configurations, however, they received rewards, negative reinforcement, or feedback about their performance. Interest was in the differences in intrinsic motivation of the experimentals and controls following the puzzle-solving period.

To obtain the dependent measure of intrinsic motivation, the experimenter left his position for a period of 8 minutes following the puzzle solving. The pretext was as follows: When a subject had completed the four puzzles, the experimenter told him that he had done all the problem solving which he had to do, but that there was one more thing which he would be asked to do, and that was to complete a short questionnaire about the way he had solved the puzzles. The subject was told further that there were four different sets of questions, only one of which would be most appropriate for him, and that, since his questions would be determined by how he had done on the puzzles, the appropriate data from the session would be fed into a computer through a teletype. To do this, the experimenter would have to leave for a short time, 5 to 10 minutes. The subject was told that he could do whatever he liked during that time, but he was asked to stay in the room. The experimenter left his position and entered the experimental room through the back door, walked past the subject, and exited through the front door. He then climbed a small set of steps outside the room and left the lab area through a door at the top of the stairs. The subject could hear him climb the stairs and open and close the door.

The subject was then alone in the room and was free to work on the puzzles, read magazines, or do anything he liked. Therefore, the amount of time out of the 8 minutes which he spent working on the puzzles was used as the dependent measure of intrinsic motivation. This measure was taken by a second experimenter who observed through the one-way window and used a stopwatch to record the time. The second experimenter was blind to the condition and also to the hypotheses of the experiments. The first experimenter signaled to the second to assume his position just after the first experimenter left the room. The second experimenter reached the outside of the one-way window through a different door which the subjects did not know about. There is no indication that the subjects suspected that they were being observed during this free-choice period.

Since any subject who was unable to reproduce a configuration within the 10 minutes allowed was shown the solution, the possibility that the Zeigarnik (1927) effect would influence whether or not he worked on the puzzle in the 8-minute free-choice period was minimized.

The two configurations whose drawings were in the pile to his right under the sample were there, so he could work on them during the free-choice period if he chose to. These puzzles were impossible to do, and that fact precluded the possibility that a subject would finish a configuration during the 8-minute period and have that be a causal factor in determining whether or not he continued working on the puzzle.

After 8 minutes the first experimenter returned to the room and asked the subject to complete the questionnaire.

Manipulation

Just as in the three-session experiment described above, experimental subjects received $1 for each of the four puzzles which they were able to solve within the time limit. Control subjects did the same puzzles for no pay.

The experimental procedure then was substantially different from the three-session procedure; however, the results were the same. Subjects who had been paid for doing an intrinsically motivated activity were less intrinsically motivated following their experience with money than subjects who had engaged in the same activity without pay. The results of this experiment, which were reported in Deci (1972a), were that paid subjects spent an average of 108.6 seconds of free-choice time working on the puzzles, whereas the unpaid controls spent 208.4 seconds.

An alternative explanation to the decrease in intrinsic motivation interpretation is that paid subjects may have worked harder during the puzzle-solving and therefore displayed a satiation effect. As a means of ruling out this alternative explanation, performance scores of the subjects were investigated. The average amount of time spent by each subject on each puzzle during the puzzle-solving portion of the experiment (as opposed to the free-time portion) was compared for the experimentals and controls in both experiments described above. The results were reported in Deci, Cascio, and Krusell (1975).

Neither difference was statistically significant; further, in one experiment, the experimentals spent more time, and in the other, they spent less. This, then, suggests that performance on the puzzle solving did not affect the amount of free-choice time which subjects spent working on the puzzles.

The finding that monetary payments when made contingent on performance decrease intrinsic motivation was replicated again by a controlled field experiment (Deci, 1971) in a college newspaper office. The subjects (who did not realize they were in an experiment) were members of two staffs of headline writers who participated for a 16-week period. Both experimental and control subjects wrote headlines according to certain quality standards. Base level rates of intrinsic motivation were taken during the first 4 weeks. The measure of intrinsic motivation was the average amount of time spent writing each headline. Since quality was controlled, it was reasoned that the faster a person worked on the headlines, the more motivated he must be. During the fifth, sixth, and seventh weeks experimental subjects were paid $.50 for each headline they wrote. They were told that there was extra money in the budget which needed to be used up by the end of the year so they would be paid only until it was used up. Then, during the eight, ninth, and 10th weeks, intrinsic motivation was assessed for both groups. Finally, during the 15th and 16th weeks, the last measure was taken.

In sum, the key difference between the two groups was that the experimental subjects were paid $.50 per headline written during three sessions. This paid group (relative to the controls) showed a decrease in intrinsic motivation after the experience with money, and this difference was evident during the follow-up eight weeks after payment stopped. In other words, this study replicated the laboratory studies and suggested that the effects are not merely short-term effects.

Change in Perceived Locus of Causality

To account for these findings Deci (1971, 1972a) used the ideas of de Charms (1968) and Heider (1958) and asserted that when subjects were paid for doing an intrinsically motivated activity there was a change in their perceived locus of causality.

Initially, subjects were intrinsically motivated and the perceived locus of causality was internal. They engaged in the behavior because it provided them with internal rewards, that is, they did it in order to feel competent and self-determining. Then, when rewards were introduced, they began to perceive that they were performing the activity in order to make money, so the perceived locus of causality became external, leaving them with less intrinsic motivation.

PROPOSITION I OF COGNITIVE EVALUATION THEORY: *One process by which intrinsic motivation can be affected is a change in perceived locus of causality from internal to external. This will cause a decrease in intrinsic motivation, and will occur, under certain circumstances, when someone receives extrinsic rewards for engaging in intrinsically motivated activities.*

This proposition implies two very important things. First, it implies that extrinsic rewards, do (in some sense, and for reasons which are not yet clear) have more salience or more impact than intrinsic rewards, since they can "co-opt" intrinsic motivation.

The second implication follows from the discussion in Chapter 1, and is that if a person perceives the locus of causality to be outside of himself, then he will behave in accord with that perception. People make choices about their behavior on the basis of their perceptions, so if they perceive that they engage in a certain activity for an extrinsic reward, then they'll do so only when they think such activity will lead to the extrinsic reward.

Threats of Punishment

Deci and Cascio (1972) reasoned that if monetary rewards would decrease intrinsic motivation by changing the perceived locus of causality, then other "controlling" extrinsic rewards should do the same. The avoidance of a punishment is a very common extrinsic reward and would be expected to decrease intrinsic motivation just as money did. The investigators reported that when subjects were threatened with punishment for poor performance, their intrinsic motivation also decreased. The experimental subjects were told that if they were unable to solve a puzzle within the 10 minutes allocated, a buzzer would sound indicating that their time was up. They were given a brief exposure (under 1 second) to the buzzer so that they would know that it was truly noxious. Hence, they were performing because they were intrinsically motivated and because good performance would allow them to avoid a punishment (the buzzer). The results indicated that those who solved puzzles with a threat of punishment were less intrinsically motivated during the free choice period than subjects who solved the same puzzles with no threat of punishment. Again it appears that their behavior had become dependent on an external control. Thus, they were left with less intrinsic motivation. These results, however, were only marginally significant, and further replication would be quite appropriate.

Contingent Awards for Children

Lepper, Greene, and Nisbett (1973) report results similar to those in the Deci experiments. Their study used groups of nursery school children who were asked by an experimenter to draw pictures using attractive materials. The subjects in the first group were told that they would receive an award for drawing, while the second group was told nothing. Several days later, all children had an opportunity to play with the drawing materials in a free-choice situation, and the measure of intrinsic interest was the percentage of time they spent working with these materials, as opposed to numerous other things available to them. The experiment was similar in design to the Deci "one-session paradigm" study described above, although here, the manipulation and dependent measure were separated by several days. The results were again the same. The children who had engaged in the activity for the reward spent less time in the free-choice period working on the activity than did the children who had been rewarded.

Change in Competence and Self-Determination

We have suggested that the important factor in understanding the effects of extrinsic rewards or feedback on intrinsic motivation is the person's phenomenological evaluation of the reward. If he comes to perceive the reward or feedback as the reason he is engaged in the activity, his perceived locus of causality will change from internal to external. However, if he does not perceive the reward or feedback as the cause of the activity, the effects will be different.

Intrinsically motivated activities are ones which a person engages in to feel a sense of competence and self-determination. Therefore, if the reward or feedback affects the person's sense of competence and self-determination, it can affect his intrinsic motivation.

PROPOSITION II OF COGNITIVE EVALUATION THEORY: *The second process by which intrinsic motivation can be affected is a change in feelings of competence and self-determination. If a person's feelings of competence and self-determination are enhanced, his intrinsic motivation will increase. If his feelings of competence and self-determination are diminished, his intrinsic motivation will decrease.*

We are suggesting that some rewards or feedback will increase intrinsic motivation through this process and others will decrease it, either through this process or through the change in perceived locus of causality process. To understand why one process will be operative sometimes and the other will be operative at others, we need to consider that rewards and feedback have two aspects.

Two Aspects to Rewards

Rewards are generally used to control behavior. Children are sometimes rewarded with candy when they do what adults expect of them. Workers are rewarded with pay for doing what their supervisors want. People are rewarded with social approval or positive feedback for fitting into their social reference group. In all these situations the aim of the rewarder is to control the person's behavior—to make him continue to engage in acceptable behaviors. And rewards often do work quite effectively as controllers. Further, whether it works or not, each reward has a controlling aspect. Therefore, the first aspect to every reward (including feedback) is a controlling aspect.

However, rewards also provide information to the person about his effectiveness in various situations. When Eric received a bonus for outstanding performance on his job, the reward provided him with information that he was competent and self-determining in relation to his job. When David did well at school his mother told him she was proud of him, and when Amanda learned to ride a bike she was given a brand new two-wheeler. David and Amanda knew from the praise and bicycle that they were competent and self-determining in relation to school and bicycling. The second aspect to every reward is the information it provides a person about his competence and self-determination.

When the controlling aspect of the reward is very salient, such as in the case of money or the avoidance of punishment, the change in perceived locus of causality process will occur. The person is "controlled" by the reward and he perceives that the locus of causality is external. On the other hand, if the control aspect is not salient, then the informational aspect of the reward will initiate the change in feelings of competence and self-determination process.

PROPOSITION III OF COGNITIVE EVALUATION THEORY: *Every reward (including feedback) has two aspects, a controlling aspect and an informational aspect which provides the recipient with information about his competence and self-determination. The relative salience of the two aspects determines which process will be operative. If the controlling aspect is more salient, it will initiate the change in perceived locus of causality process. If the informational aspect is more salient, the change in feelings of competence and self-determination process will be initiated.*

So far the studies reported have used rewards where the controlling aspect was very salient. These rewards were money, avoidance of punishment, and desired awards for children. If the reward were something, such as positive feedback or praise, where the controlling aspect was not so apparent, the effects should be different.

Positive Feedback

Deci (1971) performed an experiment to investigate the effects of positive feedback (i.e., verbal reinforcements) on intrinsic motivation. The study employed the "three-session paradigm" described earlier, and the manipulation consisted of giving positive verbal reinforcements to the experimental subjects during the second session. The reinforcements were statements such as, "Very good, that's the fastest this one has been done yet." The subjects were college students, and all of them were males except for two females in the experimental condition and two females in the control. Those subjects who received the verbal reinforcements showed an increase in intrinsic motivation from sessions I to III relative to the control subjects who received no verbal rewards. The informational aspect of the verbal reward was more salient than the controlling aspect, so the change in feelings of competence and self-determination process was invoked, and the subjects were left with more intrinsic motivation for this activity.

In a different study (Deci, 1972a) employing the one-session paradigm described above, an equal number of male and female subjects was used. Experimentals were given the same verbal reinforcements as those in the previous experiment; controls received no verbal rewards. The results indicated that males who had received verbal reinforcements displayed significantly more intrinsic motivation than males who received no positive feedback, thereby replicating the earlier finding that positive feedback increased intrinsic motivation. However, in the current experiment, there was an unexpected finding. Females who had received positive feedback showed substantially less intrinsic motivation than females who received no feedback, though this difference was not statistically significant. Nonetheless, it suggested that there may be a sex difference in the effects of positive feedback on intrinsic motivation, so another study was run to clarify this question.

This experiment (Deci, Cascio, & Krusell, 1973) used the same one-session paradigm as the study just reported. However, both a male and female experimenter were used so that it would be possible to separate the effects of an interaction between the sex of the experimenter and the sex of the subject from the effects of the sex of the subject. The results of the experiment were quite unequivocal and appear in Table III. Female subjects who received positive feedback spent less free-choice time working on the puzzles than the subjects who got no feedback regardless of whether the experimenter were a male or a female. In other words,

TABLE III. *Average Number of Seconds of "Free Choice" Time Spent Working on the Intrinsically Interesting Activity*

	Female subjects		Male subjects	
	Female experimenter	Male experimenter	Female experimenter	Male experimenter
Control (no feedback)	205.8	354.9	293.8	275.3
Positive feedback	157.5	136.5	454.5	340.3

females who received positive verbal feedback showed less intrinsic motivation following the puzzle-solving experience than females who received no feedback.

On the other hand, positive feedback increased the intrinsic motivation of males just as it did in previous experiments described above. This phenomenon was produced when the experimenter was female just as it was when the experimenter was male. An analysis of variance showed the "sex of subject X feedback" interaction to be highly significant, so this substantiated the finding that positive feedback works differently for males and females.

There was no variance accounted for by sex of experimenter, as the F value was less than 1, though there was a main effect for sex of subjects. However, this main effect is somewhat misleading, in that it was caused entirely by the positive feedback condition. The more critical test of whether males and females differ (independently of the effects of positive feedback) is done by comparing control conditions. Here we see no difference. Women control subjects spend an average of 280.3 seconds, whereas males spent an average of 257.5 seconds, of free-choice time working on the puzzles.

The main effect for sex of subject simply underscores the strength of the differential effect of positive feedback on males and females, since the entire main effect is accounted for by the feedback condition. This experiment, then, has shown quite clearly that positive feedback has different effects on the intrinsic motivation of males and females. It increases the intrinsic motivation of males, whereas it decreases the intrinsic motivation of females. This difference can be seen quite clearly in Figure 9.

For females the change in perceived locus of causality process was initiated, whereas for males the change in feelings of competence and self-determination was initiated. This implies that the controlling aspect of positive feedback is more salient for females than the informational aspect, whereas for males the informational aspect is more salient. And, indeed, that implication seems very plausible if one considers the socialization processes in the traditional culture.

Girls are taught that they are to be more dependent than boys. Frequently girls, and subsequently women, define themselves in terms of men. They assume their husbands' names, they often stay at home to take care of their homes and their husbands, and even if they work, their jobs are secondary to their husbands'. Furthermore, girls are typically taught to be more sensitive to interpersonal matters. Such seemingly insignificant matters as frequent trading of compliments about clothing, and so on, may make girls more attuned to feedback from others.

One would hope that, with the heightened concern, about women's roles and identities, the traditional picture might change, yet, as of now, it would seem that this picture has had a profound influence on many of us.

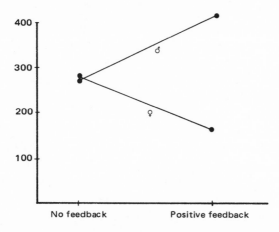

FIGURE 9. Intrinsic motivation displayed by male and female subjects who got either no feedback or positive feedback.

In light of the socialization process just mentioned it seems very reasonable that males and females will react differently to positive feedback. Women, who are more sensitive to feedback and more dependent on other people, will be more likely to become dependent on the positive feedback from the experimenter. In other words, the controlling aspect of positive feedback is more likely to be salient for women than for men, so the change in perceived locus of causality process is likely to be initiated for women. Men, on the other hand, are socialized to be more independent and less dependent on feedback. Consequently, they are less likely to perceive that they are engaging in the activity for the verbal reward, and more likely to perceive the feedback as information about their competence.

If our interpretation of these findings is accurate, one would predict that females, as well as males, would display enhanced intrinsic motivation if they received positive information about their competence and self-determination in a way which did not involve the controlling aspect of verbal praise.

Feather (1966, 1968; Feather & Saville, 1967) did a series of studies which relates to this prediction. His studies, as well as replications by Ryckman, Gold, and Rodda (1971) demonstrated that persons who experienced success at a task (e.g., anagrams) were more confident, and performed better on subsequent tasks, than subjects who failed. There were apparently no differences between males and females in these studies.

The cognitive evaluation theory interpretation of these results is that the positive feedback which was inherent in the success experience strengthened the subjects' feelings of competence and self-determination (as measured by their expressed confidence) and made them more intrinsically motivated (as reflected by better performance).

Whereas Deci, Cascio, and Krusell found decreased intrinsic motivation for females who received verbal positive feedback, presumably because the verbal feedback caused a change in perceived locus of causality, there was no decrease when the feedback was not administered interpersonally. This, therefore, supports our interpretation of the sex differences obtained by Deci, Cascio, and Krusell.

Negative Feedback

We have seen that information about a person's performance on an intrinsically motivated activity can affect intrinsic motivation by changing the person's feelings of competence and self-determination. Negative feedback should decrease a person's intrinsic motivation by diminishing his feelings of competence and self-determination. Deci, Cascio, and Krusell (1973) reported a study which tested this hypothesis using the one-session paradigm described above.

In the first experimental condition subjects were given negative verbal feedback from the experimenter. After each puzzle which the subject was able to solve in the first part of the experiment, the experimenter said something like, "Although you did solve that one, you took longer than average." When the subject failed to solve a puzzle, the experimenter said something like, "Well, most people were able to solve that one, but let's go on to the next." One can see that the design of this experiment was identical to the positive feedback experiment except for the nature of the feedback. The experimentals and controls did the same puzzles, though the experimentals were given negative verbal feedback about their performance, whereas the controls got no feedback.

The other negative feedback condition in the current experiment was a self-administered negative feedback condition. Here, experimental subjects were given very difficult puzzles and the controls the same easier puzzles as the negative verbal feedback subjects. This manipulation of hard-*vs.*-easy puzzles lead the experimentals to fail at a much higher percentage of puzzles and therefore let them see that they were not very competent at this activity. In fact, the manipulation was successful in that 79% of the puzzles given to the experimentals were unsolved, whereas only 37% of those given to the controls were not completed.

The results of this experiment are shown in Figure 10. It can be seen that negative feedback, whether given verbally by the experimenter or self-administered by the subject through failure at the intrinsically motivated task, caused a decrease in intrinsic motivation. The statistical significance of this finding was beyond

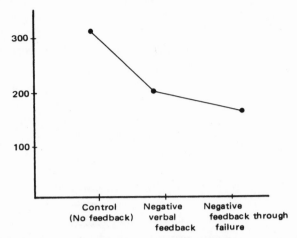

FIGURE 10. Amount of free choice time spent working on puzzles (i.e., intrinsic motivation) by negative feedback and no feedback subjects (*N* = 96).

the .01 level. The means for males and females in this experiment were virtually identical; the analysis of variance yielded an *F* of less than 1, so the data in Figure 10 have been collapsed across sex of subject.

These data present clear evidence that negative feedback decreases intrinsic motivation. This occurs through decreasing one's feelings of competence and self-determination in relation to this activity.

Dependent Measures of Intrinsic Motivation

In Chapter 2, I stated that although there are several conceptualizations of intrinsic motivation the general operational definition is that an activity is intrinsically motivated if there is no apparent external reward for the activity: The activity seems to be the reward; it is the end rather than the means to an end. In line with the general operationalization of intrinsic motivation, the studies presented so far by Deci and his associates and by Lepper *et al.* used as their measure of intrinsic motivation the amount of time which subjects spent working on the target activity in a free-choice situation where there were other things to do and where there was no external reward to be gained.

Other studies which have considered the same general question have taken different approaches to operationalizing the construct. One approach notes that intrinsically motivated behaviors are ones which are supposedly interesting and enjoyable to the actor, so the studies have used subject ratings of enjoyment as measures of intrinsic motivation (or more appropriately, intrinsic interest). Several studies have used self-report measures, and these studies have replicated the general findings of the previously presented studies.

In one study Kruglanski, Alon, and Lewis (1972) used 10- and 11-year-old children who participated in competitive games. Half of the subjects were given prizes (puzzle games in attractive wrappers) for their participation, whereas the other half received no rewards. Subjects were then asked to rate how much they enjoyed the competition. As predicted, and in line with the studies reported earlier, subjects who had received rewards reported that they liked the activity less than those who received no rewards. The data were collected at two different times: immediately following competition and 1 week later. Even 1 week after participation, the rewarded subjects still reported that they enjoyed the activity less than did those subjects who had not received rewards.

In another study, Calder and Staw (1973) had business students solve puzzles with interesting pictures for either $1 or no pay. The subjects who received pay also reported that they had enjoyed the activity less than no-payment subjects.

Additional support was found by Patty and Safford (personal communication) in a field experiment. They reported that women who volunteered to give blood and expected the reward of free basketball tickets for doing so were significantly less positive toward blood donation than were women who gave blood without expecting the reward.

The evidence from these three studies lends further support to the hypothesis that extrinsic rewards, such as pay, decreases subjects' intrinsic motivation for a task whether measured with a behavioral, "free-choice" measure or a self report of task enjoyment.

Both measures are intended to assess internal states, as is typical in social psychological experiments. Frequently, in social psychology, internal states such as attitudes are the primary topic of interest. The assumption is made that people's behaviors in a whole variety of situations will be caused by, or follow from, these internal states. I, too, believe this to be so. If someone has intrinsic motivation for an activity, I assume that he will perform the activity without rewards at various times in the future.

Some investigators have gone directly to performance measures, rather than looking at intrinsic motivation *per se*. Kruglanski, Freedman, and Zeevi (1971), for example, conducted a field experiment with teenagers in which half of those high school students who performed several tasks were rewarded with a guided tour through the psychology department of a nearby university, and half were not rewarded. The tasks involved measures of the Zeigarnik effect, creativity, and recall. All three factors showed significant differences. Subjects who were rewarded showed lower recall, less creativity, and smaller Zeigarnik ratios than nonrewarded subjects. An additional measure showed that rewarded students rated themselves as having enjoyed the experiment less than nonrewarded students.

This experiment, then, showed that extrinsic rewards not only interfere with one's intrinsic motivation for an activity, but also interfere with one's performance on that activity.

In sum, the evidence seems quite clear that, whether the dependent measure is free time spent on the target activity, enjoyment of the activity, or performance on the activity, cognitive evaluation theory seems quite useful in accounting for the effects of rewards and feedback on intrinsic motivation.

Contingent vs. Noncontingent Rewards

In all three Deci studies where money was administered as an external reward, the money was administered contingently, that is, the amount of money a person received was dependent on his performance. In another experiment using the one-session paradigm (Deci, 1972b) subjects were paid noncontingently for performing the same intrinsically motivated task. Each subject was given $2 for participating in the experiment, regardless of how well he did on the tasks. As in the previous experiments, subjects did not know until they arrived for the session that they would be paid.

This experiment was virtually identical to the Deci (1972a) study, except that in this study subjects were paid $2 regardless of performance, whereas in the earlier Deci study subjects were paid in a way that was contingent on their performance. Average earnings in the contingent payment study were $2.38 per subject. Although this is not exactly the same as $2, it is unlikely that an average difference of $.38 would affect the results. Hence, the contingency, *vs.* the noncontingency, of the reward is the critical difference.

Table IV presents the results of the noncontingent payment conditions, as well as the contingent payment conditions. The results indicated that the subjects who received $2 for participating spent the same amount of free-choice time working on the puzzles as did control subjects who received no pay, whereas subjects whose pay was contingent on their performance spent less free-choice time working on the puzzles than did control subjects.

TABLE IV. Number of Seconds of Free-Choice Time Spent by Experimental and Control Subjects When Rewards Were Contingent and Noncontingent

	Control	Experimental
Noncontingent	190.2	192.8
Contingent	208.4	108.6

The finding that noncontingent money payments did not decrease intrinsic motivation can be understood in relation to cognitive evaluation theory. When money is contingent, the subjects are more likely to perceive that they are performing for the money. Their engaging in the activity is instrumental to their receiving rewards, so they perceive the rewards as the reason for the activity. On the other hand, when rewards are noncontingent, performance is not tied directly to rewards, so the subjects are less likely to perceive that the rewards are the reason for their performance. Hence, they would be less likely to lose intrinsic motivation.

We are not suggesting that noncontingent extrinsic rewards will not decrease intrinsic motivation; rather, we are suggesting that it is less likely. The important factor leading to a decrease in intrinsic motivation is the person's perception that the reward was the cause of his behavior. When the rewards are contingent, he will be more likely to perceive the reward as the reason he is engaging in the activity.

In some situations, however, when rewards are not directly contingent on performance, the person may still perceive the locus of causality to be outside of himself, if the controlling aspect of the reward is for some reason made salient to him. In the Calder and Staw (1973) study, subjects received $1 for doing the task of assembling 15 puzzles. Although the puzzles were interesting because of the pictures on them, they were trivial to assemble. Therefore, every subject solved every puzzle very quickly. Although the $1 reward was not made contingent on performance the subjects were told that they would get the $1 when they finished the puzzles. The result of the study showed that noncontingently paid subjects enjoyed the task less than unpaid subjects.

This experiment makes it clear that contingency/non-contingency is not really a binary concept. Putting the dollar bill in plain view at the end of a line of 15 easy puzzles and telling the subjects that they could have the money as soon as they finished the puzzles created more of a contingency situation than was created by giving subjects $2 for coming to the experimental room regardless of whether they even continued the experiment, as was the case in the Deci (1972b) study. However, it constituted less of a contingency situation than did telling the subjects that they would get $1 for each puzzle solved when the puzzles were moderately difficult and subjects solved an average of 2.38 out of the 4 puzzles.

In the Kruglanski *et al.* (1971) study the reward (a tour of the psychology laboratory) was announced to the high school experimental subjects before they began the task and given to them regardless of their performance. Here we found a decrement in intrinsic motivation even though the reward was not contingent.

Greene and Lepper (1974) did a study in which they told half of their preschool subjects that the experimenter had a few rewards. These may have been perceived by the subjects as contingent payments. The other half of the subjects were not told that there were a few rewards. Their results showed a decrease in intrinsic motivation for both the noncontingent and the "contingent" groups. However, since there may have been ambiguity about whether or not the performance demand was seen as a contingency, this study does not help shed light on the importance of contingency-*vs.*-noncontingency of rewards, though the study does show that noncontingent rewards can decrease intrinsic motivation.

The simple fact of a contingent-*vs.*-noncontingent situation is not the critical variable, in and of itself, for determining whether or not extrinsic rewards will decrease intrinsic motivation. The important factor is whether or not the controlling aspect of the reward is salient. When rewards are clearly contingent, the controlling aspect will be very salient, since the reward is dependent on some qualitative factor of the person's behavior. Hence, we find a sharp decrease in intrinsic motivation. As the rewards become less contingent, the controlling aspect of the reward becomes less salient, and the decrement in intrinsic motivation is less likely to occur, since the person is less likely to perceive the change in locus of causality.

Expectation of Rewards

In the paper by Lepper *et al.* (1973) the authors asserted that an important factor in determining whether or not extrinsic rewards will decrease intrinsic interest is whether or not the subject expects to receive the reward. In other words, the authors hypothesized that if a person engages in an intrinsic activity and subsequently is given a reward for having done so, the reward will not have a detrimental effect on the person's intrinsic interest. Their study had three groups of children working with magic markers and construction paper; children in one group were told they would receive awards, children in the second were not told about the awards but were given them after completion of the activity, and the children in the third group got no rewards. Their data showed that expected-reward children displayed significantly less intrinsic motivation one week later, though there was no difference between unexpected-reward and no-reward conditions.

These data seem quite compelling and are easily interpretable in terms of cognitive evaluation theory. When a person is doing something and expects to receive a reward for it, it is very likely that he will perceive the reward as the cause of his activity. Hence, he will experience a decrease in intrinsic motivation. However, I would also predict that an unexpected reward could initiate a process of retrospective reevaluation of the activity, though this reevaluation would be less likely to occur than it would be if the rewards were expected. Further, the decrease in intrinsic motivation, if it did occur in the retrospective-reevaluation condition, would undoubtedly be less than in the expected-reward condition. Nonetheless, it is possible that a decrease would occur.

And, in fact, in the experiment by Kruglanski *et al.* (1972) in which rewards were given to children for playing competitive games, the rewards were given after the games and were not expected by the children. But there was less intrinsic interest in the unexpected-reward subjects than in the no-reward subjects immediately following the activity, and also one week later.

Furthermore, in a study by Ross (in press) which will be discussed below, one experimental group was led to expect a prize for doing an intrinsically interesting task. However, they did not show a decrement in intrinsic interest.

We see, then, that expectation of rewards is not necessarily an important determinant of the effects of extrinsic rewards on intrinsic motivation. Rather, expectation of reward may just make the causal link between the behavior and the reward more apparent to the subject and therefore will appear to mediate the effects of rewards on intrinsic motivation.

Salience of Rewards

Ross (in press) hypothesized that the reward must be salient to a person if it is to decrease his motivation for an activity. Ross added that if the reward does not provide the person with compelling evidence that his behavior is extrinsically caused, he is likely to attribute intrinsic motivation to himself. To test his hypothesis, Ross manipulated salience by altering the conspicuousness of the reward. For one third of the nursery school subjects, a surprise reward was placed under a box which was in a prominent location. The children were told that as soon as they finished playing a drum for a certain period of time they could lift the box and get their surprise. The box provided a constant reminder that the reward would follow. Another third of the children were simply told by the experimenter that they would receive a prize at the end of the time period, and for the remaining third there was no mention of a prize.

The results showed that the saliently rewarded children showed less intrinsic motivation than nonrewarded or nonsalient

TABLE V. *Summary of the Effects of Various External Rewards and Controls on Intrinsic Motivation*

Reward or control	Effect on intrinsic motivation
Money	
Contingent	
Deci, 1971, 1972 (a)	Decrease
Noncontingent	
Deci, 1972 (b)	No change
Calder & Staw, 1973	Decrease
Desired Awards	
Expected	
Lepper *et al.*, 1973	Decrease
Kruglanski *et al.*, 1971	Decrease
Unexpected	
Lepper *et al.*, 1973	No change
Kruglanski *et al.*, 1972	Decrease
Salient	
Ross, in press	Decrease
Nonsalient	
Ross, in press	No change
Threats of punishment	
Deci & Cascio, 1972	Decrease
Positive feedback	
Males	
Deci, 1972 (a)	Increase
Females	
Deci, Cascio, & Krusell, 1975	Decrease
Negative Feedback	
Deci, Cascio, & Krusell, 1973	Decrease

subjects. The same results were obtained on three different measures of intrinsic motivation: (1) amount of free-choice time spent on the activity, (2) whether or not the target activity were the first toy the children played with during the free-choice period, and (3) whether or not the children said the target activity was the most enjoyable of all the activities available to them in the room.

In a follow-up assessment 4 weeks later, boys in the salient-reward condition still played with the drum significantly less than boys in the nonrewarded or nonsalient conditions, though the effect did not last for females.

The results of this experiment show that a reward must be salient to the subject if it is to lead to a change in perceived locus of causality and, hence, a decrement in intrinsic motivation. I would argue, however, that it is not the salience of the reward, *per se*, but rather, salience of the controlling aspect of the reward, which is critical. In most cases these two will be synonymous. However, if they are not, the salience of the controlling aspect, rather than the salience of the reward, should mediate the effects of extrinsic rewards on intrinsic motivation. For example, if male subjects were given positive verbal rewards, and if these rewards were very salient, an increase in intrinsic motivation should be produced. The informational aspect would be more salient than the controlling aspect, so the salient verbal reward would not decrease intrinsic motivation.

Table V summarizes the effects of various extrinsic rewards on intrinsic motivation.

Generalizability to Other Activities

People tend to be intrinsically motivated to solve challenging puzzles, to understand novel situations, etc. Piaget (1952) and Baldwin (1967) convey the same idea by suggesting that people are intrinsically motivated to engage in activities which are assimilable but not completely so. This implies that once a person has fully understood a situation or has learned the algorithm for a puzzle problem, he may no longer be intrinsically motivated to explore that particular situation or manipulate that particular puzzle. This does not mean that he has lost intrinsic motivation for solving puzzles or for understanding novel situations, since intrinsic motivation is to some extent general to certain kinds of situations.

Although intrinsic motivation is defined in relation to a particular activity, it is to some extent generalizable. When, for example, someone is intrinsically motivated to work a crossword puzzle, he probably will also be intrinsically motivated to play Scrabble. His intrinsic motivation, though specific to an activity, is to some extent generalizable to similar activities.

Furthermore, the effects of extrinsic rewards on intrinsic motivation should be generalizable to some extent. For example, when male subjects were given positive feedback for reproducing a Soma configuration in the Deci (1972a) experiment, this did not increase their intrinsic motivations for that particular configuration, since they then knew how to achieve it; rather, their intrinsic motivation for other configurations was increased. Similarly if someone is paid for doing a puzzle, not only will his intrinsic motivation for that particular puzzle decrease, but his intrinsic motivation for similar puzzles will also decrease.

Leavitt (1962) has made the point that people tend to program themselves out of challenging and novel situations and then lose interest in those situations. Cognitive evaluation theory maintains, however, that they will be even more intrinsically motivated for programming the next challenging and novel situation they encounter.

A Jewish Fable

There are some people who assert that we never really discover anything new, but rather that we just rediscover things. Although the research presented in this chapter sheds much new light on the effects of extrinsic rewards on intrinsic motivation, the fable which appears below suggests that we may not have learned as much *new* information as we think we have (though of course the nature of the evidence is different):

> In a little Southern town where the Klan was riding again, a Jewish tailor had the temerity to open his little shop on the main street. To drive him out of the town the Kleagle of the Klan set a gang of little ragamuffins to annoy him. Day after day they stood at the entrance of his shop. "Jew! Jew!", they hooted at him. The situation looked

serious for the tailor. He took the matter so much to heart that he began to brood and spent sleepless nights over it. Finally out of desperation he evolved a plan.

The following day, when the little hoodlums came to jeer at him, he came to the door and said to them, "From today on any boy who calls me "Jew" will get a dime from me." Then he put his hand in his pocket and gave each boy a dime.

Delighted with their booty, the boys came back the following day and began to shrill, "Jew! Jew!" The tailor came out smiling. He put his hand in his pocket and gave each of the boys a nickel, saying, "A dime is too much—I can only afford a nickel today." The boys went away satisfied because, after all, a nickel was money, too.

However, when they returned the next day to hoot at him, the tailor gave them only a penny each.

"Why do we get only a penny today?" they yelled.

"That's all I can afford."

"But two days ago you gave us a dime, and yesterday we got a nickel. It's not fair, mister."

"Take it or leave it. That's all you're going to get!"

"Do you think we're going to call you "Jew" for one lousy penny?"

"So don't!"

And they didn't."   (Ausubel, 1948).

Summary

This chapter has presented a great deal of evidence from recent studies which has demonstrated that intrinsic and extrinsic motivation are not additive. Extrinsic rewards decrease intrinsic motivation in many situations, though positive feedback to males increases intrinsic motivation. We also saw that when rewards are contingent on performance they are more likely to decrease intrinsic motivation. Further, when rewards are expected before the behavior begins they are more likely to decrease intrinsic motivation. A theory was presented to account for these various results. The theory outlined two processes though which rewards can affect intrinsic motivation, a change in perceived locus of causality process and a change in feelings of competence and self-determination process. Further, it was pointed out that all rewards have two aspects, a controlling aspect and an informational aspect, and that the relative salience of the two aspects will determine which process will be initiated.

Author's Note

I have come across a number of studies since completion of the manuscript for this book which relate directly to Chapters 5 and 8. I shall therefore list them for reference.

Condry, J. The enemies of exploration. Unpublished manuscript, Cornell University, 1975.

Deci, E. L., Porac, J., & Shapira, Z. Effects of rewards on interest and intrinsic motivation for an extrinsic activity. Unpublished manuscript, University of Rochester, 1975.

Eden, D. Intrinsic and extrinsic rewards both have motivating and demotivating effects. *Journal of Applied Social Psychology*, in press.

Garbarino, J. The impact of anticipated rewards upon cross-aged tutoring. *Journal of Personality and Social Psychology*, in press.

Kruglanski, A. W., Riter, A., Amitai, A. *et al.* Can money enhance intrinsic motivation?: A test of the content-consequences hypothesis. *Journal of Personality and Social Psychology 31*, 744–750.

Kruglanski, A. W., Riter, A., Arazi, D., *et al.* The effects of task-intrinsic rewards upon extrinsic and intrinsic motivation, *Journal of Personality and Social Psychology, 31*, 599–605.

Levine, F. M., & Fasnacht, G. Token rewards may lead to token learning. *American Psychologist*, 1974, *29*, 816–820.

McGraw, K. & McCullers, J. C. The distracting effect of material reward: An alternative explanation for the superior performance of reward groups in probability learning. *Journal of Experimental Child Psychology*, 1974, *18*, 149–158.

Pinder, C. C. Goodness of fit as a moderator of the impact of contingent rewards on intrinsic motivation, satisfaction, and performance. Unpublished manuscript, University of British Columbia, 1975.

Staw, B. M. *Intrinsic and Extrinsic Motivation.* New York: General Learning Press Module, 1975.

6

Cognitive Dissonance Theory: Effects of Insufficient Justification on Intrinsic Motivation

In 1957, Festinger proposed a theory of cognitive dissonance which has probably generated more research than any other theory in social psychology. Briefly, cognitive dissonance theory asserts that if a person holds two cognitions which are discrepant, he will experience discomfort and be motivated to do something which will reduce the dissonance.

In Chapter 2 we saw that there are two general mechanisms involved in the intrinsic motivation of behavior. People seek out challenges (i.e., they seek out incongruity or dissonance) and people also attempt to conquer challenges (i.e., they seek to reduce incongruity or dissonance). Therefore, the reduction of dissonance may motivate people to engage in a wide variety of behaviors.

There are two respects in which Festinger's conceptualization differs from my view of intrinsic motivation. First, Festinger proposed that people prefer no dissonance. We have seen however, that people often seek out incongruity to provide challenge. In turn, they typically proceed to reduce that incongruity. However, focusing only on the reduction of incongruity leaves out an extremely important aspect of the picture. Secondly, I have suggested that encountering incongruity provides challenge and gives the person an opportunity to meet the challenge and then to

161

feel competent and self-determining. Festinger, however, said that dissonance is uncomfortable, so people are driven to reduce the discomfort. Therein lies a difference; I assert that dissonance is not always uncomfortable; sometimes it just represents a challenge. On the other hand, there may be times when the dissonance is quite uncomfortable. If a person attempts a task and fails, the incongruity may be very uncomfortable, whereas previously it had not been. In most dissonance studies there does seem to be discomfort because of the induction. People are induced to lie, to refrain from doing something they like, to do aversive acts, etc. Hence, the incongruity is typically created so as to be aversive rather than simply challenging. Therefore, it may be that the most meaningful way to reconcile this is to recognize that dissonance is a subset (albeit an uncomfortable one) of incongruity. Hunt's use of *incongruity* and my use of *challenge* are much broader than Festinger's use of *dissonance*. I would suggest that when a person sees that he is unable to behave so as to reduce the incongruity (i.e., to meet the challenge) he will begin to experience discomfort (i.e., dissonance). He then seeks to reduce this discomfort, most probably by changing one of his own internal states, such as an attitude, a motive, or an emotion. I submit that all of these internal states have a cognitive component and can therefore be affected by the cognitive process of dissonance reduction.

In sum, I am suggesting that reduction of incongruity (i.e., challenge) is one of two mechanisms governing intrinsically motivated behavior. Dissonance is a subset of incongruity. More specifically, it involves incongruity which the person experiences as aversive. For example, if he fails to meet a challenge, the incongruity which formerly represented a challenge becomes dissonance. Or if the incongruity exists between his perception of himself, on the one hand, and an act which he has just engaged in, on the other, he will experience discomfort (i.e., dissonance). When a person experiences dissonance, he will seek to reduce it and will do so by changing one of his internal states.

Consider this example. When Fred, who disliked roast lamb, was served, and ate, it at a formal dinner party, he would have experienced dissonance. He found himself eating lamb (the first cognition) but knew that he did not like it (the second cognition).

Since these cognitions are dissonant, he would, according to the theory, seek to reduce the dissonance, which he could do in a variety of ways. He could stop the behavior of eating lamb, he could change his attitude about lamb, or he could rationalize the behavior. Since the formal nature of the situation pretty much required that he eat what was served, he had either to decide that he really likes lamb, or to rationalize that behavior. Fortunately, the situation provided an easy out. He could easily have said to himself, "I don't like lamb, but to be polite I really had to eat it. I won't do it again." He rationalized the behavior quite easily.

Several weeks later Fred was at a smorgasbord. Standing behind the serving table was a chef who carved a roast lamb with such aplomb that Fred was intrigued. With great sensitivity the chef would carve the roast and without a break in his graceful movement would deliver the succulent meat to the customer's plate. Carried away by watching the chef perform his job so superbly, Fred found himself asking for two slices of lamb. Fred no longer had such an easy means of rationalizing. He could not write off the behavior to politeness and social pressure. He chose the lamb over several other entrees which were available to him. He would therefore have experienced greater dissonance and would have been more likely to change his attitude about lamb as a means of reducing dissonance. He would have convinced himself that he liked lamb to justify having it. (After all, who would choose a dinner he did not like, just because he enjoyed watching the chef serve it?)

The example shows a person changing an internal state (i.e., a liking for lamb) to reduce dissonance. In this chapter we will be concerned with the fact that a person may change his level of intrinsic motivation for some activity as a means of reducing dissonance. I shall attempt to show that if a person engages in a dull activity (the first cognition) for insufficient extrinsic rewards (the second cognition), he will experience dissonance, which he will reduce by convincing himself that he is intrinsically motivated toward that activity. In other words, his intrinsic motivation will increase to reduce dissonance. This proposition is derived from an area of research which is generally referred to as "the psychology of insufficient justifications" (e.g., Festinger, 1961; Aronson, 1966, 1969).

If a person performs an act which is inconsistent with one of his internal states (e.g., an attitude, a feeling, a motive) he will experience dissonance and be motivated to reduce that dissonance. If he has "sufficient external justification," the behavior will be easily rationalized, thereby reducing the dissonance almost immediately. For example, if he were forced to behave by a strong threat or if he were given a sizeable reward to behave, he would rationalize that he did it because of the threat or the reward. This would quickly reduce the dissonance. When he does something to avoid a punishment or to get a reward, it doesn't really matter if the behavior is consistent with his own internal states. When Fred ate lamb at the dinner party, the reason was obvious. Social custom and politeness dictated that he do it, so his feeling about lamb didn't really matter. There was plenty of external "justification" for the behavior, so the dissonance was readily dispelled.

It is interesting to note that there is some disagreement among dissonance theorists about whether an event for which there is adequate external justification arouses dissonance that is immediately reduced or does not arouse dissonance, at all. My position is the latter; I think that the dissonance is caused by the inconsistency between engaging in a behavior, and having no meaningful reason for doing it. Although this is something of a moot point, since the two positions are "functionally" equivalent, I think that it is an interesting difference theoretically. Dissonance is a motivational state which is aroused when a person behaves in an inconsistent way for no good reason. Frequently we behave in ways that are inconsistent with an internal state without experiencing dissonance. When someone fasts for religious reasons, or lies to save his life, there is no dissonance. As I said at the beginning of this chapter, the dissonance is the uncomfortable state which exists when a person has no apparently meaningful way to deal with an incongruity.

Consider a situation in which a person behaves in a way that is inconsistent with one of his internal states, and has insufficient justification for doing so. He will experience dissonance. In such a situation the most likely way for him to reduce the dissonance is to distort his internal state. For example, when Fred ate lamb at the smorgasbord, there was insufficient justification for doing it (no reward, no threat, no social custom), so he reduced the dissonance by convincing himself that he likes lamb. He cognitively distorted (or changed) his internal state to justify the dissonant behavior.

Dissonance and Intrinsic Motivation

Imagine a person doing a dull, boring task; doing the task is inconsistent with his internal states (he doesn't like the task and he's not intrinsically motivated to do it). If he is handsomely rewarded for doing the task, there will be no dissonance. He does the task, dull though it may be, because of the reward. There is plenty of external justification. If on the other hand he gets only a small reward, he will have insufficient justification for having done the activity, so he will experience dissonance. One way of reducing the dissonance is to imbue the task with additional intrinsic worth. In other words, the person's intrinsic motivation for the activity may increase as a means of reducing dissonance.

In Chapter 5 we saw that when a person is rewarded substantially for doing an interesting activity his intrinsic motivation will decrease. We now review evidence which substantiates the parallel proposition that if a person is insufficiently rewarded for doing a dull task his intrinsic motivation will increase. Both sets of findings suggest a negative relationship between the amount of extrinsic reward and the level of intrinsic motivation.

Studies relating to this proposition have often used "liking for the task" as the dependent measure, though a few have used "behavior in the absence of extrinsic rewards" as the dependent measure. I shall interpret both of these as measures of intrinsic motivation, though I add the *caveat* that experimental comparisons between these dependent measures is called for.

Perhaps the best known study of this kind was done by Festinger and Carlsmith (1959). In this study there were essentially three parts. First, all subjects spent an hour doing dull and boring tasks. For the first half-hour, using only one hand, they loaded spools into a tray, then unloaded the tray and began again. For the second half-hour they turned square pegs a quarter-turn at a time, again using only one hand. The purpose of this first part of the experiment was to give all subjects a common experience of doing a dull boring task.

Subjects were then asked to help out the experimenter by substituting for an experimental assistant who had been unable to work that day. Their job would be to go into the waiting room and tell the next subject (a stooge) that the experiment had been interesting, enjoyable, and exciting. Half the subjects were paid $1 for doing this, and half were paid $20.

The third part of the experiment was an interview conducted by a different experimenter to obtain the dependent measure, *viz.* how much the subjects enjoyed the experimental tasks. The prediction derived from dissonance theory was that the subjects who lied for low pay ($1) would experience dissonance and would change their attitude about the task as a means of reducing dissonance. They lied about having liked the task but they had inadequate justification for lying, so they grew to like the task as a means of justifying having lied. The people who received $20 could easily rationalize the behavior, since there was quite adequate external justification. They lied because of the $20, so they did not need to change their attitudes. The results of the experiment appear in Table VI. As predicted, attitudes of the low-payment subjects became significantly more positive, that is, these subjects evaluated the task as significantly more interesting and enjoyable. Attitudes of the high-payment subjects, however, did not differ significantly from those of the control subjects who had done the dull task but had not lied about it. Therefore, the data do support dissonance theory.

TABLE VI. *Average Attitude Toward Task of High Reward, Low Reward, and Control Subjects (Festinger &* *Carlsmith, 1959)*

Type of reward	Ratings[a]
High ($20)	−.05
Low ($1)	+1.35
Control	−.45

[a] How enjoyable the task was, based on a scale ranging from −5.0 to +5.0

This study, however, has been widely criticized. For example, Chapanis and Chapanis (1964) and Janis and Gilmore (1965) criticized the use of a $20 reward, pointing out that such a large reward is unbelievable and probably instilled guilt and discomfort in the subjects. Aronson (1966) however, contended that this was probably not the case. Each subject was asked, in turn for $20, not only to speak to the waiting "subject" but also to be on call in the future to help out, if needed. Further, the experimenter conveyed that he was rather desperate and very much needed that subject to help him out. While this question is somewhat disputable, Aronson's point does seem reasonable. Moreover, it is supported by several subsequent studies, which have replicated the findings and have involved smaller amounts of money. For example, in a study conducted among teenagers by Carlsmith, Collins, and Helmreich (1966), each subject was asked to perform a dull, boring task and then to tell another that the experiment had been very interesting. Subjects were paid either $.50, $1.50, or $5 for telling the lie. As predicted, there was an inverse relationship between amount of payment and expressed liking for the activity.

I asserted that if someone is underpaid to do a dull activity he will enhance his intrinsic motivation for the activity as a means of reducing dissonance. The Festinger and Carlsmith study, as well as that by Carlsmith *et al.*, offers indirect evidence for our assertion. It is not conclusive, however, because in these studies the payment, whether sufficient or insufficient, was given *not* for doing the task, but rather, for lying about one's enjoyment of the task.

A study which more nearly tests our assertion is a field experiment by Bogart, Loeb, and Rutman (1969) conducted in a psychiatric rehabilitation center. The subjects were patients who attended vocational workshops and received incentives for perfect and prompt attendance at the workshops. Low-reward subjects received $.25 per week for attending each day, whereas high-reward subjects received $2 per week for attending regularly. After four weeks incentive rewards were terminated and behaviors were recorded for four weeks of "extinction." In addition, behaviors had been recorded for a 4 week pretreatment period to provide a baseline measure. All measures were analyzed as change from pre- to posttreatment periods.

The predictions, of course, were that low-reward subjects would have more positive attitudes about the workshop than high-reward subjects, and also that low-reward subjects would attend the workshops more during the posttreatment period than high-reward subjects. In other words, low-reward subjects would have enhanced their intrinsic motivation for the work experience.

The predictions were upheld. Attitudes of low-reward subjects became significantly more positive, whereas attitudes of high-reward subjects decreased slightly from pre- to posttreatment periods. Similarly, attendance at the workshops showed the same pattern. For both low- and high-reward subjects attendance increased from pretreatment to treatment conditions. When subjects were paid to attend, they did so more regularly (though the investigators did not report whether or not this increase were statistically significant). The important data, however, are the data from the posttreatment period. Following removal of rewards, attendance of low-reward subjects remained constant, whereas attendance of high-reward subjects decreased markedly (i.e., absences increased). This difference, which was significant in an analysis of variance, is represented in Figure 11.

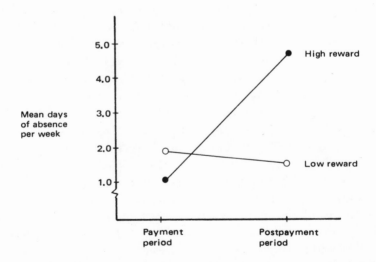

FIGURE 11. Attendance rates of low reward and high reward subjects during payment (i.e., treatment) period and posttreatment period when there was no reward (after Bogart *et al.*, 1969).

Threats of Punishment

The insufficient justification analysis has also been applied to situations where strong threats (sufficient justification) or mild threats (insufficient justification) have been used to control behavior. In one study by Aronson and Carlsmith (1963) children were told not to play with an "attractive toy." Half of the children received mild threats (the experimenter said he would be annoyed at them) and the other half received strong threats (the experimenter said he would be very angry with them and would take the toys away and not return). The investigators predicted that subjects who received mild threats for "not playing" would become more favorable toward "not playing" (i.e., they would derogate the forbidden toy), whereas the severe-threat children would not. The predictions were upheld. Severe-threat children increased their rating of the toy, whereas mild-threat children derogated the toy. Since the latter group had had insufficient external justification for refraining from playing with the target toy, they changed their evaluation of the toy to reduce dissonance. Turner and Wright (1965) replicated the findings.

Freedman (1965), using a procedure very similar to that of Aronson and Carlsmith, found that children who received mild threats for refraining from playing with an attractive toy spent less time playing with the target toy than did severe-threat children in a free-play situation several weeks after the threat manipulation. In other words, Freedman showed, not only that insufficient justification can lead to attitude change about the target activity, but that it can also lead to long-lasting behavioral changes. The Freedman study relates closely to our assertion that a person who has insufficient justification for doing an unpreferred activity will increase his intrinsic motivation for that activity as a means of reducing dissonance. If one considers "not playing with the toy" as the unpreferred activity, then the Freedman results provide direct support for our assertion. In other words, the results showed that if someone does something (refrains from play) for inadequate justification (a mild threat), he will increase his intrinsic motivation for the activity (i.e., he will be intrinsically motivated to refrain from playing) as a means of reducing dissonance. On the other hand, if the person refrains from play after receiving a strong threat, the threat provides adequate justification for refraining, so the dissonance is immediately dispelled and there is no need for him to change his interest in the toy.

In recent replications of the general findings that desired toys will be derogated more by a child when a mild threat, rather than a severe threat, is used to prevent him from playing with the toy, Zanna, Lepper, and Abelson (1973) found that the more that the child's attention can be drawn to the dissonant elements (not playing with a desired toy and having only the insufficient justification of a mild threat), the greater will be the dissonance reduction (i.e., derogation of the toy). If there is sufficient justification or if the child is not fully aware that the elements are dissonant, then he will be less likely to change his interest in the activity.

Task Enhancement

Weick (1964) proposed that if someone does a task which he's been asked to do by a person he dislikes, he will experience dissonance. The request of a disliked other is insufficient justification for doing the task, so dissonance is produced which will be eliminated if the person grows more favorable toward the task. Following this reasoning, Weick did an experiment to test the hypothesis that if subjects do a task for a negatively valued task-setter (i.e., an experimenter whom they dislike) they will reduce dissonance by enhancing the task and expending greater effort on the task. In his experiment, subjects worked on a concept-identification task. Half the subjects were given experimental credit for participating in the experiment (a desired reward) and were treated respectfully by the experimenter. These subjects had sufficient justification for doing the activity. The other subjects had been expecting credit for the experiment. However, when they arrived, an unfriendly experimenter told them that they would not be able to get credit for the experiment, since in the view of the psychology department of that university he had illegitimately lured the subjects into participating. Then, with a rather brusque manner, he said that he could not force them to stay, but that it would be convenient for him if they stayed (50 out of 54 stayed and participated). Clearly, these subjects had insufficient justification for participating; there were no rewards and they were working for an experimenter whom they undoubtedly disliked.

The results of this experiment are quite compelling and provide strong support for our assertion that intrinsic motivation may be enhanced as a means of reducing dissonance. Using several dependent measures, Weick found that insufficient-justification subjects performed better on the task than rewarded subjects. The nonrewarded subjects solved more problems, requested less help from the experimenter, persisted more at impossible tasks, and remembered more information than did rewarded subjects. Further, the nonrewarded subjects found the task significantly more interesting than did rewarded subjects.

Dissonance and Attitudes

As we have seen, there is some support for our assertion that insufficiently justified, boring activities may lead to enhanced intrinsic motivation for participating in them. The psychology of insufficient justification, however, has been far more often applied to the area of attitude-change than to intrinsic-motivation-change. Since these studies derive from the same reasoning as does my assertion, we shall review some of them. This will provide us with the opportunity of outlining some of the conditions under which we might expect dissonance findings and others where we are likely not to find them. Although these restraining conditions have been tested for changes in attitudes, it is reasonable and compelling to think that they will also hold for changes in intrinsic motivation.

The basic hypothesis of these "counter-attitudinal advocacy" studies is that if a person argues in favor of a position which is counter to his own, he will experience dissonance. If he has sufficient external justification (high pay, strong threats, etc.) for this behavior, he will be able to rationalize the behavior and experience little discomfort. If he has insufficient justification he will experience dissonance which he will reduce by becoming more favorable toward the position which he advocated. In short, if there is insufficient justification he will change his attitude to bring it more in line with his counter-attitudinal behavior.

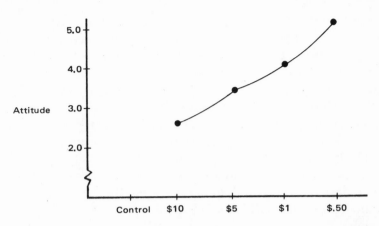

FIGURE 12. Relationship between payment for espousing a counter-attitudinal position and attitude following espousal (after Cohen, 1962). The higher the attitude value the more favorable toward the police: hence, the more attitude change toward the espoused position.

Cohen (1962) asked college students to write a counter-attitudinal essay supporting the actions of New Haven police during a disturbance at Yale. Students were paid \$.50, \$1, \$5, or \$10 for doing this. The results showed clear support for dissonance theory; there was an inverse relationship between the amount of pay and the amount of attitude change. The subjects who had been paid only \$.50 became more favorably disposed toward the police action, whereas the \$10 subjects became slightly less favorably disposed. The results for each condition appear in Figure 12. As can be seen, the relationship between payments and attitude change is monotonic and inverse. Numerous other studies have also demonstrated a negative relationship between amount of justification and amount of attitude change; e.g., Aronson and Mills (1959), Smith (1961), Brock and Blackwood (1962), Freedman (1963), Nuttin (1964), Zimbardo (1965), and Gerard and Mathewson (1966). We see, then, that dissonance theory and the insufficient justification prediction which is derived from it have received substantial experimental verification. Yet, as we mentioned earlier, dissonance theory has not been without its adversaries. When dissonance theory was first introduced in 1957, its predictions, on the face of it, seemed to contradict an enormous body of data which showed a positive relationship between size of reward for engaging in counter-attitudinal behavior, and amount of attitude change. These studies, part of what is known as the *Yale communication studies*, were summarized by Hovland, Janis, and Kelley (1953). More recently, Rosenberg (1965) and Elms and Janis (1965) have also found results which they claim are contradictory to dissonance theory. We will now review this controversy briefly and report various attempts to reconcile the seeming discrepancies. We will see that the two sets of findings are reconcilable; under certain conditions one effect appears, and under other conditions the other appears.

Dissonance vs. Incentives

The reinforcement theory of attitude change as proposed by Hovland *et al.* (1953) was derived primarily from learning theory principles (Hull, 1943; Miller & Dollard, 1941). When a subject is exposed to a persuasive communication, his attitude will change toward the view which was expressed in the communication, if he attends to, comprehends, and accepts the espoused attitude. If the subject has attended to, and comprehended, the communication, his acceptance will depend primarily on the incentives or reinforcements associated with the communication. The greater the incentive, the greater the attitude change. This theory applies to the attitudes of both the listener and the communicator. For counter-attitudinal advocacy, then, the prediction is that there will be a positive relationship between the inducement or reward which a person receives for espousing positions he doesn't believe in, and the amount of change in his attitude toward the espoused position. (Recall that dissonance theory leads to the prediction of a negative relationship.)

Scott (1959) showed that cash prizes given to winners of a debate who argued counter-attitudinal positions produced attitude change toward the argued position, and that the change was still evident 10 days later. Bostrom, Vlandis, and Rosenbaum (1961) demonstrated that students changed their attitudes more toward the position they expressed in a counter-attitudinal essay if they received an A for the essay (large reward) than if they received a D (low reward). Thus, we see that incentive effects are sometimes produced in counter-attitudinal advocacy.

Later studies which support this position have argued that the dissonance effect was artifactual (Rosenberg, 1965; Janis & Gilmore, 1965). As we pointed out previously, Janis and Gilmore argued that the $20 reward paid to subjects in the Festinger and Carlsmith (1959) study was probably unbelievable and induced in the subjects guilt and discomfort which interfered with their attention to their arguments and therefore prevented attitude change. Since the dissonance effect has been produced by amounts much smaller, however, their explanation seems implausible.

Rosenberg (1965), in discussing the Cohen (1962) experiment, argued that Cohen's results were artifactual. He asserted that, since the experimenter who induced compliance was the same person as the post-tester who assessed the attitudes, the subjects probably perceived the experimenter to be evaluating them. If so, the subjects would have resisted changing their attitudes to show the experimenter that they could not be bribed into changing their attitudes. Rosenberg then did a study where he used two different experimenters and found an incentive effect.

Although Rosenberg did not find a dissonance effect, it is quite clear that dissonance effects cannot be explained away by his artifactual explanation. Numerous studies have separated the two experimenter functions of performing the manipulation and assessing the attitudes and still have found a dissonance effect (e.g., Festinger & Carlsmith, 1959; Carlsmith *et al.*, 1966; Linder, Cooper, & Jones, 1967; and Sherman, 1970). Further, Aronson (1966) pointed out that Rosenberg inadvertently lowered the prestige of the second experimenter in his study, so his results may have been artifactual.

The obvious conclusion from all of the studies seems to be that both dissonance effects and incentive effects in counter-attitudinal advocacy are valid phenomena and that the important task for experimenters is to elaborate the conditions under which each is likely to occur.

It seems clear that attitudes associated with rewarded behavior may be strengthened, but that this will happen only when the situation is not dissonance producing. Several studies have been done which have produced both a dissonance effect and an incentive effect under slightly different conditions.

In one such study Carlsmith *et al.* (1966) argued that when a person is espousing a counter-attitudinal position, anonymous essay writing might not be dissonance producing while face-to-face role playing would be. In an anonymous situation the person would be less committed to the discrepant statement. "No one knows he wrote it, so he can forget about it." However, if he has committed himself to the position in the presence of another, he can't forget it. He is committed to it, and hence he experiences dissonance. The investigators used high school boys in an experiment in which they performed the dull task of striking out numbers from a random list. Then, they either reported face to face to a waiting subject (actually a confederate) that the experiment had been interesting and fun, or they wrote an essay reporting that they had enjoyed the task. The results showed very striking effects. As predicted, the private essay condition produced an incentive effect over the three reward levels ($.50, $1.50, $5) whereas the public role playing condition produced a dissonance effect (see Figure 13).

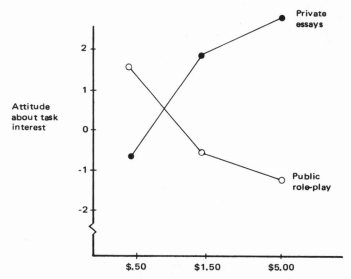

FIGURE 13. Attitude about how interesting the task was as a function of inducement for lying (after Carlsmith *et al.*, 1966).

Choice

Linder *et al.* (1967) suggested that unless subjects perceive themselves to have had a choice about whether or not to engage in the counter-attitudinal behavior, it will not be dissonance producing. If they had no choice about complying with the request for counter-attitudinal behavior, they could easily rationalize the behavior: "I did it because I had no choice." However, if they chose to engage in the dissonant behavior, there is no escaping the dissonance. Linder *et al.* did a study in which one group of subjects was given no choice about whether or not to write an essay, whereas those who comprised another group were told that they were free not to write it, since they had not committed themselves to do so when they volunteered for the study. The results showed an incentive effect in the no-choice conditions and a dissonance effect in the choice conditions.

Linder *et al.* then pointed out that subjects in the Rosenberg (1965) experiment had been given no choice about complying, and hence, the incentive effect. To show this conclusively Linder *et al.* replicated the Rosenberg procedure. Subjects reported to the experimenter and were told that there would be a delay of 15 minutes or so. Then, offhandedly, the experimenter said there was another little experiment which they could do while waiting, and that they could earn money doing it. The choice subjects were told that they were not committed to do the task and that they should withhold deciding about whether to participate until after they heard what the task was. The no-choice subjects were not told this.

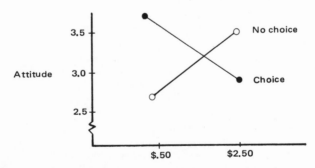

FIGURE 14. Attitudes as a function of incentive under choice and no-choice conditions (after Linder *et al.*, 1967).

Again, the results showed an interaction between choice and magnitude of reward. Those results are shown in Figure 14. When there was choice, there was a dissonance effect, and when there was no choice, an incentive effect.

Holmes and Strickland (1970) and Sherman (1970) have reported replications of the Linder *et al.* results.

Consequences

Collins (1969) suggested that the consequences of one's actions must be considered in understanding counter-attitudinal behavior. If the consequences to oneself of one's actions are aversive, then dissonance will be induced. Therefore, a counter-attitudinal behavior should produce attitude change only if the negative consequences are sufficient. Several studies (Chase, 1970; Cooper & Worchel, 1970; Nel, Helmreich, & Aronson, 1969; Cialdini, 1971; Goethals & Cooper, 1972) have substantiated this by demonstrating that if listeners seem persuasible or persuaded (high consequences) there will be dissonance which will lead to attitude change on the part of the counter-attitudinal communicator. However, if the audience seem unaffected by the communicator (low consequences) there will be no dissonance and no attitude change. Similarly, Cooper, Zanna, and Goethals (1974) showed that lying to a disliked other (low consequences) is not so dissonance producing as lying to a friend (high consequences), so attitude change will occur only when the speaker likes the person whom he lies to and convinces.

Consequences and Responsibility (Choice)

Collins and Hoyt (1972) claimed that neither choice nor consequences alone could adequately integrate the forced compliance literature but that the two together could. They stated that a person must feel personal responsibility for a behavior with meaningful consequences in order to experience dissonance. Choice is seen to be a special case of personal responsibility. If one chooses to do something he will feel greater personal responsibility about it.

Collins and Hoyt further suggested that the public role play *vs.* anonymous private essays of Carlsmith *et al.* (1966) could be considered as a question of consequences, rather than public/private. In the private condition, since the essay was to be rewritten by the experimenter before others read it, the subjects were less likely to associate negative consequences with their actions. The public subjects, however, actually saw the listener face to face and were therefore more aware of the negative consequences. This interpretation does seem plausible, though it seems even more reasonable to us that personal responsibility (rather than consequences) is more adequate in reinterpreting the public/private variable. When a person faces another and lies to him, he would be hard pressed not to accept responsibility. In the essay condition, no one even sees his essay, so he feels less responsible. The consequences of the essay may be fully as unfortunate as the consequences of the face-to-face arguments, but he will undoubtedly accept less responsibility for them.

In line with the Collins and Hoyt assertion, Hoyt, Henley and Collins (1972) demonstrated the dissonance effect in counterattitudinal essay writing about not brushing one's teeth only when subjects felt personally responsible for negative consequences. When subjects were told that the readers would get pro- as well as antitoothbrushing arguments and that their essays would not actually influence toothbrushing behaviors, there was no dissonance effect.

Collins and Hoyt (1972) then hypothesized that responsibility for consequences could reconcile the dissonance and incentive findings. When there are high personal responsibility and high aversive consequences, there should be a dissonance effect; when there are low consequences and low personal responsibility, there should be an incentive effect. The experiment was a $2 \times 2 \times 2$ design (high/low personal responsibility; high/low negative consequences; high ($2.50)/low ($.50) reward). Subjects wrote counterattitudinal essays about 24-hour open visitation policies in the U.C.L.A. undergraduate dormitories. Results revealed a dissonance effect in the high responsibility, high consequences conditions (i.e., more attitude change in the $.50 condition than the $2.50 condition). However, there was not an incentive effect in the low responsibility/low consequences condition.

At about the same time that the Collins and Hoyt study was done, Calder, Ross, and Insko (1973) did a study that was conceptually almost identical. Calder *et al.* manipulated choice, rather than responsibility, yet as we mentioned above, the two seem closely connected. The paradigm in this study was the paradigm "dull task and lie that it was interesting" used by Festinger and Carlsmith (1959), rather than the essay paradigm. The choice manipulation was done by the experimenter who told subjects that they had a choice about lying; the consequences manipulation was done by the confederate listener who was either persuaded or not persuaded that the task would be interesting; and the reward manipulation was $\frac{1}{2}$ hour of experimental credit *vs.* 2 hours.

The results of this study were very similar to those of Collins and Hoyt (1972). In both studies, when aversive consequences were high there was an interaction between reward and responsibility (choice) such that with high responsibility (choice) there was a dissonance effect and with low responsibility (choice) there was an incentive effect. The results for both experiments in the high consequences conditions appear in Figure 15. The conclusions

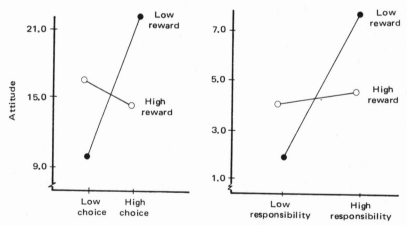

FIGURE 15. Attitudes as a function of responsibility (choice) for high and low rewarded subjects in *high consequences* conditions (after Calder *et al.*, 1973 and Collins & Hoyt, 1972). In both studies, the higher the attitude, the closer the match between the attitude and the counter-attitudinal behavior. In the low choice and low responsibility conditions there is an incentive effect (i.e., more attitude change in the high reward conditions). In the high choice and high responsibility conditions there is a dissonance effect.

from these two studies seem quite clear and useful in integrating the forced-compliance literature.

For attitude change to occur—either as a dissonance effect or as an incentive effect—there must be negative consequences to one's counter-attitudinal behavior. If consequences are low there will be no predictable attitude change. Collins and Hoyt predicted an incentive effect under low responsibility/low consequences, and when they did not find it, they stated that more work is necessary to determine when there will be an incentive effect. We think, however, that the answer appears in their data and identically appears in the data of Calder *et al.* An incentive effect occurs when consequences are high and there is no choice (responsibility) about the counter-attitudinal behavior.

The main conclusion, then, seems quite clear. When consequences of a counter-attitudinal behavior are sufficiently negative, there will be an inverse relationship between reward and attitude change (i.e., a dissonance effect) if there is high responsibility (choice) for the behavior and consequences, and there will be a direct relationship between reward and attitude change (i.e., an incentive effect) if there is low responsibility (choice) for the behavior and consequences.

This conclusion seems to integrate the forced-compliance literature quite satisfactorily. Since, as Collins and Hoyt pointed out, there were aversive consequences in the experiments by Linder *et al.* (1967) and Sherman (1970), the choice X reward interaction which they obtained was replicated by the Calder *et al.* and Collins and Hoyt experiments.

In the consequences studies of Cooper and Worchel (1970) and Cooper *et al.* (1974), the subjects were given direct choice, and in the Nel *et al.* study, there also appeared to be choice, so these studies also were replicated by Calder *et al.* and by Collins and Hoyt.

Finally, if the Carlsmith *et al.* study is reinterpreted as a manipulation, primarily, of responsibility rather than of consequences, then their results also fit the same pattern as those of all the other studies.

Hence, high negative consequences seem to be a necessary condition for attitude change, and responsibility/no responsibility (choice/no choice) seems to mediate the relationship between rewards (justification, incentives, etc.) and attitude change. Personal responsibility leads to a dissonance effect, and low responsibility leads to an incentive effect. This interpretation seems to be the most adequate of all those offered to date to account for all the various findings in the forced compliance literature.

Intrinsic Motivation

All of the studies which have attempted to determine the conditions under which a dissonance effect will be produced have used attitudes as the dependent measure. However, these seem to have close relevance to our concern about changes in intrinsic motivation. For one thing, many of the studies used the dull task paradigm and measured liking for the task. As we said previously, it is quite reasonable to expect that liking for a task and intrinsic motivation for a task are very highly correlated. We saw, for example, in Chapter 5 that the effects of rewards on a person's intrinsic motivation for an interesting task were the same whether the dependent measure were a behavioral measure of intrinsic motivation or an attitude measure of liking for, interest in, or enjoyment of the task.

Therefore, it seems reasonable to make the following conclusions for intrinsic motivation: If a person engages in a dull and boring activity for inadequate justification (rewards), and if he feels personally responsible for performing the behavior, his intrinsic motivation for the activity will increase as a means of justifying the behavior. It might be noted that if a person is engaging in an activity (i.e., giving his time and energy for inadequate reasons), the consequences to him would seem to be high. After all, his time and energy are worth a lot to him.

The notion of personal responsibility ties in closely to the personal causation and self-determination which we've asserted is the psychological basis of intrinsic motivation. For a person's intrinsic motivation to be affected by his behavior and the justification for that behavior he must feel personally responsible for having engaged in that behavior (i.e., he must feel self-determination). If he feels personal responsibility, and if he has insufficient extrinsic justification, he will enhance his intrinsic motivation for the activity, that is, he will come to see the activity as something he does to feel competent and self-determining.

Dissonance and Motives

Zimbardo (1969) edited a collection of papers, the aim of which was to demonstrate that cognitive dissonance reduction could affect a person's biological drives and social motives. If, for example, a thirsty person chose to continue playing ball rather than to go to the corner tavern, he might well convince himself that he's not thirsty as a means of reducing the dissonance created by having chosen not to go for a drink. The fact that a number of studies have supported the assertion that one's biological or social motives will change as a means of reducing dissonance helps to buttress our assertion that one's intrinsic motivation may be affected by dissonance reduction processes. Therefore, we will very briefly review some of the studies reported by Zimbardo (1969).

Biological Drives

Brehm (1962) and Brehm, Back, and Bogdonoff (1964) have demonstrated that dissonance reduction can affect a person's hunger drive. In these experiments subjects who had foregone food for many hours and who reported being very hungry agreed to fast for an additional period in order to allow further testing. In the Brehm (1962) study half the subjects were offered no rewards for doing so, and half were offered $5. The subjects were told they did not have to do this, thus there was choice (personal responsibility) involved. After they committed themselves to forego dinner they rated how hungry they were. Then, they were told that after the evening testing session they would be served sandwiches, milk, and cookies, and were asked how many of each they wanted. The results showed that the high dissonance subjects (i.e., those who were offered no reward to continue fasting) reported that they were less hungry and ordered less food than those who were paid $5. The cognition, "I will forego dinner for no good reason," was dissonant with the cognition, "I am hungry," so, to reduce this dissonance, subjects convinced themselves that they were less hungry. In the $5 condition, however, there was external justification for not eating, so there was no need to adjust their hunger to reduce dissonance.

Brehm *et al.* (1964) reported that when hungry subjects agreed to fast without pay, they were less hungry and showed a lower free fatty acid level than hungry subjects who agreed to fast for substantial rewards. This essentially replicated the Brehm (1962) results and showed that a physiological correlate of hunger was also responsive to the dissonance manipulation.

In addition to the findings that dissonance can affect one's hunger, studies have shown that it can affect food preferences. Two studies have shown, for example, that when people were induced to eat a disliked food (grasshoppers) for insufficient justification, their liking for the food increased. Smith (1961) had a friendly experimenter request that soldiers eat grasshoppers, and an unfriendly one order soldiers to do it. The experimenters reasoned that, when someone eats a disliked food for an unpleasant person, he will experience dissonance, whereas if he does it for a pleasant person, there will be less dissonance, since he would be doing the act as a favor to the pleasant other—hence, those who did it for unpleasant other should increase liking for the food to reduce that dissonance. Their results tended to support their reasoning. Zimbardo, Weisenberg, Firestone, and Levy (1965) replicated the Smith results and showed stronger, more convincing evidence of the effect.

In these studies relating cognitive dissonance to hunger, subjects were given choice about doing the behaviors. With choice, there was a negative relationship between the amount of inducement and the changes in motivation (i.e., a dissonance effect). This is consistent with the counter-attitudinal advocacy studies reported above. Unfortunately, the studies did not run groups with no choice, hence we are left only to speculate that there would have been no change in motivation if there had been no choice.

Thirst

Brehm (1962) also explored the effects of dissonance on thirst. Assuming that thirst has a cognitive component and that cognitions can affect one's thirst, Brehm reasoned that if a thirsty person voluntarily abstained from drinking for inadequate justification he would experience less thirst as a means of reducing dissonance than would someone who abstained for adequate justification. Using a paradigm very similar to that of the hunger study reported above (Brehm, 1962), Brehm found that there was a significant difference between subjective reports of thirst in the high dissonance (inadequate justification) conditions. High dissonance subjects reported less thirstiness than did low dissonance subjects.

In a study by Brock and Grant (1963) subjects with experimentally induced dry mouths—created by eating crackers with "hot sauce"—were told (while they were under hypnosis) that they were water satiated and had bloated stomachs. This, of course, was a high dissonant situation, and the results of the study showed that these subjects reported less thirst and also drank less than low dissonance subjects who had not been told of bloated stomachs. Further, the high dissonance subjects reported less thirst than nonhypnotized subjects who role-played bloated stomachs. This latter finding showed that the dissonance, rather than the suggestion of being bloated, in and of itself, caused the decreased thirst and water consumption.

Mansson (1965) also showed that thirsty subjects who voluntarily committed themselves to 24 hours of water deprivation for low justification reported less thirst than those with adequate justification. Further, the insufficient justification subjects behaved more like nonthirsty controls than thirsty controls on projective techniques.

In summation, we can see from the data on hunger and thirst that biological drives seem to have a cognitive component and that a person's cognitions can influence his experience of hunger or thirst, as well as his eating and drinking behavior. We turn now to a brief look at the effects of cognitions on one's social motives.

Motive for Success

In Chapter 5 we saw that failure at an intrinsically motivated activity led to decreased intrinsic motivation, poorer performance and lowered expectations about future performance. A study by Schlachet (1965) has shown that when subjects volunteer to do a task with high probability of failure and with low external justification, they will lower their success motivation to reduce the dissonance. The subjects in the study apparently convinced themselves that they did not need to succeed, as a rationalization for agreeing to fail. Further, they exhibited less negative affect about failure, and they recalled more failure stimuli—interpreted by Schlachet as a reversal of the repression hypothesis (Rapaport, 1961) thus indicating less fear of failure—than did subjects who had adequate justification for agreeing to fail.

This study of success motivation (related to need for achievement, though measured differently), coupled with the earlier studies on hunger and thirst, shows quite clearly that motives can, indeed, be affected by one's cognitions and the need to reduce dissonance between cognitions.

Summary

In this chapter we have reviewed evidence which shows that cognitive dissonance reduction can affect a person's motivation. I hypothesized that if a person engages in a dull, boring activity for which he has insufficient justification, he may enhance his intrinsic motivation for the activity as a means of reducing dissonance between the cognitions "I am doing a dull activity" and "I have little justification for this activity." He convinces himself that the activity is interesting and that he's intrinsically motivated to engage in it. Some studies were reviewed which bear directly on the hypothesis. Further, numerous studies were reviewed which considered the related hypothesis that, when a person expresses a counter-attitudinal position for little justification he will change his attitude in the direction of being more favorably disposed toward the espoused position, as a means of reducing dissonance.

We saw however, that this dissonance phenomenon seems to hold only if there are negative consequences which follow the behavior and if the person feels personal responsibility for the behavior.

Further, we saw that cognitive dissonance reduction can also affect one's biological drives of hunger and thirst, as well as the social motive for success. It was asserted that these findings make more plausible the hypothesis that dissonance reduction will affect intrinsic motivation.

7

Inequity and Intrinsic Motivation

Kevin, who has always loved to act, got his first job in a 3-month run of a new play. He was further pleased to find out that the theater paid well above the going rate. However, 4 days before the scheduled closing the manager discovered that she'd be unable to pay the cost for the remainder of the run. Attendance had been down and there just wasn't any money. Either the show would have to close or the cast would have to work without pay.

In Chapter 5 we reviewed research which has some bearing on this problem. The general findings were that when someone is rewarded extrinsically for doing an intrinsically interesting activity, the experience of being rewarded will cause the person to lose intrinsic motivation for the activity. This suggests that Kevin would be less likely to continue working than if he had gotten lower wages, since the high pay would have decreased his intrinsic motivation for acting.

Danielle, on the other hand, worked doing makeup for the cast; she experienced this job as dull and boring. She did it, even though the pay to the crew was bad, because she could not find another job. What might she have been expected to do in response to the announcement that there would be no pay for the last 4 days?

In Chapter 6 we saw that when a person does a dull, boring task for inadequate extrinsic rewards he may enhance his intrinsic motivation for the activity as a means of justifying to himself having done an uninteresting task for insufficient rewards.

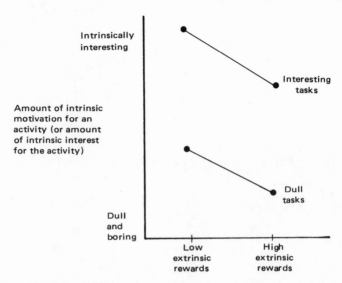

FIGURE 16. Relationship between extrinsic rewards and intrinsic motivation for an interesting and a boring task.

That research on dissonance theory suggests that Danielle might have continued to work for the last 4 days without pay. Having been insufficiently rewarded, she would have developed an interest in the activity as a justification for doing it, so with her newfound interest she would have been willing to work for the intrinsic satisfaction which she now derived from the job.

The general findings from work in cognitive evaluation theory (Chapter 5) and cognitive dissonance theory (Chapter 6) are presented in Figure 16. One can see that the findings are complementary. Both sets of findings suggest a general negative relationship between extrinsic rewards (or controls or justifications) and the amount of intrinsic motivation (or interest) which a person has for the activity. The differences, however, are in the processes which cause the phenomena. In the case of overly sufficient justification (a term suggested by Nisbett & Valins, 1971), it is proposed that when a person receives both intrinsic satisfaction and extrinsic rewards, there is a decrease in intrinsic motivation owing to a change in perceived locus of causality. The intrinsically motivated person who gets no extrinsic rewards is assumed to experience no change in his intrinsic motivation. In the case of insufficient justification, the person who gets no (or low) extrinsic rewards increases his intrinsic motivation as a means of reducing dissonance, whereas the person who did the dull task and got sufficient rewards is assumed not to experience a change in intrinsic motivation.

Adams (1963a, 1965) proposed a theory of inequity which makes opposite predictions in the Kevin/Danielle example from those of cognitive evaluation theory and cognitive dissonance (insufficient justification) theory. We will first review inequity theory and then look at the differing predictions.

Finally we will consider a means for reconciling the apparent contradictions. In discussing the discrepant predictions and means of integrating the theories, we will first discuss overly sufficient justification and then insufficient justification.

Inequity theory has been proposed in slightly differing forms by Homans (1950, 1961), Sayles (1958), Jacques (1961), Patchen (1961), and Adams. Since Adams's theory has generated by far the greatest number of empirical investigations related to inequity, we shall discuss his theory.

Equity Theory

Adams proposed that when one person is in an exchange relationship with another, the person will be concerned about what he puts into (inputs) and gets out of (outcomes) the relationship. Outcomes are all of the compensations a person gets from the relationship, for example, money, comfort, independence, friendship, personal satisfaction, and so on. Inputs are all of the things he brings to the situation which he believes to be relevant—things like training, effort, material expenditures, and so on.

Adams argued that the person will evaluate his own ratio of outcomes to inputs and compare it to the other person's ratio. If the two ratios are unequal, the person will feel inequity and will be motivated to reduce this inequity. Inequity will exist for a person both when he is overcompensated (i.e., when his ratio of outcomes to inputs is greater than the other's) and when he is undercompensated (i.e., when his ratio is less than the other's).

This model has been most frequently discussed and tested in relation to work situations (see reviews by Lawler, 1968; Goodman & Friedman, 1971), though a recent paper by Walster, Berscheid, and Walster (1973) has extended the formulation into interpersonal situations where one person harms another. The theory is applicable for a "Person" either when he is in a direct exchange relationship with an "Other" (e.g., his employer) or when Person and Other are both in a relationship with a third person (usually an employer).

In the typical experimental paradigm, Person is in a direct exchange relationship with an employer. However, the comparison Other is often ambiguous. None of the literature refers to the employer as the one with whom Person compares his ratio of outcomes to inputs, but, of course, it is the employer who gives the compensation. Generally a third person, often hypothetical, is invoked in the experimental instructions as the comparison Other.

Using Other to mean (a) the one with whom Person is in an exchange relationship, (b) someone engaged in a comparable activity, or (c) a hypothetical Other can lead to considerable confusion. To reduce this confusion, I shall use the term Other to refer to the one with whom Person is in a direct exchange interaction and the term *Colleague* to refer to someone else, whether real or hypothetical, who Person thinks is a suitable comparison person. Hence, the typical situation is that Person feels that his exchange with Other is either equitable or inequitable depending in part on the comparison of his outcomes/inputs ratio with that of some Colleague (either real or imaginary).

Adams (1965) mentioned that the Person may also use an internal standard as his comparison Other. Pritchard (1969) elaborated this point by defining *internal standard* as "the amount of outcome Person perceives as being commensurate with his own inputs, *without regard to any comparison person*" (p. 205). He suggested that "feelings of inequity arise *first* and *foremost* from the correspondence between Person's own inputs and outcomes. If his inputs are greater than (his) outcomes, he will experience inequity, which will lead to feelings of dissatisfaction" (p. 206). Similarly, if his outcomes are substantially greater than his inputs, he will experience inequity.

According to Adams, when a state of inequity exists for Person, he will be motivated to bring about psychological equity (which may or may not coincide with some "objective" equity) in one or more of the following ways: (1) by changing his inputs, (2) by changing his outcomes, (3) by cognitively distorting his inputs or outcomes, (4) by leaving the field, (5) by acting on the other party, or (6) by using a different comparison other (i.e., a different Other or a different Colleague).

Further, Person will seek to reduce inequity in a way which will maximize his own outcomes. This assertion is in agreement with cognitive theories of motivation and with the widely held beliefs that persons behave in ways which maximize their own utility. Walster, Berscheid, and Walster (1970) made a similar assertion, that Person will restore equity in the least costly manner. Pritchard *et al.* (1972) suggested also that Person would restore equity in ways which are least costly. They suggested that over the short run, Person might restore equity from overpay inequity by increasing his inputs, but that this would not persist. Over time, he would distort his cognitions about equity, redefine outcomes and inputs or use some similar manner of maintaining equity in the least costly manner.

The experimental investigations of inequity have generally focused on changes in inputs (as reflected by the dependent measures of quantity or quality of work). However, we will see that cognitive distortion is also a common response under certain circumstances. Indeed, changes in one's attitude toward a task or one's intrinsic motivation for a task are examples of cognitive distortion in situations where there were apparently "inequitable" payments. In this chapter I shall attempt to specify some of the circumstances wherein one might expect changes in inputs *vs.* cognitive distortion.

Studies of the effects of inequity on inputs (as reflected in productivity) have been of four kinds: overpay hourly, overpay piece rate, underpay hourly, and underpay piece rate. We will consider the overpayment situation first and in so doing will compare it to the overly sufficient justification effects.

Overpayment Inequity

In an overpayment situation, Person is made to feel that he is being overpaid for the task he is performing. Inequity theory asserts that if he feels overpaid he will experience discomfort (or dissonance) and seek to reduce this discomfort by increasing his inputs and/or decreasing his outcomes. There are, of course, other ways to restore equity. However, the empirical studies have generally considered only these two. If Person is being paid a set rate per hour of work there is no way to change his outcomes (at least, his financial outcomes), so it is predicted that he will increase his inputs by producing more, or by giving a higher quality of performance. However, if he is being paid on a contingency- or piece-rate basis (e.g., $1 per puzzle solved, or $.50 per interview conducted) he cannot restore equity be increasing quantity of production, since increased quantity means still higher pay. Therefore, he is expected to decrease his outcomes by producing fewer items but of higher quality.

In most of the overpayment studies, feelings of inequity have been induced by paying Person a reasonable rate for the job but having Other (i.e., the employer and/or experimenter) tell Person that he is much less qualified than Colleague (generally a hypothetical person or group of people). Person then is assumed to feel "overpaid," since he is getting more than he deserves as an unqualified performer. The use of this induction has been criticized by writers who offer an alternative explanation, namely, that Person's self-esteem is devalued by the induction and that he therefore increases his inputs to prove to himself and to Other that he is well qualified. It is not my purpose to discuss this controversy. The interested reader is referred to Goodman and Friedman (1971), who concluded a review of the argument by saying that the inequity interpretation seems more tenable than the self-esteem interpretation. Further, a study by Pritchard, Dunnette, and Jorgenson (1972) showed overpayment inequity effects without devaluing Person's qualifications. Their study induced the feelings of overpayment by increasing Person's payments, and therefore induced inequity without consideration of a comparison Other.

Four studies of hourly overpayment support the theory: Adams and Rosenbaum, 1962; Arrowood, 1961; Goodman and

Friedman, 1968; Pritchard, *et al.,* 1972. Six studies which considered piece rate overpayment also tended to support the hypothesis by showing decreased outcomes; Adams, 1963b; Adams and Jacobsen, 1964; Adams and Rosenbaum, 1962; Goodman and Friedman, 1969; Lawler, Koplin, Young, and Fadem, 1968; Wood and Lawler, 1970.

Hourly

In the first of two experiments reported by Adams and Rosenbaum (1962) Person was hired by Other to do interviewing at an hourly rate of pay. Half the subjects (Persons) were told that they were unqualified to do the work in relation to a hypothetical Colleague, but they were paid the standard rate. Thus, they were being overpaid. The other subjects were told that they were appropriately qualified and would be paid accordingly (i.e., equitably paid). The prediction was made and supported by the data that overpaid subjects would conduct more interviews.. Presumably, since they felt inequitably overpaid, they increased their own inputs to bring them in line with their outcomes.

Arrowood's (1961) study was similar to that of Adams and Rosenbaum. Subjects were made to feel either equitably paid or overpaid in relation to hypothetical Colleagues using the same qualifications manipulation and hourly pay. In addition, however, there were public and private conditions. Half the subjects sent the results of their inverviews to another city very far away (private) and the other half of the subjects (public) gave their results to Other (i.e., the employer/experimenter). Thus, he had a 2×2 design such that public/private crossed with equitable/inequitable. The results showed two main effects. Overpaid subjects in both public and private conditions produced more interviews than did equitably paid subjects. Also, public subjects produced more than did private subjects. Private subjects were led to believe that Other would not see their results. Hence, apparently, some portion of inequity is interpersonal (e.g., approval seeking or norm conforming). A person who feels inequitably overpaid is motivated to restore equity, both for his own internal satisfaction, and to present himself favorably to Other (or to conform to a norm). Hence, if Other does not know he's restored equity, he will lose some of the motivation to do so. A recent study by Reis (1975) adds further support to this notion. He found that maintaining equity for *Person* was due in large part to norm conformity of which Other and Colleagues were unaware, though Person's desire for equity (irrespective of Other's or Colleagues' awareness) was also operative.

Goodman and Friedman (1968) also did an overpay, hourly manipulate-qualifications study and reported results similar to those above. However, they added a group of subjects who were told they were not qualified and hence would receive less pay. Therefore, they, too, were supposed to feel equitably paid. The overpaid subjects produced more than did these subjects. The addition of this group helps to rule out the alternative interpretation that overpaid (qualification manipulated) subjects produce more to raise their own self-esteem, which had been inadvertently lowered by the experimenter who told them they were unqualified. The unqualified–overpaid produced more than the unqualified–equitably paid, yet there is no reason to expect a difference based on the self-esteem explanation.

Pritchard *et al.* (1972) did a study which lasted for 7 days—thereby making it a more true-to-life situation. Their study was on a larger scale and was somewhat more definitive than the previous ones. This study looked at overpaid, equitably paid, and underpaid situations using both hourly and piece-rate payments.

The overpay hourly induction was done without making references to qualifications. Rather, subjects were told that people generally got only \$1.65 per hour for this job and that \$2 was really too much, but that they would get the \$2 because the advertisement which they responded to when applying for the job mistakenly listed \$2 as the pay. Therefore, this study rules out the "devalued self-esteem" interpretation of some earlier studies.

In addition to the experimental manipulation of overpayment, there was a "natural" manipulation, in that halfway through the experimental period, the basis of pay was changed. As a result, some subjects received increases in pay. They were therefore being overpaid because of a natural occurrence.

The results tended to show that hourly overpaid subjects produced more than did equitably paid subjects. In the experimental manipulation the significance did not reach customary levels, but there was a trend in the predicted direction. Then, when pay systems were changed, the equitably paid subjects showed a large decrease in performance, whereas the overpaid subjects did not decrease. Therefore, this effect, which was significant, does support the hypothesis.

In sum, then, the Pritchard *et al.* data do offer some support for the overpayment hypothesis under hourly conditions, and these, coupled with earlier data, do support equity theory predictions.

Overpay Piece Rate

In the second experiment by Adams and Rosenbaum (1962) subjects were overpaid on a piece-rate basis. The induction was done by devaluing their qualifications, as was the case in the first experiment by these investigators, which was reported above. The prediction was that subjects would try to decrease their outcomes. Since increasing inputs (i.e., producing more), which is the common means of decreasing hourly overpayment inequity, would also increase outcomes (i.e., pay), it would not restore equity. Therefore, it was predicted that subjects who were overpaid on a piece-rate basis would produce less in order to get smaller outcomes. This prediction was upheld.

There is, however, a difficulty with this prediction. Since piece-rate payments tie pay directly to output, the ratio of pay to units of output (which is Person's inputs to the exchange) is constant. Therefore, if only pay and units of production are considered in the outcomes/inputs ratio, the ratio never changes. Consequently, the prediction that overpaid piece-rate workers will produce less to get less pay is not a clear-cut prediction unless other factors are considered.

Adams (1963b) reasoned that subjects overpaid by piece rate would lower productivity so that they could increase the quality of their work. Increased quality implies increased inputs without increased outcomes, so this is a means of reducing inequity. The data do support the hypothesis, though there is an artifact in the experiment. Overpaid subjects were told that they were not fully qualified and that therefore they should pay particular attention to quality. This suggestion was not made to equitably paid subjects. Therefore, subjects were essentially being told what to do. In the

Adams and Jacobsen (1964) study the same results were found, but the same artifact existed.

Goodman and Friedman (1969) did an overpaid-piece-rate study which showed that overpaid subjects would adjust either quantity or quality as a means of reducing inequity, depending on suggestions made by the experimenter.

Lawler *et al.* (1968) replicated the finding that overpaid piece-rate subjects would lower quantity and increase quality following an induction which devalued their qualifications. However, the authors suggested that this would not persist over time since people prefer more money to less money. Hence, they found that over time there was not a difference in output and pay, but rather that overpaid subjects cognitively distorted their inputs. They believed themselves to be more qualified than the experimenter said, so the higher pay was equitable.

Finally, Wood and Lawler (1970) showed that overpaid subjects whose qualification had been devalued decreased their productivity (i.e., inputs) without necessarily increasing quality.

In summation, therefore, several studies have supported the proposition that if a Person is made to feel inequitably overpaid he will be motivated to reduce this inequity by increasing his inputs or decreasing his outcomes. There have been some studies which have failed to support the hypothesis; however, as Goodman and Friedman (1971) pointed out, there are difficulties with these studies which suggest that they were unable to induce feelings of inequity. Since studies of inequity have been reported and reviewed in so many places, they will not be discussed at length here. Goodman and Friedman (1971) provided one of the most complete yet parsimonious reviews. Our purpose here is not so much to review the inequity research as to view it in light of the overly sufficient justification studies.

Consider once again the case of Kevin who was substantially overpaid to do something which he liked very much (acting). When the money ran out would he continue to work without pay? The answer from equity research is clear. He would continue to work because he felt inequitably overpaid and working without pay would help him to restore equity.

As we saw in Chapter 5, the cognitive evaluation theory prediction is that he would be less likely to continue to work, because the experience with money made him dependent on the money and decreased his intrinsic motivation to perform. Therefore, the two theories make conflicting predictions. However, it will now be proposed that the theories are not conceptually discrepant.

In cognitive evaluation theory, it is suggested that when a person performs an intrinsically motivated task for money, his perception of the reason for performing the task shifts from "it is intrinsically motivated" to "it is motivated by the money." Since the person is then performing for money (and therefore has less intrinsic motivation), the principle of inequity will certainly be relevant. In other words, in the example above, Kevin would continue to perform after the money stopped if he were feeling inequitably overpaid. However, he would not perform if he felt equitably paid. In either case his intrinsic motivation would have decreased, and he would have had less intrinsic reason to perform, so that continued performance predicted in the first case would occur because of inequity in his own mind, not because intrinsic motivation increased. This additional performance would last only until equity was restored.

Therefore, the two theories, inequity and cognitive evaluation, are not incompatible. A person who is paid for an intrinsically motivated activity may lose intrinsic motivation because of a change in locus of causality, and at the same time experience himself as having been overpaid.

In one study reported in Chapter 5 (Deci, 1971), several subjects were paid as much as $4 for about 20 minutes of work on an interesting puzzle. It was only at the time that the subjects were actually handed the money that they appeared to feel "uneasy" and "inequitably overpaid." During the session when the experimenter said things like, "You have now earned $3," or "You have now earned $4," the subjects said nothing and did not appear to feel discomfort. However, when they were actually handed the money, they became very uneasy, and many of them said things like "That's a lot of money for what I did," or "I feel funny taking all this money."

Therefore, in the Deci (1971) study, the decrease in intrinsic motivation was demonstrated and at the same time anecdoctal evidence indicated that subjects felt overpaid.

Deci (1972a) attempted to show both effects experimentally. Imagine a laboratory experiment wherein a subject is intrinsically motivated to perform an activity for overpayments, and then has an opportunity to continue performing with no additional pay. If the subject were actually given the money before he had the free time to continue working (i.e., the period with no pay), it seems likely that he would experience inequity (since he would have the money as an initiating stimulus), so he would be more likely to make additional inputs to restore equity. However, if he knew he were going to be paid, but payment were withheld until the end of the free time, he would not experience the same inequity (since he would not yet have the initiating stimulus money), so he would be less likely to do more work. He would no longer be as intrinsically motivated, and he apparently would not experience inequity from overcompensation, so he would be less likely to continue to make inputs. Thus, the timing of the payment may determine whether the change in performance is governed by the process of inequity or that of cognitive reevaluation.

I am not suggesting that timing of the reward has any particular theoretical significance. All I am suggesting is that one will observe an inequity effect only when feelings of inequity have been induced. Since the feelings of inequity seemed, in the Deci (1971) experiment, to have been induced only after subjects received the money, Deci (1972a) predicted that the timing of reward would mediate the effects of monetary rewards on behavior during the no-pay free-choice period which followed the payment period.

To investigate this, Deci (1972a) used the one-session paradigm outlined in Chapter 5. Subjects were paid $1 for each of four puzzles that they were able to solve in 10 minutes. Next, one third of the subjects were given their earnings in cash immediately. Then all subjects had an 8-minute free-choice period while the experimenter was allegedly away at a computer terminal. Without the knowledge of the subjects, however, a second experimenter observed them during this period and recorded the amount of time they spent working on the puzzles.

The prediction was that subjects paid before the 8-minute free-choice period would spend the most time working on puzzles in order to "work off" their feelings of overpay inequity, whereas

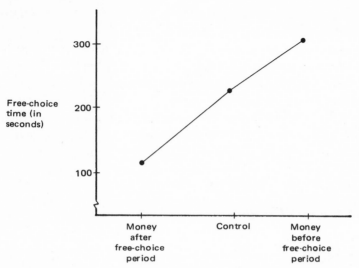

FIGURE 17. Effects of rewards and timing of rewards on the amount of time spent by subjects during free-choice period working on puzzles [after Deci, 1972 (a)].

paid subjects who were promised the money, but had not yet received it, would work least. They would have lost intrinsic motivation and would not yet be experiencing inequity. Control subjects who did the puzzles without pay would be intermediate. In Chapter 5 data were reported from this same experiment which looked at the effects of verbal reinforcements. Therefore, only data which consider the effects of rewards and timing (without verbal reinforcements) will be reported here. The results are shown in Figure 17. As predicted, subjects paid "before" spent the most time, subjects paid "after" spent the least time, and control subjects were intermediate.

Calder and Staw (1975) have criticized this experiment by saying in essence that the conclusions cannot be validly derived from the data.

I recognize that the use of the same dependent measure to show resolution of overpayment inequity and amount of intrinsic motivation causes some ambiguity. It would be a more conclusive tests of the assertion to have separate measures. Nonetheless, the predictions were derived from the theories and the data supported the predictions. This gives some support to the predictions, though a more conclusive demonstration of the effects would be appropriate.

The essence of my position is that inequity theory and cognitive evaluation theory are not incompatible. There are situations in which the *behavioral* predictions of the two theories may be in contradiction, yet the theories are easily reconcilable. We saw in the above experiment that there are some conditions in which the inequity prediction is more likely to appear and others in which the cognitive evaluation prediction will be apparent.

Underpayment Inequity

So far we have considered only situations where Person was inequitably overpaid. We will now discuss underpayment inequity.

Inequity theory asserts that if a Person believes that his outcomes-to-inputs ratio is less than that of Other or a Colleague, he will be dissatisfied and will experience discomfort, which will motivate him to restore equity. Pritchard's extension proposed further that if Person perceives that his inputs are greater than his outcomes he will experience inequity without regard to a comparison Other. In either case, Person will be motivated to restore equity, and research indicates that this will be most likely to occur in the form of decreased inputs or increased outcomes. The most desirable way to restore equity for Person would undoubtedly be to increase his own outcomes. Unfortunately, however, the situation frequently does not allow him to affect his level of outcomes, so in those situations he will have to bring his inputs in line with his outcomes.

Four studies give support to the Adams hypothesis that underpaid subjects will experience inequity and be motivated to decrease it by changing inputs and/or outcomes. These studies fall into two categories, piece-rate underpayment (Andrews, 1967; Lawler & O'Gara, 1967) and hourly underpayment (Evan & Simmons, 1969; Pritchard *et al.*, 1972). In piece-rate underpayment the results have shown that subjects produced a larger number of lower quality outputs, i.e., more low quality interviews (Andrews; Lawler & O'Gara), in order to increase their own total outcomes without substantially increasing their inputs. In hourly underpayment, however, outcomes are set and cannot be increased, so the results indicate that subjects lowered their own inputs, i.e., did fewer pages of proofreading (Evan & Simmons) or did less searching through a catalogue (Pritchard *et al.*).

The inequity predictions for underpayment are intuitive. It is only common sense to expect that if a person is underpaid he'll be unhappy and try to alter that. Overpayment, on the other hand, is more counterintuitive. Common sense would tend to predict that overpaid people will like it, and even if they do not like it, they will not lower their own outcomes. Probably because of the counterintuitive nature of overpayment in equity, that area has produced more research than underpayment inequity.

The underpayment studies reported above are more straightforward than the overpayment studies. There were no manipulations which devalued qualifications. Instead, the investigators generally induced in Person a feeling of inequitable underpayment by having Other pay him less than the going rate, i.e., less than hypothetical, but comparable, Colleagues were getting, (Andrews, 1967; Evan & Simmons, 1969) or by having Other pay him less than that of a real Colleague doing the same work (Lawler & O'Gara, 1967).

One can now see clearly the analogy between the situations in insufficient justification research and in equity research. In both, Person is interacting with Other (the experimenter, an employer, etc.) and is doing a task requested by Other, for which he feels undercompensated (i.e., for which he feels he has insufficient justification). In the case of inequity research, this feeling of insufficient reward generally comes from a belief that some Colleague has a higher outcomes/inputs ratio, whereas in insufficient justification it comes from a variety of sources (see Chapter 6 for a review).

A Discrepancy? An apparent contradiction between the findings and predictions of insufficient justification and inequity theories has been alluded to by Opsahl and Dunnette (1966), Lawler (1968) and Goodman and Friedman (1971) and is illustrated by the Danielle example at the beginning of this chapter. Recall that Danielle had been doing a job which she considered to be dull and boring and which gave here inadequate rewards. Then the management of the theater where she worked asked her to work for a few days without pay. Proceeding from the notion of insufficient justification, one would have predicted that she would imbue the task with additional intrinsic worth while receiving inadequate pay (i.e., insufficient justification). Thus she would have been more likely to continue working after the pay stopped, since she enjoyed the task or considered it important and was intrinsically motivated to do it. On the other hand, one would predict from inequity theory that Danielle would have felt underpaid for what she had already done, so that she would surely not have been inclined to make more inputs without additional outcomes. That is, she would have been less likely to agree to work without pay.

When a person feels inconsistency between what he is doing and what he feels he should be doing, he can either change his behavior to make it more consistent with his attitudes about the activity or he can change his attitude (or intrinsic motivation) to make it more consistent with his behavior. Of course, a change in attitude or in intrinsic motivation might be expected to lead to subsequent behavior which is consistent with the new attitude. The inequity prediction for Danielle would involve changing behavior (i.e., stopping the task) to make it more consistent with an attitude (i.e., a feeling of being underpaid for what she has already done), whereas the insufficient justification prediction would involve changing an attitude (i.e., imbuing the task with additional worth) to make it more consistent with the behavior (i.e., doing the task for inadequate extrinsic rewards).

I will now propose that the predictions related to insufficient justification and inequity are not contradictory; rather, there are certain situational factors which will determine which prediction, change in attitudes and/or intrinsic motivation (insufficient justification prediction), or behavior change affecting one's ratio of outcomes to inputs (inequity prediction), will follow from a situation of inadequate justification.*

The following framework attempts to specify some of the determinants of whether Person will enhance his intrinsic interest

---

* This framework was developed in discussions with David Landy. David deserves half the credit but less than half the blame (because he probably would not have made it public).

in an activity or will decrease his inputs as a response to undercompensation.

(I) When Person is in a situation in which he experiences dissonance because he is doing something for which he has inadequate justification, he will reduce the dissonance by selecting from the alternatives which *he perceives* to be open to him. Many experiments have been structured in ways which limit the alternatives open to Person, and this could be one reason for the seemingly discrepant results in these areas. Goodman and Friedman (1971) made a similar point by suggesting that in inequity experiments the induction often provides subjects with an instrumental way to restore equity.

In experiments related to insufficient justification, the typical paradigm is that experimenter asks subjects to enage in certain counter-attitudinal behaviors. The subjects then experience discomfort or cognitive inconsistency, because they observe themselves behaving in ways which are dissonant with their attitudes. The results of most of the experiments are that the subjects change their attitudes to bring them more into line with their behaviors.

In this research the subjects are aware that they are participating in an experiment. The norm in experiments is one of cooperation with the experimenter (for persuasive evidence on this see Orne, 1962). Hence, when the experimenter asks a subject to perform an activity, he will almost surely perform it and will put considerable effort into doing it well. Consequently, if the activity causes dissonance, he really has only two alternatives open to him, to tolerate the dissonance or to change his attitude toward the activity or referent. It is unlikely, because of demand characteristics (Orne, 1962) and evaluator apprehension (Rosenberg, 1965), that he would stop engaging in the activity requested by the experimenter or that he would perform the task very inadequately (i.e., that he would make low inputs to correspond to the low outcomes.)

An example of this can be seen in the Festinger and Carlsmith (1959) experiment which we discussed in Chapter 6. In that experiment subjects performed a dull, boring task and then lied to one another that they had enjoyed it. Following the lying and before the final attitude was assessed, the experimenter thanked each subject for participating, said he hoped the subject had enjoyed it and pointed out that most subjects did find the task interesting. The experimenters said in the experimental report that they did this to make it easier for the subjects to persuade themselves that they had liked it.

The fact that insufficient justification experiments are designed so that attitude change is the most instrumental alternative for dissonance reduction does not vitiate the findings. Rather, it merely suggests that Person might choose a different alternative, such as lowering his inputs, if he perceived it as a viable alternative and thought it would maximize his outcomes. Research on inequity is customarily conducted outside of a laboratory setting, and since the subjects aren't aware that they are participating in an experiment, there are not likely to be the same demand characteristics present. As a result, Person feels freer to do low-quality or slow work. In other words, he feels freer to reduce dissonance caused by underpayment through lowering his inputs instead of enhancing his attitudes.

To summarize the points related to proposition (I) of the framework, the research on insufficient justification is often done in such a way that the option which Person perceives to be most readily available for reducing dissonance is change in attitudes or intrinsic motivation, whereas in inequity research changes in inputs (which may or may not also affect outcomes) is the most viable alternative.

(II) The degree of ambiguity which exists about whether or not there is inconsistency between what Person is doing and what he thinks he should be doing is a determinant of the mode of dissonance reduction which Person will choose. The more unequivocal the inequity, the more likely Person will be to respond by changing his behavior, e.g., by decreasing his input or by refusing to engage in the behavior. This is consistent with the Walster *et al.* (1970) proposition that the less distortion of reality which derogation or denial requires, the more likely it is that Person will use these methods.

In the inequity research, the instructions frequently point out that Person is getting less than standard compensation (Andrews, 1967; Evan & Simmons, 1969), or else that there is a Colleague present who is getting more (Lawler & O'Gara, 1967). Furthermore, inequity studies generally use a work situation, and there is a widely held cultural norm about a fair day's pay for a fair day's work. In insufficient justification research, it is generally less explicit that a person is doing something for which he has inadequate justification. He is not told that he has insufficient justification, nor does he have a Colleague present with whom he can compare himself. It seems, therefore, that in the typical insufficient justification experiments the inequity of the reward is more equivocal.

Aronson (1966) noted that insufficient justification studies require that there be enough justification for the person to commit himself to the behavior and engage in it enthusiastically, but at the same time there must be sufficiently little justification so that he is left wondering why he was committed to the behavior. This suggests that there will be some ambiguity about the sufficiency of justification for the subjects.

(III) The extent to which *Person* believes he has choice about, and is personally responsible for, engaging in the behavior at the specified level of reward is a determinant of the dissonance-reducing technique he will choose. In Chapter 6 we discussed the importance of choice and self-responsibility in producing the insufficient justification effect. Linder *et al.* (1967) showed that when people write counter-attitudinal essays for inadequate rewards they will become more favorably disposed toward the espoused position only if they chose to engage in the behavior for that reward. Collins and Hoyt (1972) suggested that choice was important because it made the subjects feel personally responsible for the consequences of the behavior. If subjects had no choice about engaging in the behavior and hence, no feeling of personal responsibility for the consequences, they would not need to justify the behavior. Hence, we are asserting that, in situations of under-compensation, if a person has chosen to work for a stated wage and therefore feels personally responsible for the consequences of his behavior (i.e., the small wage), he will be more likely to enhance his attitude and motivation toward the task, whereas, if he has no choice and does not feel responsible, he will be more likely to lower inputs and be dissatisfied.

In insufficient justification experiments, subjects are normally given a choice about whether to participate in the activity (e.g., Weick, 1964; Linder *et al.*, 1967). In the Weick (1964) experiment, for example, the subjects were told by the experimenter that he obviously could not force them to stay and that they could leave if they had to. Fifty out of 54 stayed, and consequently these subjects enhanced their intrinsic motivation for the activity.

In the inequity studies, however, the people go to a job committed to doing the job but unaware of the amount of compensation (e.g., Andrews, 1967). In these studies, a Person makes his choice to participate without having all of the dissonant cognitions (*viz.*, the inadequacy of pay). Hence, he does the task because he had committed himself to do it before he knew how much pay he'd get. Nonetheless, he can still feel inadequately compensated, and thus he will feel dissatisfied and will respond in accord with an inequity prediction, probably by lowering inputs.

Summary

Inequity theory proposes that when a person is in exchange relationships with another, he will seek equity between (a) his own ratio of outcomes from the relationship and inputs to the relationship and (b) the other person's ratio of outcomes to inputs. An extension of the theory asserts that the person even seeks equity between his own outcomes and inputs without regard to the other's ratio.

If the person perceives inequity in a relationship he will experience distress which will motivate him to restore equity. He is most likely to do this by changing his outcomes, changing his inputs, or distorting the situation in such a way that he achieves psychological equity. This chapter reviewed studies which support equity theory and pointed out discrepancies between inequity theory, on the one hand, and cognitive evaluation theory (Chapter 5) and insufficient justification (Chapter 6), on the other hand. It was suggested that the theories were not irreconcilable, but rather, that situational variables determine which effect is most likely to be observed at any given time. One experiment was reported which demonstrated both an inequity effect and a cognitive evaluation effect. Also, a framework was outlined for predicting when the inequity effect *vs.* the insufficient justification effects might be expected to occur.

8

Implications and Applications

The main finding of the work reported in Chapters 5 and 6 is that there tends to be a negative relationship between the amount of extrinsic reward an individual receives for engaging in an activity and the amount of intrinsic motivation he has for that activity. Extrinsic rewards which are more than sufficient tend to decrease intrinsic motivation, and insufficient extrinsic rewards tend to increase intrinsic motivation, though we've seen that there are limiting conditions to this. For example, verbal reinforcements do not decrease the intrinsic motivation of college males (Chapter 5), intrinsic motivation will not be enhanced by insufficient extrinsic rewards unless the person feels personally responsible for the outcomes of his action (Chapter 6), and a need for a feeling of equity sometimes leads to behavior which seems inconsistent with the negative relationship assertion (Chapter 7).

In spite of the limiting conditions, we now consider the possible implications of this negative relationship. Does it mean that extrinsic rewards do not motivate behavior or should not be used?

The answer to the first question is quite clearly "No!" There is probably no postulate more firmly established in the experimental literature of psychology than the notion that extrinsic rewards (reinforcements) motivate behavior (increase the likelihood of a response). Further, the introduction of extrinsic rewards often improves performance, although we did see in Chapter 5 that the introduction of extrinsic rewards impaired performance in a study by Kruglanski *et al.* (1971).

The importance of the work reported in Chapter 5 is not that extrinsic rewards are not effective motivators, but rather, that they have some unintended negative consequences which people have not previously been aware of. Rewards can motivate behavior extrinsically, but at the same time they will very likely be decreasing intrinsic motivation. Therefore, whether or not extrinsic rewards are appropriate depends on what the rewarder is attempting to do.

If one is trying to motivate a person to engage in a particular activity on a one-shot basis and is not concerned with the person's intrinsic motivation for the activity, the extrinsic-rewards route may be the best one to travel. Further, since extrinsic rewards have been shown to be effective motivators, it would seem that extrinsic control systems would be appropriate so long as the system remains operative, that is, so long as the rewards never stop, quality is rigidly controlled, etc. However, there may be some difficulties even if the system remains operative. Since extrinsic rewards will be co-opting the person's intrinsic motivation by making him dependent on the rewards, he may become more concerned with the rewards than with the activity, in which case he may attempt to "psych out" the rewarder to get the most rewards for the least effort. Furthermore, if the rewards stop, the activity will stop.

So, if one is primarily interested in performance and is not concerned with intrinsic motivation, then extrinsic reward systems, if properly administered, may be quite effective.

But if one is concerned about long-term consequences, the answer may be different. For example, if one is concerned with children's learning, he undoubtedly will want the children to enhance, rather than diminish, their intrinsic motivation, and this would seem to be more important than immediate performance on some task. The appropriate route here becomes the intrinsic one. Yet, as we will see later in this chapter, the problem of rewards in education is a very knotty one and the use of intrinsic motivation is very complex.

Another consideration regarding the use of extrinsic rewards is whether or not the person would perform the activity without the rewards. Rewards work effectively to induce a person to do something he would not do otherwise. It may even be something he would like very much (i.e., would have high intrinsic motivation for) if he tried it, but which he would not try without the reward. You probably know of examples, such as the math major who would never have considered taking a course in French literature unless forced to do so by a distribution requirement, but who became fascinated by it once he was in the course. This, then, is a situation in which extrinsic rewards (or controls) are necessary to produce the behavior in the first place, and to make the person aware that he is intrinsically interested in the activity. That serves as a *caveat* that the negative relationship findings in Chapters 5 and 6 should not be applied blindly in real world situations.

Further, there are undoubtedly many situations in which it is important to get things done but there is no one who would find the activity intrinsically motivating. To get the task done, rewards will have to be used. Of course, in these situations, the findings of the insufficient justification research become applicable. Small rewards will be more likely to enhance intrinsic motivation than large rewards.

It is important to remember that the dependent measure in the studies reported in Chapters 5 and 6 was intrinsic motivation, not performance. The two must be kept distinct. Although they are related, the relationship between them is not perfect.

In general, then, we see that the question of whether or not to use extrinsic rewards is a very complicated one. Rewards affect performance and intrinsic motivation differently, so one must be clear about whether he is interested primarily in immediate performance or in the maintenance or development of intrinsic motivation. Further, we know that intrinsic and extrinsic motivation are not additive. But, even more than that, it is not just a question of whether or not "intrinsic plus extrinsic" increases total motivation, because extrinsic and intrinsic rewards may actually motivate different behaviors. Extrinsic rewards can lead to a redefinition of the activity, so the behavior itself and the quality of the activity may be different.

Let us now look at the application of this research in a more detailed way to the field of education, and then to the field of organizational motivation.

Intrinsic Motivation and Education

One of the most endearing qualities possessed by children is their curiosity (although their parents might fail to find it endearing after they've become weary from an unending stream of questions). Children are intrinsically motivated to learn; they want to understand about themselves and the world around them; they want to feel effective in dealing with their environment.

Yet these curious children often turn into uninterested students who are bored and angry about school. What has happened to their intrinsic motivation for learning? This question has been addressed by a number of persons who have worked in schools, and, as we will see, their answers turn out to be quite compatible with cognitive evaluation theory and the experimental results presented in Chapter 5.

Bruner (1962) asserted that one of the most important ways to help a child think and learn is to free him from the control of rewards and punishments.* Providing children with rewards and punishments too easily gets them into a pattern of doing what they think will lead them to the rewards. Their so-called "learning" becomes dependent on the rewards; they define "learning" as something they do to get rewards. In other words, according to cognitive evaluation theory, the locus of causality of the learning activity which was originally internal becomes external, leaving them with less intrinsic motivation for learning.

Bruner suggested that overachievers are children who learn how to satisfy the teacher by doing what he or she rewards. However, these children do not develop the capacity to transform learning into useful cognitive structures. They memorize well, but they do not develop their capacity to think creatively.

Bruner stated, " . . . to the degree that one is able to approach learning as a task of discovering something rather than 'learning about' it, to that degree there will be a tendency for the child to

---

* There is very little *experimental evidence* on the relative effectiveness of intrinsic *vs.* extrinsic motivation in education. The references here to Bruner, Holt, and others are essays rather than reports of experimental investigations. Therefore, the comments on education which precede the token economy section should also be considered primarily an essay representing my views.

work with the autonomy of self-reward or, more properly, be rewarded by discovery itself" (1962, p. 88).

Bruner subscribed to the notion that behavior may be motivated by competence (i.e., intrinsic) motivation, and he emphasized the importance of not using rewards and punishments in learning situations, since they interfere with competence motivation.

He further believed that allowing individuals to be motivated by the need for competence strengthens the extent to which they will be motivated by that intrinsic need. In other words, Bruner was suggesting the importance of providing children with intrinsically interesting activities (e.g., learning about things that fascinate them) and then refraining from using extrinsic rewards. The activity will become its own reward and thus will produce more creative and meaningful learning.

A child who is being intrinsically motivated will also, according to Bruner, have the capacity to interpret success and failure as information, rather than as rewards and punishments. This bears close relationship to the proposition in cognitive evaluation theory which suggests that positive information, which is not controlling (i.e., in Bruner's terms, is not a reward), can lead to strengthened intrinsic motivation. The research data on females who receive information about their competence at a task is a case in point. When women were told by an experimenter that they had done very well on an intrinsically motivated activity, they lost intrinsic motivation (Deci, Cascio, & Krusell, 1975). The activity became dependent on the praise. However, when females succeeded at a task, hence got self-administered positive information, their intrinsic motivation increased (Feather, 1966, 1968). The information strengthened their sense of competence and self-determination, leaving them with more intrinsic motivation, whereas the praise in the Deci *et al.* study changed their perceived locus of causality, leaving them with less intrinsic motivation.

The philosophy which embodies intrinsic motivation to learn has been the basis of many experimental schools, sometimes referred to as progressive schools, free schools, etc. The well known Summerhill School of England is one example. Neill, the founder and long time head of the school, discussed the role of rewards and punishments as motivators in his expose on the school and its philosophy (Neill, 1960). He said that even though rewards are not as dangerous as punishments, nonetheless, "to offer a prize for doing a deed is tantamount to declaring that the deed is not worth doing for its own sake" (Neill, 1960, p. 162). He has predicted precisely what the research reported in Chapter 5 has shown. Neill added that effective learning will be most likely to occur when the reward is the satisfaction in the accomplishment (i.e., when the reward is intrinsic).

Holt (1964), an outspoken critic of American education, has made a similar point. He stated, "We destroy the ... love of learning ... in children by encouraging and compelling them to work for petty and contemptible rewards—gold stars, or papers marked 100 and tacked to the wall, or A's on report cards, or honor rolls, or dean's lists, or Phi Beta Kappa keys ..." (Holt, 1964, p. 168).

Montessori (1967), who has also contributed much to progressive education, has indicated that rewards are not necessary and are potentially harmful for the intrinsically motivated child.

In a recent study by Benware (1975) college students learned material either (1) to take an exam on it or (2) to teach it to other students. The results indicated that those who learned to teach others did better on both recall and understanding of the material. When students learned in order to pass tests, they did not seem to learn the material very well.

The conclusion from all these sources seems clear. Children are intrinsically motivated to learn; the activities of learning and discovery are rewarding in their own right because they allow a child to feel competent in relation to his environment. The use of rewards or punishments to encourage this learning will only interfere with the learning because it will make the child's learning dependent on the reward and cause him to do things that will lead him to the reward in the easiest way. This, in turn, will undoubtedly leave him having "learned" less.

The implication of all this, then, seems to be that we should not use the plethora of extrinsic rewards currently being used by schools. However, that implication is somewhat premature, since the implication assumes a number of things. It assumes that schools will provide students with the opportunity to learn what is interesting to them. If schools insist on having children learn (or more realistically, memorize) certain things, then they may have to use extrinsic rewards. Otherwise kids probably would not do many of the things which they are told they have to do in schools. This, however, raises a larger question and one which is more a question of values than science. "What is it that we want schools to be doing?" Do we want children to be memorizing a host of different facts and operations? If that is important, we will probably have to use extrinsic rewards. However, as numerous writers such as Bruner and Holt have pointed out, they will probably forget most of that, anyway.

On the other hand, if we are interested in having them develop viable cognitive structures (Bruner, 1962) which relate meaningfully to the rest of their lives, then intrinsic approaches to learning are preferable. A by-product would be that the children might not learn what the teachers have previously decided they should learn, but as Holt suggested, this question of "what children should learn" deserves some consideration. In all likelihood they do not need to "learn" most of what teachers think they need to learn.

Token Reinforcement Programs

The approach to education which focuses on intrinsic motivation stands in contrast to another recent development in education, token reinforcement programs. This approach focuses on extrinsic rewards (a token which can usually be exchanged for some desired commodity). The idea is to identify desired behaviors and reinforce those behaviors.

This system has developed out of the behavioristic, operant conditioning framework. It assumes no intrinsic motivation. Behavior is believed to be determined by reinforcements and the contingencies within which they are administered.

When a token program is introduced into a classroom, (1) the program is explained to the children in order to make clear what behaviors will be reinforced, and (2) the rules for exchanging tokens for other rewards (e.g., candy, extra minutes of lunch period, etc.) are explained. The token, itself, is generally a neutral object, such as a poker chip (see Kazdin & Bootzin, 1972, for a detailed discussion of token economies).

The token programs are formalized systems for administering extrinsic rewards. Grades, stars, praise from teachers, and other rewards which are commonly used in classrooms represent the same basic approach to motivating learning, but they are generally given in a much less controlled and systematic way than are token reinforcements.

Token reinforcement programs have been shown to be quite effective for achieving certain goals in the classroom. O'Leary and Drabman (1971) have reviewed several studies which have demonstrated that while tokens are being given in classrooms, children are led to be more orderly, to display more task-oriented behavior, and occasionally to improve performance on a memory type of test.

The most impressive results (e.g., O'Leary & Becker, 1967; O'Leary, Becker, Evans, & Saudargas, 1969; Michenbaum, Bowers, & Ross, 1968; Kuypers, Becker, & O'Leary, 1968; Martin, Burkholder, Rosenthal, Tharpe, & Thorne, 1968) have been found when token reinforcement systems have been used with emotionally disturbed or disorderly children.

The clearest conclusion from the data seems to be that token programs improve the social behavior, and in some cases the task-oriented behaviors, of disturbed or disorderly children while they are in the token programs. The improvements in learning are less frequent and tend to be the "memory" type of learnings.

These kinds of improvements in classrooms are very important. A classroom full of disorderly children whose teacher is trying in vain to bring about order is not a pleasant place for anyone.

However, caution should be used in generalizing these results. As we will see below, the behavioral improvements typically do not carry over to times and places where there are no rewards. In addition, orderly classrooms certainly do not represent the objectives of education, so the results do fall short of educational objectives.

Furthermore, in a larger sense, one might wonder if the current educational systems have played some part in causing the disorder, in the first place. Holt, for example, has asserted that children become bored and unruly in part because of the trivial, meaningless activities which they are forced to engage in when they are not interested. They experience little freedom of choice and many of their activities require no resourcefulness or creativity. They are not intrinsically motivated.

Of course, the answer to the question of whether of not schools, themselves, play a part in creating the disorder is not clear, though it certainly is appropriate to investigate whether or not broad changes in the system would bring about less disorder and more meaningful learning.

Token economies are one approach, and free schools are another. Token economies achieve certain results; free schools accomplish others. Which is more appropriate depends on what results one is trying to achieve. I suspect that both are appropriate, but in different situations. Free schools allow greater freedom of choice and allow the child to play a major part in directing his own education. However, it is also clear that these approaches work better with children who have developed some responsibility for self-direction than they do with disorderly children. It may be that with disorderly children, more controls are necessary, at least at first. However, the goals of self-direction and meaningful learning should not be lost sight of.

In sum, token reinforcements seem quite effective in controlling children's behaviors, especially the behaviors of disorderly children. This, in itself, is very important, particularly in a traditional classroom setting. However, it is not at all clear that they aid in development of cognitive structures or problem solving, though they may improve memory tasks.

Further, on the basis of the experimental results presented in Chapters 5 and 6, showing a negative relationship between extrinsic rewards and intrinsic motivation, I would predict that a token reinforcement program will decrease children's motivation for learning while it is controlling their behavior.

This conclusion actually has received some support from token reinforcement studies. For example, in classes where tokens were given only during part of the day there was no improvement in the children's behavior during nontoken periods (O'Leary *et al.*, 1969; Broden, Hall, Dunlap, & Clark, 1970). In fact, Meichenbaum *et al.* (1968) reported that the behavior of their subjects was worse during nontoken periods than it had been before tokens were introduced.

Greene (1974) did a study to test the assertion that token economies decrease children's intrinsic motivation for activities. Proceeding from earlier studies (Lepper *et al.*, 1973; Greene &

Lepper, 1974; Lepper & Greene, in press) which demonstrated that rewards and adult surveillance decrease the intrinsic motivation of children, Greene set up a token economy in a public school classroom to investigate the effects of tokens on children's intrinsic motivation for engaging in mathematics activities. There were three observation periods in the study: a baseline period, a reward period, and a withdrawal period. Children were free to work on four possible activities, and records were kept of the amount of time they spent working on each during baseline. Then there were four separate groups for the reward period. One group served as controls and received rewards for all activities. The other three were experimental conditions and all received rewards, though each group received a reward for just two of the four activities.

Each person in the "High-interest" activities group was rewarded for working on the two activities'which he had spent the most time on during baseline. The members of the "Low-interest" activities group received rewards for working on the two activities which they had spent least time on during the baseline, and the people in the "Choice" group were rewarded for whichever two activities they chose.

The controls for each of the experimental conditions were the same subjects; however, different ones of their scores (i.e., time spent on the target activities) were compared to the different experimental groups. The scores for the two activities which the controls spent most time on during baseline were compared to the

TABLE VII. *Average Number of Minutes per Day during Baseline, Reward, and Withdrawal Periods Spent by Subjects on Target Activities (Ns Range from 8 to 11 per Cell)*

Condition	Baseline	Reward	Withdrawal
High-interest experimentals	19.3	25.6	14.7
Matched controls	17.8	15.0	13.0
Choice experimentals	14.5	21.9	6.8
Matched controls	13.8	14.8	16.1
Low-interest experimentals	6.7	22.4	3.5
Matched controls	6.1	10.6	11.7

"High-interest" experimentals. The scores for the two activities which the controls spent least time on during baseline were compared to the "Low-interest" experimentals. And the controls' scores which provided comparisons for the Choice group were the two activities which represented the same relative preference during baseline as the activities chosen by the Choice subjects.

The results of this experiment appear in Table VII. Looking at each of the experimental conditions, one observes the same pattern. The amount of time spent by subjects on the target activity during the reward period was substantially greater than during baseline. This, of course, is to be expected. Rewarding someone for performing activities increases the amount of time he spends on them. Then, after rewards were removed, all three groups dropped below baseline in time spent on the target activities. This is precisely what would be predicted from cognitive evaluation theory and all of the studies reported in Chapter 5.

The largest within-group drop from baseline to withdrawal was for the Choice group (7.7 minutes), and the second largest was for the High-interest group (4.7 minutes). Both decreases were statistically significant. The smallest drop was for the Low-interest group (3.2 minutes) and did not reach significance, though there was a floor effect, so it is difficult to interpret the nonsignificance.

These relative sizes of decreases in intrinsic motivation from baseline to withdrawal are quite readily explained. The largest drop should be for the Choice group. First, the fact that they chose the activities to be rewarded for should make the reward manipulation very salient. Second, when subjects chose which activities to be rewarded for they would have been experiencing substantial self-determination, and hence substantial intrinsic motivation, in relation to those activities, so they would be most susceptible to decreases.

The second largest drop should have been in the High-interest group. The subjects comprising this group were obviously very intrinsically motivated for those activities and hence susceptible to a decrease, since they had spent a lot of time on them. However, since there was no choice, the reward manipulation would not have been as salient, so there should not have been as large a drop as in the Choice group.

The smallest drop should have been in the Low-interest group, since its members were not very intrinsically motivated, in the first place.

Although these results are quite neatly compatible with cognitive evaluation theory and the experimental results presented in Chapter 5, they are not quite so neat when the experimentals are compared to the control subjects.

Just as was the case with the within-group comparisons mentioned above, the Choice group displayed the largest decrease in intrinsic motivation relative to controls. Again, this would be expected, since intrinsic motivation was high and the reward manipulation was very salient.

In the High-interest group, however, the effect did not hold up in relation to controls. Although the High group spent less time on the target activities following reward than before reward, when compared to controls this was not significant, since the scores of controls also decreased from baseline to withdrawal. I, of course, would have predicted a significant decrease in intrinsic motivation for the High-interest experimentals (in relation to controls), and it is difficult to explain precisely why there was none. It is probable that this was due to the fact that the manipulation was not particularly salient. The High-interest experimentals continued on doing the same activities that they'd been spending the most time on, anyway, so the introduction of rewards was not nearly as salient as it was for the group that chose the activities to be rewarded for.

Finally, the Low-interest group showed a significant decrease in relation to controls after rewards were removed. Whereas the drop in intrinsic motivation was not significant in the within-group analysis, it was significant when compared to controls. Although this decrease would have been expected, there should have been a larger decrease among the High-interest experimentals. However, the manipulation for the High-interest group was not very salient, though it was quite salient for the Low-interest group. They were rewarded for engaging in the activities which they least preferred, so the rewards would be rather prominent.

This interpretation, based on salience, is, of course, only speculative, and the failure to find a significant decrease in intrinsic motivation for the High group is unfortunate, yet in general the results of the Greene study do provide support for the notion that extrinsic rewards decrease intrinsic motivation for learning activities.

In concluding the discussion of token reinforcement programs, we see that the findings suggest that whether or not it is appropriate to use token reinforcement systems depends on what one is trying to achieve. If he is trying to make unruly children (whose intrinsic motivation for learning may already have been co-opted) behave in a more orderly fashion, tokens would seem to be appropriate. They will not increase intrinsic motivation, and they will necessitate careful, consistent, and continued administration, but they will improve social and task-oriented behavior.

On the other hand, if one wishes to help children learn to think creatively, to develop lasting cognitive structure, and to be intrinsically motivated to learn, token reinforcement programs will interfere with these goals and therefore will be inappropriate.

Of course, the use of extrinsic rewards need not be an all-or-none matter. It may be appropriate to use extrinsic rewards to elicit certain behaviors which would not otherwise be evinced. If a child is expected to perform an activity in which he has no intrinsic interest, he will have to be motivated extrinsically. This should be done with the minimum amount of extrinsic reward which will produce the desired behavior (O'Leary, Drabman, & Kass, 1973). On the other hand, even though one uses extrinsic rewards to elicit some behaviors, he can generally provide a supportive environment in which children may explore and engage in other intrinsically motivated activities.

Organizational Motivation

Managers, whose job it is to motivate employees, face much the same situation as school administrators and teachers whose job it is to motivate students. The desired behaviors are different, and the goals of the organizations are different, but the motivational questions cut through these differences.

Just as in education where there are two separate approaches to motivating students—intrinsic in free schools, extrinsic in token economies—in management the same two approaches are apparent. These approaches are represented most clearly in two schools of management (extrinsic in Scientific Management and intrinsic in Participative Management). While there have been other systems of management for motivating employees (see Vroom & Deci, 1970, or Lawler, 1973 for reviews), we will focus only on the two which highlight most clearly the intrinsic–extrinsic distinction.

Scientific management (Taylor, 1911) assumes that workers are indolent, lazy, and need to be told what to do, and how to do it. McGregor (1960) referred to this approach as *Theory X Management.* The aim of this system is to establish such careful controls that the workers will do precisely what the managerial elite has planned for them to do.

It assumes that a person will perform effectively to the extent that his rewards are made contingent upon effective performance. The way this assumption is operationalized is through piece-rate payments, with each worker receiving a set amount of pay for each load of pig iron he moves or each batch of widgets he produces. Sales commissions and bonus plans are other examples. Workers' extrinsic rewards are tied to, or made contingent upon, performance.

One can see that this approach to motivation is very consistent with a behavioristic orientation (see Chapter 1) and with the token economy application of behavioristic theory. People are thought to have no intrinsic motivation; instead, it is assumed that their behavior is entirely under the control of the reinforcements and contingencies in the environment. Hence, to motivate people, one must establish control mechanisms whereby rewards are dispensed by the environment only when the person performs effectively (i.e., evinces the desired behaviors). This system, then, is essentially an application of the Law of Effect, which asserts that behaviors which are reinforced will be strengthened and those which are not reinforced, or which are punished, will be weakened.

The use of piece-rate payments can also be defended by the psychological literature on expectancy theories of motivation. The basic assumption of those theories is that human behavior is goal directed, in other words, that people will engage in behaviors which they believe will lead them to desired end states. Piece-rate payments and other contingency-payment systems are structures whereby people can achieve desired rewards for effective performance.

To make a contingency-payment system work effectively, a number of factors must be considered. Standards of performance must be carefully developed and communicated to workers. In scientific management these standards are very precise and focus on how the job is done, as well as on the results which are achieved. In other words, the workers are expected to do things in very specific ways. All of the planning is done by superiors, and the workers simply do what they are told to do, when and how they are told to do it.

It is, of course, possible to use a contingency-payment system without specifying in such detail how things should be done. Scientific management is very precise about how to do things, whereas newer systems which are based on the assumption that people will perform effectively to the extent that they are rewarded extrinsically for performance tend to focus only on the results, rather than on the details of how things are done.

Profit centers are often used as part of a contingency-payment system which focuses only on results. A profit center is a subgroup of an organization which is accountable only for results (i.e., profits) and is free to attain those results in any way it chooses. Then, the managers of a profit center are often rewarded in accordance with the profits they have achieved. Here, then, rewards are contingent, as in scientific management, but the focus is on "ends" rather than "means."

Regardless of how the system is operationalized, the standards for payment must be clear and must be communicated clearly to the participants if the system is to operate effectively. Once the standards have been developed and communicated, the behavior of the workers must be monitored so that management will be able to administer rewards in accordance with the standards which they have established. The rewards must be administered consistently or the system will soon fail.

Although these systems do seem to have substantial support from the psychological literature, there are serious limitations to them. One problem is that any system which is based on external controls can easily break down if the controls are not always operative. If "no one is looking," people tend not to do what they are supposed to do. Just as with token economies, people tend to learn strategies to get rewards as easily as possible. Rather than doing what management wants, they do whatever they can to get rewards easily. The focus shifts from the activity to the rewards. Often, in fact, people will satisfy their intrinsic need to be creative and competent by devising ways to beat the system. They tend to resent the control, and they are likely to react against their loss of freedom (Brehm, 1966). This may take the form of subtle sabotage and will certainly manifest itself in people's trying to get the greatest rewards from the organization while giving the least effort to the organization.

According to cognitive evaluation theory (Chapter 5) people's locus of causality becomes external when they are paid contingently. Since the cause of the behavior is the reward, the behavior itself is only incidental and hence, whatever behavior achieves the results with the least cost will be used. From the organization's viewpoint, this will be unfortunate, since the resultant behaviors are often not in the best interests of the organization.

Participative management, on the other hand, focuses on an intrinsic, rather than extrinsic, approach to motivating employees. This orientation assumes that situations can be structured so that people will motivate themselves. Underlying this approach is the belief that humans have intrinsic motivation to deal effectively and creatively with their environment, and that performing effectively is rewarding in its own right. People can become committed to doing their jobs well, and they can derive satisfaction from evidence that they are being effective.

This approach to management, sometimes referred to as *Theory Y Management,* or *management by objectives,* is discussed in detail by McGregor (1960) Likert (1961, 1967), Argyris (1957), Maslow (1965), and Marrow, Bowers, & Seashore (1967). Unlike scientific management, this approach integrates planning and doing. The people who carry out the operations are given greater freedom to decide the most appropriate ways of doing the job; they are given broad objectives and allowed substantial discretion in determining how the objectives will be achieved. This discretion, it is believed, will provide the workers with additional challenge which will serve to elicit their intrinsic motivation.

Such an approach to management minimizes the use of extrinsic controls and minimizes the differences in authority between the supervisor and subordinates; the supervisor becomes more of a consultant than a boss. He helps to create conditions within which the subordinates will motivate and reward themselves.

We have stated frequently through the book that the basis of intrinsic motivation is one's need for competence and self-determination. The two primary mechanisms utilized by management theorists to motivate employees intrinsically relate directly to this need.

Participative management places great emphasis on the participation of employees in making decisions which affect them. Making decisions which affect one's work life allows one to experience a sense of self-determination and are therefore intrinsically rewarding. When people have some say about what they will do and how they will do it, they become ego involved and committed to doing it.

The other mechanism for motivating workers intrinsically is often referred to as *job design* (Myers, 1970; Lawler, 1969). Jobs are redesigned to be more challenging and to require greater resourcefulness and creativity. The scope of a person's responsibilities becomes greater, and often he will do more tasks than before. His job may be structured so that he can do enough tasks to see some completed end-product. Rather than sitting on an assembly line and adding one bolt to an assembly, he may now assemble the entire mechanism, or at least some discernible subassembly. He not only has greater variety and autonomy; he also has a finished product in which he can take pride.

Clearly, then, this enlargement or enhancement of jobs relates to people's need for competence or effectiveness, and calls on their creativity and curiosity.

Participative management advocates believe that this approach is the most effective way of achieving high performance (e.g., Likert, 1961) and also that it is more conducive to mentally healthy employees (e.g., Maslow, 1965). There are some experimental results which indicate that organizations which have implemented these practices are more productive and have higher levels of employee satisfaction (Likert, 1967; Marrow *et al.*, 1967). Further, Kornhauser (1965) found that there is a positive relationship between employees' reports of the degree to which they get to use their special abilities on the job and mental health.

Intrinsic Plus Extrinsic?

Most theories of work motivation have assumed that the effects of intrinsic and extrinsic rewards are additive. Porter and Lawler (1968), for example, have asserted that satisfaction is a function of the sum of the effects of intrinsic and extrinsic rewards, mediated by one's perception of equity.

Porter and Lawler suggested that extrinsic rewards should be made contingent upon performance in order to maximize the effectiveness of extrinsic rewards for motivating employees, and also that the situation be structured so that intrinsic rewards will accrue to the person who performs effectively. This would lead to the most productive organization; people would be working for intrinsic and extrinsic rewards at the same time. And since Porter and Lawler assume that the effects of intrinsic rewards and extrinsic rewards are additive, this situation maximizes motivation. The relevant aspects of their model appear in Figure 18.

The evidence presented in Chapters 5 and 6 calls their assumption of the additivity of intrinsic and extrinsic motivation into serious question. The two do not seem to be additive; they are interactive. Extrinsic rewards affect intrinsic motivation; in general, the greater the extrinsic rewards the greater the decrease in intrinsic motivation.

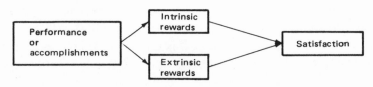

FIGURE 18. Aspects of the Porter–Lawler model (1968) highlighting their additivity assumption about intrinsic and extrinsic motivation.

Specifically, studies have shown that contingent monetary payments, threats of punishment, negative feedback, and verbal reinforcements to females decrease intrinsic motivation. Verbal reinforcements to males, positive information about one's competence either to males or females, and insufficient extrinsic rewards when the person has chosen to work for those meager rewards, all increase intrinsic motivation. Noncontingent extrinsic rewards may decrease intrinsic motivation, though they are less likely to do so than are contingent rewards.

What do these results mean for motivating employees? What are the implications?

Some antagonists have asserted that the logical implication of these results is that workers should not be paid. Whether or not that is the logical implication, it is clearly unworkable. People would not work if they were not paid. But I do not think that that is the logical implication. I am not asserting that people should not be paid. All that I mean to imply is that while contingent rewards can motivate a person extrinsically, they appear to be doing so at the expense of intrinsic motivation. There will be unintended consequences to the use of contingent extrinsic payments.

Whether or not that means that contingent payments should not be used is not clear. We need more research which looks at the relative effects of extrinsic rewards. For example, consider the following situation. A person is engaging in an activity which he enjoys, and he finds intrinsic rewards in doing it well. The person can be paid either contingently or noncontingently. Contingent payment will probably be a more effective use of extrinsic rewards than noncontingent payment. So contingent payments tend to be more effective in increasing extrinsic motivation. But at the same time, they are more likely to interfere with intrinsic motivation. Whether or not they should be used, then, depends on whether the increment in extrinsic motivation is greater than the decrement in intrinsic motivation. That is, of course, an empirical question and deserves the attention of interested researchers.

My hunch is that contingent payment systems tend to do more harm than good, although there are some situations where they may be necessary. If a job has to be done and there is no one who finds it intrinsically interesting, then it may be necessary to pay people contingently in order to get it done efficiently. However, even this prescription is questionable, since recent work on job design suggests that a more appropriate strategy in many of these cases would be to redesign the job so that it is more interesting. In short, contingency payments may be necessary in certain situations, though I suspect that, in general, they are not the most satisfactory means of motivating employees.

The evidence on the use of piece-rate payments suggests great difficulties in utilizing this approach. For example, in response to Deci (1972b), the manager of personnel research of a large American corporation wrote, "I have observed over the years that 'pay for performance' plans do not seem to operate as effectively as they should if we accept a simple law of effect principle. On the other hand, I have found it difficult to explain why such programs are not effective. This work [on the effects of rewards on intrinsic motivation] provides an excellent explanation for this" (Meyer, personal communication).

On the basis of the following line of reasoning, I would suggest the use of intrinsic approaches to motivating employees. However, I acknowledge that there is not yet unequivocal empirical support for the position.

It is important to distinguish between the use of rewards to keep a person on the job, and to motivate him to perform effectively on that job. To attract and keep someone in an organization it is necessary to satisfy his needs (Ross & Zander, 1957). He will have to be paid a competitive salary and given other comforts. However, satisfying a worker does not guarantee that he will be motivated to perform well on the job (Brayfield & Crockett, 1955; Kahn, 1960; Vroom, 1964).

Let us, therefore, consider how payments and intrinsic factors relate to satisfaction on the one hand and effective performance on the other. Paying workers is necessary to attract them to jobs and keep them satisfied with those jobs. However, if money is to be used as a motivator of performance, the performance has to be perceived by the worker as being instrumental to his receiving the money (Vroom, 1964; Lawler, 1971). This is generally accomplished by making pay contingent upon performance. In other words, it is not the money *per se* which motivates performance, but rather, it is the way that it is administered. If money is to be used as an extrinsic motivator (or controller) of behavior, it has to be administered contingently. However, we have seen that, not only are there many difficulties in making such a system work effectively, but that, also, such a system decreases intrinsic motivation.

On the other hand, a system for motivating employees such as participative management which—through participation and job enlargement—attempts to arouse intrinsic motivation, appears to motivate effective performance at the same time that it satisfies intrinsic needs. It seems to me, on the basis of evidence showing the effectiveness of participative management and job enlargement (e.g., Marrow *et al.*, 1967; Likert, 1967; Myers, 1970) that these intrinsic approaches would work most satisfactorily.

Wages could be paid noncontingently to attract people to the job and keep them satisfied, and then intrinsic factors would be the dominant motivators.

In Chapter 3 we discussed Maslow's (1943, 1954) need-hierarchy theory, pointing out that needs seem to be ordered in a hierarchical fashion. The most basic and prepotent needs are physiological needs. Then, in ascending order, come safety needs, love needs, esteem needs, and the need for self-actualization. A person progresses through this hierarchy, beginning with physiological needs. When they are satisfied, safety begins to emerge as the prepotent motivator. Satisfied needs do not motivate, so people are primarily motivated by the lowest unsatisfied need. Considering this hierarchy in relation to our present discussion, we see the importance of pay. It satisfies lower order needs, so that higher order needs for self-esteem and self-actualization are prepotent. Therefore, if money is paid noncontingently, it attracts people to the organization, keeps their lower order needs satisfied (thereby making higher intrinsic needs more salient), and is less likely than contingent payments to decrease intrinsic motivation.

In short, I favor a work environment which is challenging, is interpersonally supportive, and allows for a considerable amount of self-determination. In such an environment people would receive information about their competence and they would be encouraged to engage in self-evaluation. Self-evaluation programs are now being used by a few organizations and fit nicely with approaches that emphasize intrinsic motivation. Bassett and Meyer (1968), for example, have reported experimental results which indicate that such systems have important potential for motivating and satisfying workers.

Summary

In this chapter we have considered the implications of the results showing a negative relationship between amount of rewards and intrinsic motivation. We saw that external rewards can motivate a person extrinsically but at the same time they decrease the person's intrinsic motivation. Whether or not they are appropriate, therefore, depends on whether or not one is seeking immediate performance on a particular activity. If so, extrinsic rewards may be necessary. But, if one is seeking more creative work or learning, intrinsic approaches without the interference of external rewards seem more appropriate. We looked at this distinction in some detail in relation to education and work motivation.

III

RELATED ISSUES

9

Pro-Attitudinal Advocacy: Effects of Extrinsic Rewards on Attitudes

Cognitive evaluation theory (Chapter 5), derived in part from the work of Heider (1958) and de Charms (1968), distinguishes between an internal and external locus of causality. This distinction, which will be considered in greater detail in Chapter 10, is illustrated by the following example. Imagine a person who attempted to persuade his neighbor to support a referendum blocking the construction of an expressway through a nearby game preserve. If he did it because he believed strongly in wildlife conservation, the perceived locus of causality would be internal: he tried to persuade his neighbor because of his attitude about conservation. However, if he had a neutral attitude but was hired by the Conservation Society to campaign for the referendum, the perceived locus of causality for the behavior would be external: he did it because of the payments.

The situation is more complicated when a believer in conservation espouses the belief and receives payments for doing so. Will the perceived locus of causality be internal or external? Further, will the experience of being paid for expressing an opinion which one supports affect his opinion?

In Chapter 5 we saw that if a person engages in a behavior for which the perceived locus of causality is internal (e.g., he believes in conservation) and he then begins to receive an external reward such as money for engaging in that behavior, the perceived locus of causality will change from internal to external. This suggests then, that if the person who believes in conservation is paid to argue for the referendum, the perceived locus of causality will change from internal to external.

Numerous studies reported in Chapter 5 have shown that when a person is rewarded for doing an intrinsically motivated task, his intrinsic motivation will decrease. I have asserted that this is because of a change in the perceived locus of causality. Similarly, other studies have shown that rewarding an intrinsically motivated activity leads people to change their attitudes about the task, so that they find it less interesting and enjoyable than they did before the payments.

These findings relate closely to the example of the conservation espouser mentioned above, yet the two are slightly different questions. We turn now to the question of what happens to a person's attitude if he is paid to espouse that attitude.

There is sufficient evidence to allow one to predict with confidence that the perceived locus of causality of the behavior (espousing the attitude) will become external. There is less evidence, however, about whether or not this will affect the attitude. Nonetheless, it seems reasonable to assert that one's attitude will change to a less favorable one toward the espoused position when one is paid to espouse it. Once a person perceives that he is espousing the attitude for the reward, the reward becomes the primary justification so that he no longer needs to hold the attitude to justify the behavior. Hence, the attitude may weaken.

Implicit in much of the work on cognitive consistency is the notion that people attempt to maintain a balance between their behaviors and the justification for those behaviors. When there is imbalance, people may alter their internal states to achieve this balance. I am asserting, therefore, that the paid espouser may experience more justification than necessary, since the reward provides adequate justification. Thus, his attitude will change to restore balance between the behavior and the justification.

There is some evidence from attribution studies to support the notion that, when one cause provides adequate justification for a behavior, other potential causes will be downplayed. Deci, Benware, and Landy (1974) found that subjects' attributions about others' intrinsic motivation decreased when extrinsic rewards provided an adequate justification for the behavior, and Kun and Weiner (1973) found that subjects assumed that a second potential cause did not exist when one cause was adequate to account for the behavior.

The question of the effects of rewards on pro-attitudinal advocacy is closely related to the question of the effects of rewards on counter-attitudinal advocacy. In Chapter 6 we reviewed several studies which showed an inverse relationship between amount of rewards and attitude change. People paid a small amount to espouse a counter-attitudinal position changed their attitudes toward the espoused position. The current question is parallel, and my prediction is parallel, namely, that there will be an inverse relationship between amount of pay and attitude change.

The reason underlying attitude change for espousing a counter-attitudinal position is somewhat more compelling than that for pro-additudinal advocacy. In the former case there is immediate discomfort set up by stating an opinion contrary to one's own without having adequate justification for doing so. Lying is dissonance producing, and people are readily motivated to reduce that dissonance. With pro-additudinal advocacy, however, there is no necessary dissonance induced when a person is paid for saying what he believes. The assertion of a need for balance between justification and behavior, while implicit in dissonance (insufficient justification) theory, is more subtle than dissonance reduction. I am asserting that when a person comes to perceive that he is saying something to get a reward, the reward becomes the primary justification, because the perceived locus of causality has become external, so the balancing of behavior and justification leads to a weakening of attitudes. However, since this process is more subtle than dissonance reduction, one might expect a smaller effect (i.e., less change in attitudes) in the pro-attitudinal advocacy than in the counter-attitudinal advocacy situations.

Benware and Deci (1975) did an experiment to test the prediction that paying someone for espousing a pro-attitudinal communication will weaken his attitude.

In their study, attitudes about student control of university course offerings were collected as part of an attitude survey, three months prior to the actual experiment. All subjects favored student control. Then, during the experiment, subjects were asked to try to convince others that students should have control of course offerings. The subjects were led to believe that the (nonexistent) listeners were actually the subjects, and that they themselves were experimental assistants.

Half the subjects were paid $7.50 for five readings ($1.50 per reading) of a pro-attitudinal communication favoring student control of course offerings, and the other half of the subjects received no pay for reading the communication five times. After they had completed the communications, their own attitudes were assessed and compared to their previous attitudes on that topic taken three months earlier. Results showed a significant attitude change among the paid subjects in relation to the unpaid controls. The attitudes of the paid subjects toward student control became less favorable.

Thus, this study constitutes the first empirical demonstration that payments for pro-attitudinal advocacy can undermine attitudes. The effect, however, was relatively small, even though significant at the standard .05 level. The experimental effect was .44 on a scale ranging from 1 to 7. This small effect is not surprising since, as I said, this effect in pro-attitudinal advocacy might reasonably be expected to be less strong than the insufficient justification effect in counter-attitudinal advocacy.

One other study (Kiesler and Sakumura, 1966) has also investigated the effects of rewarding someone for espousing a pro-attitudinal position. In their study, subjects were given an attitude survey with a key item which assessed their attitudes about lowering the voting age to 18. They were then induced, by the payment of either $1 or $5, to read into a tape recorder a communication which was consonant with their own attitudes about this issue. Next, they were asked, allegedly as part of a different experiment, to read a communication which was counter to their own attitudes, and finally, they were given a second attitude survey which included the same key item. In a control condition, subjects were paid either $1 or $5 to read the consonant communication but were not given the counter-communication. This allowed the authors to examine separately the effects of the consonant communication and the effects of the counter-communication. The rationale given to the subjects for reading the consonant communication was that they were helping in a study of speech patterns in mass media communications.

The results indicated that there was no significant attitude change for either the $1 or $5 control subjects who read only the consonant communication.

Although these results seem inconsistent with the Benware and Deci results, Nisbett and Valins (1971) offered an explanation which can account for this apparent inconsistency. Their explanation was based on a study by Kiesler, Nisbett and Zanna (1969) in which subjects were asked to argue against air pollution. These subjects were in one of two conditions, either a belief-relevant, or a belief-irrelevant, condition. The induction of belief-relevance/irrelevance was done by a confederate who was to argue for auto safety and to tell the subject that he would do so because he believed strongly in the issue (belief relevance) or because it was important for science (belief irrelevance). The results indicated that belief-relevant subjects opposed air pollution more strongly than belief-irrelevant subjects. Apparently then, the more one perceives one's behavior and the justification for the behavior as relevant to his attitude, the more likely it is that the attitude will be affected.

In the Kiesler and Sakumura study, the induction was belief-irrelevant, since subjects were told that they were reading the consonant communication as part of a study on speech patterns. Therefore, in the subjects' phenomenologies, the behavior of reading the communication was not very relevant to their attitudes about lowering the voting age, so the behavior did not lead to attitude change.

In the Benware and Deci study, subjects attempted to persuade others to adopt the espoused positions. Hence, the behavior was belief-relevant, and the investigators found attitude change in the paid subjects. Presumably, therefore, the reason why Benware and Deci found attitude change but Kiesler and Sakumura did not was that the Benware and Deci induction was belief-relevant whereas the Kiesler and Sakumura induction was not. If there had been belief relevance in the Kiesler and Sakumura study, there would probably have been attitude change about the voting age.

In the Kiesler and Sakumura study the subjects who had been paid $5 showed significant attitude change toward the counter-communication during the second part of the experiment, whereas the $1 subjects did not change. Apparently, then, even though the induction was belief-irrelevant, the experience of reading the pro-attitudinal communication for a substantial reward has some weakening effect on the attitude, even though there was no attitude change *per se.*

This would seem to be a further instance of what Heider (1958) has termed "the behavior engulfing the field." The fact of "espousing a position for a large reward" seems to have some affect on one's attitude, even if the act is belief-irrelevant. If the act is belief-relevant, it will have a still greater effect on the attitude; in fact, Kielser *et al.* found that simply committing oneself to doing an act can lead to attitude change if the induction is belief-relevant.

In the $1 condition of the Kiesler and Sakumura study, the $1 reward apparently did not provide adequate justification for the behavior of reading the communication, so the attitude did not appear to be undermined by the behavior. It is possible, though there is not enough data to substantiate, that reading the communication may even have strengthened the attitude. Espousing a position without rewards or for meager rewards, may, since the attitude is the justification for the behavior, tend to strengthen the attitude. According to Kiesler's (1972) interpretation, the person becomes more committed to the attitude when he expresses it for small rewards.

Self-Perception Theory

Bem (1972) used his self-perception theory to analyze the question of the effects of rewards on pro-attitudinal advocacy. He referred to it as *the over justification question.*

Self-perception theory asserts that, to some extent, people infer their own internal states (attitudes, motives, feelings) from their observations of their own behavior and the contingencies which are present when the behavior occurs. Bem therefore proposed that people observe themselves and infer their internal states in much the same way that they observe others and infer the others' internal states.

Using this theory, Bem (1967) has offered an alternative interpretation of the insufficient justification effect (see Chapter 6 for a detailed account of the effect). Bem asserted that if someone does a dull, boring task, or delivers a counter-attitudinal communication for inadequate rewards, he will infer that he must like the task or that he believes the communication. Otherwise, why would he be doing the task or delivering the communication?

Considering the question of overjustification (*viz*, liking a task or believing a communication and also being paid for doing the task or delivering the communication), Bem (1972) predicted a decrease in one's liking for a task or attitude toward some position. Bem stated that the prediction of this affect, using his theory, necessitates the assumption that when there are strongly apparent external contingencies of reinforcement, a person will infer that he did not like the task or did not believe in what he said.

Therefore, one would predict, using Bem's self-perception theory, the same results which Benware and Deci reported.

Psychological Reactance

Reactance theory (Brehm, 1966, 1972) asserts that if a person's freedom is threatened or eliminated he will be motivated to restore the freedom. Further, his attitudes about the "forced" alternative or "eliminated" alternative will be affected. For example, if a person is choosing between going to Mexico and going to Trinidad for a winter vacation, and a friend tries to persuade him to go to Mexico, proffering a bribe and some friendly persuasion, the person will experience his freedom of choice to be threatened and therefore reactance will be aroused. The theory suggests that Trinidad (the threatened alternative) will become more attractive, and Mexico less attractive.

Reactance exists to greater or lesser extents depending on several factors. There will be greater reactance: (1) the more certain the person was that he had freedom, in the first place, (2) the more important that freedom was to him, (3) the greater the extent to which the freedom was eliminated, and (4) the more this reduction in freedom implies that similar occurrences will happen in the future.

Numerous studies have substantiated the basic postulate of reactance theory. For example, Brehm and Sensenig (1966) did a study which ostensibly looked at subjects' abilities to make sensitive judgments. The subject was asked to select five pictures of people—one each from five pairs of pictures—and to make judgments about these people. In addition, he was asked to select five pictures—which could be the same ones—for another (bogus) subject to make judgments about.

While he was selecting, the experimenter delivered a note from the other (bogus) subject, saying either that "he'd like picture X" or that "he thought both of them *should* take picture X." The second case, of course, was the condition where the subject selecting the pictures was threatened with loss of freedom.

The results showed that when the bogus subject stated his own preference, the subject actually selected the same alternative for himself in 73% of the cases, whereas when the bogus subject told the subject what he should select, the subject selected that one in only 40% of the cases. Apparently the threat to his freedom made him react by preferring the threatened alternative.

In another experiment, Sensenig and Brehm (1968) asked subjects to write a short essay advocating one side of a particular topic. Subjects were told that another (though bogus) subject would select which position the pro or con position, each subject would take in his essay, but that each subject would have some influence on that decision. Then half the subjects received a note from the (bogus) other telling them what side they had to argue, whereas the other half of the subjects got a note from the (bogus) other saying which side he preferred the subject to take if it were okay with the subject. In the former case, the subject's freedom to influence the decision was eliminated. In both conditions, the "forced" or the "suggested" side was the side which the subject agreed with. The subjects who were told that they had to write on a topic they agreed with became less favorably disposed toward that topic than subjects who experienced some choice about the decision.

This study suggests an additional interpretation of the finding that paying subjects to espouse a position which is consonant with their attitudes causes a weakening of those attitudes.

When subjects in the Benware and Deci experiment were offered $1.50 to read a short communication in order to try to persuade a listener to adopt the position, they may have perceived the reward to be a restriction of their freedom. If so, they would be expected to react against that restriction by becoming less favorably disposed toward the espoused position. This explanation is less compelling than those of cognitive evaluation theory and self-perception theory, since it is not really clear what choice was being threatened or eliminated. Subjects were simply asked to read a communication and were rewarded for doing so. Nonetheless, the results are consistent with reactance theory, even if they are not readily predicted by it.

I agree with Brehm about the importance of personal freedom to make choices. Indeed, this is very close to the need for self-determination which underlies intrinsic motivation. Hence, we see that if people are denied the opportunity to be self-determining, they will react against this loss.

Summary

This chapter has reviewed a study by Benware and Deci which showed that paying people for trying to convince others of a position which they themselves believe in leads to a weakening of their attitude. This prediction was derived from cognitive evaluation theory and was seen to be consistent with self-perception theory and reactance theory. The results were compared to results from a study by Kiesler and Sakumura (1966) wherein paying people for reading a pro-attitudinal communication did not lead to attitude change, and it was suggested that the differing results can be accounted for because the Kiesler and Sakumura induction was belief-irrelevant, whereas the Benware and Deci induction was belief-relevant.

10

Attribution and Motivation

So far in this book we have been concerned with questions related to a person's own internal states, such as intrinsic motivation or attitudes. We turn now to the question of how a person infers the internal states of another. If Ken watched Nancy build a table, how would he decide whether or not she liked what she was doing? Or if Judy watched David type a manuscript, how would she decide whether or not he was motivated primarily by the pay or by his interest in typing? These are questions of attribution. How does one person make causal attributions to another?

As first discussed by Heider (1958), attribution involves the linking of some event with the conditions which underlie it, through a process of considering personal and environmental forces. This process of attribution stems from a person's desire to undertand his world as somewhat ordered and nonrandom. He can, through attribution, predict and control his own relation to the world, which in turn plays a part in his feeling a sense of competence and self-determination.

According to Heider, events can be accounted for by personal forces and environmental forces. Personal forces include "trying" and "power." Trying is of course a motivational concept and is determined by intentions and exertion. Power is synonymous essentially with ability. Environmental forces include barriers to the occurrence of the event (typically thought of as task difficulty) and luck. This appears in Figure 19. It follows that whether a person "can" cause an event to occur depends on whether or not his power outweighs the barriers. Whether or not he does achieve this

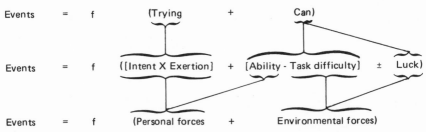

FIGURE 19. The forces in Heider's conception of the causes of events.

depends on one of two sets of circumstances: (1) the facts that he can, and also, that he tried; and (2) the fact that he was lucky. The first set of circumstances typically involves personal causality—his power outweighed the barriers, and he tried to bring about the event. In the second set of circumstances, it makes no difference whether he has power or not, nor whether he tried hard or not; the environment delivered the event. There was impersonal or environmental causality.

If a person fails to bring about an event, it may mean that (1) his power was not as great as were the barriers, (2) he did not try, or (3) he was unlucky. The third case is clearly one of environmental or impersonal causality, and the second is clearly one of personal causality, though the first could be either. If he had substantial power but the barrier were overwhelming, one would typically attribute that failure to the environment. The barrier was too great, so the causality was impersonal. However, if the barrier were small, but his ability were smaller still, the attribution would probably be lack of ability. The cause of the failure would be personal.

Weiner and his colleagues (Weiner, 1972; Weiner, Frieze, Kukla, Reed, Rest, and Rosenbaum, 1971) have pointed out that trying (a personal factor) and luck (an environmental factor) are both relatively instable forces which change and fluctuate over time, whereas ability (a personal factor) and task difficulty (an environmental factor) are relatively stable over time.

Personal Causality

Let us consider the concept of personal causality more carefully, since this is particularly relevant to our central concern of intrinsic motivation. Heider (1958) and Jones and Davis (1965) in elaborating this concept have employed the notion of intentions. Heider submitted that personal causation implies that the actor *intended* to bring about the event. This concept is essentially a motivational one, since motivated behavior is behavior which a person chooses to engage in, in order to achieve some desired end state. Ability is necessary, though it is not a sufficient condition for achieving the end state. Intention must be present to have motivated behavior, i.e., to have personal causality. If the person has intention but is lacking sufficient power (i.e., he cannot do the thing desired), there may be motivated behavior, but the desired end state will not be achieved. The desired end state was the intended *effect*; however, it was not achieved. The failure would be attributed to the "can" dimension and would be either personal, if his ability were very low, or environmental, if the barrier were very large.

In the process of attribution, one begins with an observed event. This may include the desired effect and/or an unintended or accidental effect. If the observer concludes that the event included the desired effect, he will infer intention and will attribute personal causation. If he concludes that it is an undesired outcome, he will infer no intention, and will therefore attribute either impersonal causality (bad luck, large barrier) or lack of ability.

Intention is the most critical factor in personal causation. According to Heider there cannot be true personal causality without intention. Even if a failure were due to one's lack of ability (a personal force), rather than to the overwhelming size of the barrier (an environmental force), the event would not be a case of personal causality. Personal causality assumes intention to produce the observed effects; that is, it involves one's being motivated to achieve the end state.

Heider proposed that there are two conditions which characterize personal causation, "equifinality" and local cause. In that they operationally define personal causation, they necessarily imply intention. *Equifinality* (cf. von Bertalanfly, 1950) means simply that there is one end state but a variety of possible paths to that end. For example, if Sandy intends to get to her office, she can do that through several means; she may drive, walk, ride her bike, and so on. The end state can be achieved even when the most preferred path is blocked by some barrier (her car won't start) which outweighs her power (her ability to fix the car). The alternative path to the same goal may require more power, but if her power outweighs the barriers, then the desired end state will be achieved.

Heider pointed out, however, that although equifinality is necessary for personal causality, it is not sufficient to produce it. He used the example of a marble in a bowl, to show that the marble can arrive at a unitary end state (i.e., being at rest in the bottom of the bowl) through a variety of paths. Yet this is not personal causality. In addition, there must be a local cause; that is, the causal path must be controlled by part of the system. In the marble example, the force leading the marble to its final outcome is gravity, a force outside of the system. In the example of Sandy's reaching her office, the cause is in the system. The cause is Sandy's intention to reach the office. Her intent initiated the activity, her exertion persisted at it, and her ability assisted her in producing the desired end state of reaching the office.

For our purposes, we can interpret "local cause" as meaning that the person sets a goal and chooses a path which he thinks will lead to that goal. This choice will typically be made so as to minimize "trying" while still achieving the desired end state.

Jones and Davis (1965) expanded Heider's work in their theory of correspondent inferences. Their theory begins with the observation of one action (which may, of course, have many effects) and attempts to account for the attribution of that action to a particular intention and subsequently to a dispositional characteristic of the actor. They asserted that for an action to be attributed to a disposition of the actor (i.e., personal causality), an observer must infer intention on the part of the actor. To do this the observer must believe that the actor had the ability to cause the effect and had knowledge that the behavior would lead to the effect. If there were not ability and knowledge, there was no intention so the Jones and Davis model is not applicable. Their model, then, attempts to predict *which* personal cause will be attributed; it is not intended to determine *whether or not* personal causation will be attributed.

The attribution of causality in their model is determined by the desirability of an effect. They assert that an observer will pick the most desirable effect of an action as the reason for the action (i.e., as the actor's intent). Then that effect will be used to infer a disposition. The more unique the effect (i.e., the less common the effect, or the more unusual the effect), the more likely that it will be attributed to the disposition. For example, if Sandy ran to her office, the observed effects would be that she arrived at her office on time but was out of breath. Her intention was to arrive at her office on time, since being out of breath is less desirable and so, not considered the intent. The observer then determines how unusual that effect is; it is not too unusual to arrive at one's office on time, so the dispositional attribution would not be too strong.

Kelley (1967, 1971) took quite a different approach to expanding and elaborating Heider's theory. His version of the attributional process was patterned after an analysis of variance framework. Kelley's model differed from that of Jones and Davis (1965) in two primary ways. First, Kelley's analysis allowed for making attribution not only to the personal dispositions of the actor (e.g., Sandy's compulsive promptness), but also to the entity in question (e.g., a strict boss) or the particular circumstances (e.g., there is an important meeting that day). To determine which of these potential causes will be inferred, the observer decides whether or not all people would get to the office on time (*consensus information*), whether or not Sandy gets to most other places on time (*distinctiveness information*), and whether or not Sandy is on time to her office nearly every day (*consistency information*).

If Sandy's behavior were inconsistent (she's seldom on time), that would imply a circumstantial explanation (an important meeting); whereas, if her behavior were consistent (she's always on time), the explanation would probably be a personal cause (her compulsiveness) or an entity cause (a strict boss). If Sandy were consistent (always on time to her office), low on consensus (other people are seldom on time to the office), and low on distinctiveness (she's on time every place she goes), the cause would seem to be personal (her compulsive promptness). On the other hand, if she were consistent, but high on consensus (other people are on time to the office) and high on distinctiveness (she's seldom on time to other places), then the cause would seem to be in the entity (something about the office causes her promptness to the office).

We can see from this that Kelley's model is more general, in that it attempts to account for environmental (entity or circumstances) attributions as well as personal ones. The Jones and

Davis model is a more precise means of assigning causality to a particular personal cause, whereas Kelley's model allows for causality to be assigned to other causes. Jones and Davis' model would not be operative if the evidence suggested an environmental cause.

As I said, the Jones and Davis model is primarily concerned with the uniqueness of effects. The more desirable the effect (i.e., the less unique the effect), the less confident would be the dispositional attribution. So, if most people would get to their offices on time, the Jones and Davis model would assign a disposition with low confidence. The Kelley model, however, would, since there is high consensus, attribute the act to the entity if it were distinctive behavior, or it would make a weak attribution either to the entity or to Sandy if it were not distinctive.

The second major regard in which the two models differ is that the Jones and Davis framework provides the basis for attributions to be made from only one event, whereas Kelley's model tends to require more information than would ordinarily be available from observing one act and its effects. Kelley's model works most effectively when several events have been observed. The primary process for making attributions, according to Kelley, is the *co-variation principle*. Over time, what dimension co-varies with the event? For example, does Sandy run to her office everytime her car won't start in the morning? If not, the primary cause is not attributed to a disposition of hers. Or does being on time co-vary with her office? If everyone who works there is always on time, but people from other offices aren't, then the entity would seem to be responsible, since the behavior co-varies with the entity.

Kelley (1971) also recognized that people often have minimal data available and cannot rely on several observations, so he offered two other principles to help in making attributions based on fewer data.

The *augmentation principle* asserts that if a behavior occurs in the presence of inhibiting environmental forces, the personal attribution will be augmented (i.e., made more strongly). For example, if Sandy had to run three miles through very cold weather (inhibiting environmental forces), the personal attribution would be stronger than if the weather were beautiful and she had to run only one mile through the park. The latter case would be one of facilitating environmental forces, so there is greater ambiguity in determining the cause.

The *discounting principle* proposes that when behavior occurs in the presence of multiple plausible causes, the attribution will be discounted, that is, the observer attributes the effect less to any one cause than he would if only that cause were plausible. The attributor will be less confident of his attribution and he will make a less extreme attribution than he would make if there were only one plausible cause. This implies that if a behavior occurs in the presence of a facilitating environmental force, internal factors will be discounted. For example, if Sandy were on time and ran through the beautiful park in nice weather, the attribution to her disposition would be discounted.

Enzel, Hansen, and Lowe (1975) reported that environmental forces take precedence over personal ones. Thus, if both personal causes and environmental causes are plausible explanations, there is causal ambiguity and the attribution is most likely to be to the environmental force.

Lowe (1975) has presented a model which elaborates the attributional process and is based in part on the earlier work of Kelley and Jones and Davis. The model, which is shown in Figure 20, begins with the observation of behavior and its effects. This behavior is then analyzed for consensus, distinctiveness, and consistency. From this analysis inferences are made about ability and intent, which in turn lead to causal attributions and finally to dispositional attributions and behavioral reactions on the part of

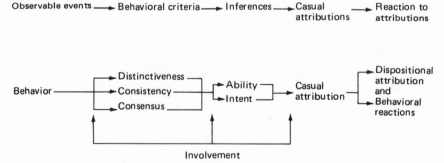

FIGURE 20. Lowe's attributional model.

the observer. An important aspect at each link is the observer's *involvement*, which is a global individual difference variable that makes the attribution process partly subjective. For example, when Judy watches David type a manuscript, her attributions are likely to be affected by whether or not she's a secretary, whether or not she wrote the manuscript which he's typing, whether or not she's friendly with him, and so on. These and other such factors will influence her perceptions, as well as her interpretations, attributions, and reactions.

The Attribution of Motivation

This section is about the attribution of intrinsic and extrinsic motivation. How does an observer make an attribution of intrinsic *vs.* extrinsic motivation to an actor?

Intrinsically motivated behaviors are ones for which the rewards are internal to the person. The actor engages in them to feel competent and self-determining. Extrinsically motivated behaviors are ones which the actor engages in to receive some extrinsic reward. If David typed a manuscript in order to make money, he was extrinsically motivated; if he did it because he enjoyed typing and he felt competent and self-determining when he did it, he was intrinsically motivated.

In either case, the behavior is the same. However, the desired effects are different. In the case of extrinsic, the desired effect is the receipt of the money. In Kelley's terms, if David were doing it for money, there would be high distinctiveness (David would type only in response to an entity that involved money), low consensus (only people high on the disposition of extrinsic motivation would type for pay), and high consistency (he'd generally be willing to type for money). Using Kelley's model there would be some ambiguity, but the attribution would tend to be environmental. The high distinctiveness puts the causality in the entity, though the low consensus would weaken the attribution.

In the case of intrinsic, the desired effect is to engage in the behavior. The rewards are internal, so the attribution would be to a personal disposition, *viz.*, intrinsic motivation. In Kelley's terms, if

David were intrinsically motivated, there would be low distinctiveness (David would still type if the entity changed), low consensus (only the people intrinsically motivated to type would do it) and high consistency (he'd probably type a lot if it were intrinsically rewarding). Hence, the attribution would be personal.

Internal and External Causality

In both the intrinsic and the extrinsic cases, however, there would be both ability and intention on the part of the actor. Heider (1958) and Jones and Davis (1965) have emphasized the central role of intentions in personal causality. In the case of extrinsic motivation, David intended to get the money. He performed the act to achieve that effect. Further, he'd undoubtedly do many other things to achieve that desired effect, so there would be equifinality. Further, the cause is in the system. The cause is David's intention to get the money. So this implies personal causality, though Kelley's model would attribute the behavior to environmental forces.

I am therefore pointing to an issue which has heretofore been somewhat hazy in the attribution literature, namely, the relationship among personal, impersonal, and environmental causality. The essential difference between personal and impersonal causality is intention. If there is intention, there is personal causality.

Personal causality exists when a person intends something whether the ostensible cause is in him or in the environment. Hence, some events which are attributed to the environment, could be attributed to the person and thereby provide a more meaningful account. Sometimes when an observer attributes environmental causality, he could go beyond that to learn a good deal about the actor. For example, when David types a manuscript for money, one could simply say that the money is the cause (*ergo,* an environmental attribution). However, I am asserting that David's intention to get the money is the real cause. Hence, when David types for money, we learn something about his extrinsic motivation. Similarly, when Sandy walks in the beautiful park, we can learn something about Sandy (e.g., she loves nature). Therefore, I would propose to modify Kelley's notion of personal causality and environmental causality. I suggest that there are personally caused

intentions and environmentally caused intentions. It seems to me
that this distinction is a very important one to make. Heider spoke
of environmental forces as being task difficulty and luck. Neither of
these involves intention; each represents impersonal causality.
Therefore, to speak of environmental causality as Kelley does
seems to me to confuse environmentally caused intentions with
impersonal causality.

Impersonal causality refers to situations where there is (1)
global causality (a person is believed to have caused an event if he
had any connection to it, e.g., because I am a man I'm held
responsible for the supression of women); (2) accidental causality
(a person was instrumental to the occurrence of an effect but in no
way intended it or had reason to suspect that it would happen); or
(3) incidental causality (the person engaged in behavior X inten-
tionally and event Y followed from it, but he had no way of
knowing that Y would follow X).

I am suggesting that the attributional process would not end
when an attribution is made to environmental causality. Rather,
the next step would be to determine whether or not that behavior
was really caused by the person's intention *vis-a-vis* the environment.

This has a number of advantages. First, it clarifies the question
of environmental causality as it relates to personal and impersonal
causality. I propose to speak of *internal* and *external* causality.
Internal relates to personally caused intentions, and *external* relates
to environmentally caused intentions. Both would constitute personal causation, since both involve intentions. "Impersonal
environmental" causality does not involve intentions. I am proposing, then, that there are three broad classes of causality: *internal*
(personally caused intentions), *external* (environmentally caused
intentions, which still constitute personal causality), and *impersonal-
environmental* (where there are no intentions).

In Chapter 5, cognitive evaluation theory utilized the notions
of internal and external causality. These terms, which were taken
from de Charms, were used in the fashion just outlined and
represent the crux of the intrinsic–extrinsic distinction.

The use of internal and external causality also allows the
observer to relate the causality to himself. Heider said that one's
desire to understand his own environment is the underlying cause

of the attributional process. If one attributes external causality (i.e., environmentally caused *intentions*) and subsequently a personal disposition, he will learn more about people in relation to the environment than he would if he attributed environmentally caused *behavior,* and left it at that.

My assertion that people desire this information is a direct corollary of Heider's proposition and also fits with my concern for the concepts of personal knowledge, and intrinsic motivation.

Let us now consider when, within Kelley's and Lowe's frameworks, the three attributions would be made. We will consider the conditions leading to (1) personal, internal, (2) personal, external, and (3) impersonal environmental.

Personal internal results when there is high consistency (David types a great deal because he likes it), low consensus (only intrinsically motivated people type without being paid for it), and low distinctiveness (David would still do it if the entity were changed because he likes typing). Personal external causality is attributed when there is high consistency (David always types if he gets paid), low consensus (only extrinsically motivated people will type to get paid), and high distinctiveness (David does it only if he is being paid). Hence, the distinguishing factor between internal and external causality is the distinctiveness of the behavior.

Intrinsically motivated behavior is less distinctive than extrinsically motivated behavior. The cause in the latter case is the intention to get the extrinsic reward, so the person will engage in the behavior only for money.

Now consider impersonal environmental causality. The person involved is irrelevant, since the environment is the cause, so there is high consensus, and there will be high consistency. Further, there will be high distinctiveness, since the environment (i.e., the entity) causes the particular behavior being observed.

The difference, therefore, between external causality (i.e., environmentally caused intentions) and impersonal environmental is that external causality has low consensus, (only people who are extrinsically motivated to make money would engage in the behavior), whereas impersonal has high consensus (everyone would do it in that situation). Table VIII shows the conditions for the three kinds of attributions.

TABLE VIII. The Conditions for Attributions of Internal, External, and Impersonal–Environmental Causality

Internal causality	External causality	Impersonal–environmental
High consistency	High consistency	High consistency
Low consensus	Low consensus	High consensus
Low distinctiveness	High distinctiveness	High distinctiveness

Now consider the situation wherein a trait held by all (or most) people causes intentions, and subsequently, behavior. In such a case there will be high consensus. A trait which is possessed by everyone or nearly everyone (e.g., social desirability) gives us little information about any particular person. Hence, a behavior which is caused by an intention stemming from a universal trait is functionally equivalent to environmental impersonal causality. Therefore, the attribution will be the same when there is an intent that was caused by a universal trait, and when there is impersonal causality (with no intent). While, in some sense, it would be incorrect to attribute environmental impersonal causality when there is intent, in pragmatic terms, such an attribution would be quite appropriate. For example, imagine analyzing a situation in which someone refused to drive his car into a brick building to try to knock it down. Virtually everyone would refuse to do that. Hence, it makes little difference whether or not there were impersonal environmental causality (e.g., whether or not the task were impossible) or whether or not a universal trait (e.g., desire not to kill oneself) caused the behavior. It is reasonably attributed to impersonal environmental.

Weiner *et al.* (1971) have distinguished between internal and external *locus of control* (a concept introduced by Rotter, 1966). They suggested that ability and effort are internal, so that an event caused by one of those two factors would have an internal locus of control, whereas luck and task difficulty are external, so that an event caused by one of those factors would have an external locus of control. That distinction is analogous to the personal/impersonal distinction and should not be confused with *locus of causality.* Internal locus of control as used by Weiner *et al.* and Rotter, involves intention (hence, personal causality) and can be either internal causality (e.g., intrinsically motivated) or external causality (e.g., extrinsically motivated). External locus of control, on the other hand, implies impersonal causality.

In sum, intrinsically motivated behaviors are characterized by *internal* causality. The cause of the behavior is the intent to receive the internal rewards of the activity, i.e., feelings of competence and self-determination. Extrinsically motivated activities are characterized by external causality. The cause of the behavior is the intent to get an external reward. Yet both of these involve personal causation. The person intended to bring about the desired effect. He tried to do it, and he was able to do it. On the other hand, events which are caused by luck or by environmental forces such as large barriers (e.g., failure at a very difficult task) are impersonally caused. The primary causality is in the environment, and there is no intention on the part of the actor to bring about that event. These distinctions are shown graphically in Figure 21.

In considering the attribution of intrinsic and extrinsic motivation, we assume both "can" and "trying." These elements distinguish personal from impersonal causality; however, we must find what factors allow us to distinguish internal from external causality.

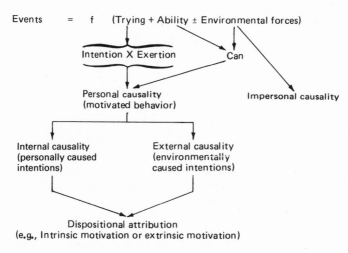

FIGURE 21. The relationship between impersonal and personal (i.e., internal, external) causality of events.

Thibaut and Riecken (1955) conducted a study which has bearing on the attribution of motivation. In their experiment subjects asked for a favor and got compliance from a high-status other and a low-status other. After the experiment, subjects were more likely to attribute internal causality to the behavior of the high-status other than to the low-status other. When the low-status other complied, he was perceived to have done it because of external pressure from the subjects; therefore, the perceived locus of causality was external. On the other hand, when the high-status other complied, he was perceived as having done it for internal reasons, presumably because a high-status other would be freer of the pressure from the subject. In this case, the perceived locus of causality was internal. In both cases the causality was personal. Both subjects chose to perform the activity; it was intentional behavior. In one case, the causality was perceived to be external, and in the other it was perceived to be internal. Although their study did not deal directly with intrinsic and extrinsic motivation, it suggests that when a person is seen as being subject to external forces, his behavior is perceived to be externally motivated, but if he is seen as being less subject to external forces, his behavior is perceived to be internally motivated.

In short, I am suggesting that when plausible external causes are present, the attribution will tend to be external. This is supported by several studies (e.g., Enzel *et al.*, 1975; Nemeth, 1970; Lowe & Enzel, 1974).

Level of Extrinsic Reward

Applying these results to the attribution of motivation, one would expect that if a person engaged in an activity for no apparent external cause (i.e., no apparent extrinsic reward) he would be perceived as intrinsically motivated. Conversely, if he received large extrinsic rewards for performing the activity he would be perceived to be more extrinsically motivated and less intrinsically motivated. Numerous studies presented in Chapter 5 relate to this proposition. These studies (Deci, 1971, 1972a, 1972b; Deci & Cascio, 1972; Lepper, Greene, & Nisbett, 1973) demonstrated that when extrinsic rewards, such as money, the avoidance of punishment, or a desired award, were given to subjects for engaging in an intrinsically motivated activity, their intrinsic motivation decreased.

These studies suggest a negative relationship between the amount of extrinsic reward which a person receives for an activity and the amount of intrinsic motivation he has for performing that activity. When he received high rewards for doing an intrinsically interesting task he displayed a low level of intrinsic motivation. When he received low rewards, he displayed greater intrinsic motivation.

The studies by Deci and by Lepper *et al.* were concerned with a person's perception of his own intrinsic and extrinsic motivation. It is not unreasonable, however, to expect that if one person observes another engaged in an activity, he is likely to make attributions of intrinsic motivation and extrinsic motivation in accord with this notion of a negative relationship between the amount of extrinsic rewards and the amount of intrinsic motivation, and, indeed, this is consistent with the work on internal/external causality cited above.

This leads to the prediction that observers will attribute greater extrinsic motivation and less intrinsic motivation to performers who receive a high level of monetary rewards for doing a task than to performers who receive a low level of monetary rewards.

This same prediction can be derived from Kelley's (1971) *discounting principle.* This principle, you will recall, asserts that when there are multiple plausible causes for an event, the role of any one of the causes will be discounted. This suggests that if a person did an interesting task and were paid a lot, the plausible cause of intrinsic motivation would be discounted. He would be judged to be less intrinsically motivated because the money would represent an alternative plausible cause. If he were paid a small amount, however, the pay would not be a plausible cause, so the intrinsic cause would not be discounted.

Level of Output

It was asserted that the conditions within which a person behaves (*viz.*, the extrinsic rewards he receives) will influence the attributions which others make about his motivation. The behavior itself will also influence the perceiver's inferences. If a person is producing some commodity or performing some service, the number of units he produces or the number of services he renders will affect the attributions an observer makes about his motivation. If the person is receiving a set amount of payment (i.e., a salary, as opposed to piece-rate payments) and is performing under constant conditions, his output will directly reflect his intrinsic motivation. The more he produces, the more intrinsically motivated he will be perceived to be.

Now consider attributions of extrinsic motivation and recall that an extrinsically motivated person is someone who engages in the behavior in order to get a reward. If there's no reward, there'll be no behavior. If a person is getting a set amount of pay which cannot be affected by his output, he will be likely to produce as little as he can get by with. Performance doesn't get him rewards, so he won't perform much. Hence, low output suggests high extrinsic motivation. On the other hand, if his output is high, he will be seen as low in extrinsic motivation, since he wouldn't be producing so much if he were motivated primarily to get money. This leads to the prediction that a person will attribute greater intrinsic motivation and less extrinsic motivation to performers who produce a high level of output than to ones who produce a low level of output, when rewards are not tied directly to output.

Deci, Benware, and Landy (1973) did a study which tested these two predictions. The subjects were each given a booklet which described an experiment alleged to have been conducted the previous semester (although it was a bogus study) and which purportedly tested the developmental trends of color perception in humans. It was explained to the subjects exactly what procedural steps these "color perception subjects" (to be called *actors*) had gone through. Essentially, the subjects were told that the actors had been given a large stack of uncolored pictures and had been asked to color pictures for three hours, coloring as many pictures as they wished and the kinds of pictures which they liked best.

The two manipulated variables in this study were: a) the amount of monetary reward ($2.50/hr *vs.* $.50/hr) received by the actor, and b) the level of output produced by the actor (25 pictures completed in three hours *vs.* 5 pictures completed). All subjects were told that the average number of pictures completed by all actors was 15, although each actor had had 100 different pictures available to color. In summary, the four experimental conditions were: low output, low reward (5 pictures, $1.50/three hours); high output, low reward (25 pictures, $1.50/three hours); low output, high reward (5 pictures, $7.50/three hours); and high output, high reward (25 pictures, $7.50/three hours). Subjects were randomly assigned to the four conditions by being provided with one of the four different booklet forms corresponding to the four conditions. Each subject was asked to judge the probable attitudes of *one* actor after having been provided with reward/output information peculiar to that actor.

The scale of attributed intrinsic motivation ranged from 1 (least enjoyable) to 10 (most enjoyable) in response to the attitude statement, "Was motivated by the enjoyment of performing the task." The scale of attributed extrinsic motivation ranged from 1 (money least important) to 10 (money most important) in response to the statement, "Was motivated by the monetary reward received."

The results of this experiment are presented in Table IX.

The prediction, that there would be a direct relationship between level of reward and extrinsic motivation, and that there would be an inverse relationship between level of reward and intrinsic motivation, was supported. For intrinsic motivation the F value was 9.88, which is significant at the .003 level, and for extrinsic motivation the F value was 42.5, which is significant at the .001 level.

TABLE IX. Mean Attributions of Intrinsic and Extrinsic Motivation

	Intrinsic		Extrinsic	
	High rewards	Low rewards	High rewards	Low rewards
High output	6.46	7.92	6.81	3.54
Low output	3.92	5.38	7.58	4.85

The second prediction, that there would be a direct relation between level of output and intrinsic motivation and that there would be an inverse relation between level of output and extrinsic motivation, was also supported. For intrinsic motivation the F value was 29.8, which is significant at the .001 level, and for extrinsic motivation the F value was 5.09, which is significant at the .03 level.

There was no interaction between output and reward on either dependent variable. Clearly, the predictions received strong support from the data. When a person performs a task for which he receives large extrinsic payments he will be perceived by an observer to be more extrinsically motivated and less intrinsically motivated than someone who does the same activity for small extrinsic payments. Further, if he produces high output on the task he will be perceived to be more intrinsically motivated and less extrinsically motivated than someone who produces low output.

The experiment just presented considered the effects of monetary rewards on attributions of intrinsic and extrinsic motivation. What might be the effects of other extrinsic rewards or controls?

Kite (1964) did a study which allows a partial answer to this question. His study showed that when one person punished another by fining him for poor performance, attributions about the causes of his compliance behavior were very highly external. The cause of the behavior was attributed to the punishment. In another condition where subjects were rewarded with monetary payments for doing well, attributions were also external, that is, the cause of the behavior was in large part attributed to the reward. However, in the punishment condition the causality was more strongly attributed to the external control than in the reward condition.

Combining these results with those of the Deci, Benware, and Landy study, one would expect that, not only extrinsic monetary rewards, but also other external controls, would lead to decreased attributions of intrinsic motivation.

Reward Contingency

The monetary rewards administered in the Deci, Benware, and Landy experiment described above were hourly payments that were not contingent on output. Imagine now a situation where extrinsic rewards are made contingent on performance. A set amount of reward is paid per unit of output, so the greater the output the greater the rewards and the lower the output the lower the rewards. What attributions would an observer make about the motivation of a performer in a contingent payment situation?

An important piece of information to be considered in making predictions about the attributions in contingent *vs.* noncontingent situations is the fact that in a contingent situation the rewards are, to a much greater extent, under the control of the performer. He determines the magnitude of monetary payments which he receives, whereas in the noncontingent situation the rewards are fixed and the performer has no effect on them.

To derive the predictions for the attributions of motivation in a contingent and noncontingent situation, consider a 2 × 2 experimental design with high output/high reward and low output/low regard on one dimension and noncontingent and contingent payments on the other. Imagine that the contingent payment is set so that both output and rewards are constant across the contingent/noncontingent conditions and within the output/reward conditions. It is now possible to compare performers whose output and rewards are the same but whose basis of rewards is different. (Table X which appears later in the chapter shows the 2 × 2 design.)

Rewards are a direct function of output when they are contingent, so rewards and output will necessarily co-vary. Hence, to make meaningful comparisons between the contingent and noncontingent conditions, rewards and output will have to co-vary in the noncontingent conditions, as well.

First, look at extrinsic attributions, and consider the low output/low reward conditions. If a person is contingently paid, he will be perceived as less extrinsically motivated than the person who is noncontingently paid, because the contingently paid person *chose* to get low rewards. He could have made more if he had been extrinsically motivated, so he must be very low in extrinsic motivation since he did not choose to make more. While the noncontingently paid person also received low pay, he did not determine his own level of pay, so that although he should be perceived as low in extrinsic motivation (as was shown in the Deci *et al.* experiment mentioned above), it will not be as low as the contingently paid person. Now for the high output/reward conditions. The contingently paid person should be perceived as more extrinsically motivated than the noncontingently paid person, since he determined his own level of reward. He worked to get a lot of money, so he must be highly extrinsically motivated. In sum, we are predicting that there will be an interaction between the output/reward variable and the contingency/noncontingency variable such that the high output/high reward contingent cell will be most extrinsic, the low output/low reward, contingent cell will be least extrinsic, and the two noncontingency cells will be moderately extrinsic.

Now consider the predictions for intrinsic motivation and look first at the high output/high reward conditions. In the noncontingent cell, the rewards are fixed so the performer's output does not affect his rewards. Therefore, it is clearer that his high output reflects his intrinsic interest in the activity. However, when the rewards are contingent, it is not clear whether his high output stems from his attempts to increase his rewards or from his intrinsic interest in the task. Therefore, he will be perceived as more intrinsically motivated in the noncontingent condition. Now consider the low output/low reward conditions. When a performer is paid noncontingently, his rewards don't depend on his output, so low output suggests lower intrinsic motivation. For the contingently paid subject it is not clear whether his low performance is due to low intrinsic motivation or to low extrinsic motivation (i.e., a lack of interest in making money). Therefore, the attributions of intrinsic motivation will be lower for the noncontingently paid performer than for the contingently paid performer. This, then, predicts an interaction between the output/reward variable and the "nature of payment" variable such that high output/high reward, noncontingent will be the most intrinsic and low output/low reward, noncontingent will be the least intrinsic.

Deci, Benware, and Landy (1974) conducted a study to test these two predictions, using a methodology which was virtually identical to that described above, the only difference being that the payments in two of the conditions were said to have been contingent on performance. In the contingent payment conditions, subjects were told that the actor received $.30 per picture colored. Therefore, in the high output conditions 25 pictures meant that the actor earned $7.50, which is the same amount that was earned by the high producer (noncontingent) who received $2.50 per hour. In the low output condition, the actor colored five pictures and therefore received $1.50, which was the same amount as that earned by the actor who received $.50 per hour. Clearly then, the amount of output and rewards was the same in the two high output/high reward conditions, and also in the two low output/low reward conditions. The only difference was that in two conditions payments were contingent on performance, and in the others they were not contingent.

The important question, then, is whether or not contingent payments affect attributions differently than do noncontingent payments.

To summarize, there were four conditions in the experiment. They were: (1) high output/high reward, noncontingent; (2) high output/high reward, contingent; (3) low output/low reward, non-contingent; and (4) low output/low reward, contingent.

The data for attributions of extrinsic motivation are presented in Table X, and for intrinsic motivation in Table XI. One can see from Table X that, as predicted, subjects in the high output/high reward conditions attributed greater extrinsic motivation to the performer when payment was contingent than when it was non-contingent, and in the low output/low reward conditions, subjects attributed less extrinsic motivation when payment was contingent than when it was noncontingent. The predicted interaction was highly significant ($p < .0001$).

TABLE X. *Mean Attributions of Extrinsic Motivation for Subjects in High and Low Output/Reward Conditions and Contingency and Noncontingency Conditions (n = 30/cell)*

	Noncontingent (Hourly pay)	Contingent ($.30/picture)	Marginals
High output/high reward (25 pictures, $7.50)	6.03	8.33	7.18
Low output/low reward (5 pictures, $1.50)	4.53	2.37	3.45
Marginals	5.28	5.35	

TABLE XI. *Mean Attributions of Intrinsic Motivation for Subjects in High and Low Output/Reward Conditions and Contingency and Noncontingency Conditions (n = 30/Cell)*

	Noncontingent (Hourly pay)	Contingent ($.30/picture)	Marginals
High output/high reward (25 pictures, $7.50)	7.00	5.63	6.32
Low output/low reward (5 pictures, $1.50)	4.63	5.10	4.87
Marginals	5.82	5.37	

Looking now at the data for intrinsic attributions, we see that, as predicted, subjects in the high output/high reward conditions attributed greater intrinsic motivation to the performer when rewards were noncontingent than when they were contingent, and subjects in the low output/reward conditions attributed less intrinsic motivation when rewards were noncontingent than when they were contingent. The interaction was significant at the .05 level.

The results of this experiment are also quite readily predictable from Kelley's theory which utilizes the augmentation and discounting principles. Contingent rewards are facilitating environmental forces. Noncontingent rewards can also be seen as facilitating environmental forces, but they are less clearly so, since there is no direct link between the behavior and the rewards.

With high contingent rewards, the money is observable and is a sufficient cause, so the personal force (intrinsic motivation) will be discounted and attributions will be strongly extrinsic. When rewards are noncontingent, however, the high rewards are not such a clear-cut facilitative force, so intrinsic will be discounted less, and attributions of extrinsic will not be so strong. When rewards are contingent, output gives little information about intrinsic motivation, since it is necessary to get the rewards. However, when rewards are noncontingent, output does not affect rewards, so it is seen to be a reflection of intrinsic motivation.

With low contingent rewards (hence, low pay), the person must be very low in extrinsic motivation. A facilitative force is available, yet even with this he still doesn't produce a lot; obviously, then, the facilitative force is not important to him, so the dispositional attribution would be low extrinsic. Also, there is no evidence of intrinsic interest, since output is low.

With low noncontingent rewards, the money is not so clearly a facilitative force, since it is not tied to output. Hence, the low output does not indicate that the external force (money) is not important to him, so there is greater ambiguity for extrinsic attributions. For intrinsic, again, there is no indication of interest. However, here the intrinsic would be seen as lower, since in the contingent case there are two plausible explanations for low output—either low intrinsic or low extrinsic—so low intrinsic would be discounted as the cause. Therefore, the person would be seen as not quite so low. With noncontingent, since rewards aren't determined by output, low extrinsic motivation is not a plausible account of the low output, so the personal cause (low intrinsic) will be seen as the unequivocal cause, and the lowest intrinsic attribution will be in this condition.

Relation of Intrinsic and Extrinsic Attributions

In Chapters 5 and 6 we discussed the relationships between extrinsic rewards and intrinsic motivation. Research evidence indicated that when rewards were high, intrinsic motivation decreased, and when rewards were low, intrinsic motivation increased (Aronson, 1966; Deci, 1972a). The evidence from the first Deci, Benware and Landy experiment substantiated that in interpersonal attribution the same principle holds. When a performer received high rewards, an observer attributed less intrinsic motivation than when the performer received low rewards.

A closely related, though different, question has to do with whether or not the attributions of extrinsic motivation and intrinsic motivation which an observer makes to a performer are also inversely related. Deci *et al.* (1974) presented evidence from studies of interpersonal attribution which address this question. In one study a significant relationship existed between attributions of intrinsic and extrinsic motivation ($r = -.40$), and in a second study there was a significant, though smaller, correlation between the two attributions ($r = -.21$). Attributions of intrinsic motivation and extrinsic motivation seem to be consistently, though moderately, negatively related. When the external cause is sufficient to account for the behavior, the internal cause is likely to be discounted or down-played. In fact, Kun and Weiner (1973) found that when one cause was sufficient to account for a behavior, other possible causes were assumed not to exist. People seem to balance the behavior with the causes of that behavior and resist attributing too much causality. This notion is similar to the assertion in Chapter 9 that people tend to balance their own behaviors and the justification for those behaviors. Nonetheless, the negative correlation between internal and external causes accounted for only 16% of the variance in the first Deci, Benware, and Landy study and only 4% in the second. This suggests that there are probably both internal and external forces operating much of the time. People are seen to be (and may, in fact be) both intrinsically and extrinsically motivated at the same time.

The Deci, Benware, and Landy studies have shown that both output and rewards provide information to an observer to use in making attributions of both intrinsic and extrinsic motivation. In the second study there were not only significant interactions between output/rewards and "nature of payments" but there was also a significant main effect on extrinsic motivation for the output/reward variable ($F = 83.04$; $p < .0001$) and a significant main effect on intrinsic motivation for the output/reward variable ($F = 10.27$; $p < .02$). High output/high rewards was more extrinsic than low output/low rewards, and high output/high rewards was also more intrinsic than low output/low rewards.

Consider first the case of extrinsic, and recall from the first experiment that extrinsic attributions vary directly with rewards and inversely with output. Therefore, the two variables work in opposite directions on extrinsic attributions. However, it seems reasonable that when one is asked to make attributions about a performer's extrinsic motivation the more salient piece of information will be the person's extrinsic rewards, so the attributions should be based primarily on the information about his rewards. Therefore, a person with high output/high reward will be perceived as more extrinsically motivated than a person with low output/low reward, even though output is inversely related to attributions of extrinsic motivation. This, then, would account for the main effect on extrinsic motivation of the output/reward variable.

Now consider the case of intrinsic motivation. Here attributions vary directly with output and inversely with money. If one were asked to make attributions about a performer's intrinsic motivation for an activity, he would be most likely to observe the performer's behavior. The person's behavior at the activity is the thing that's most likely to convey information about his intrinsic interest in the activity. So the output variable should be more salient than rewards in making attributions of intrinsic motivation. If this were the case, one would expect the main effect which can be observed in Table XI, namely, that high output/high reward would be more intrinsic than low output/low reward.

In sum, the amount of extrinsic rewards which a person receives seems (both intuitively and empirically) to be the most salient information when an observer makes attributions about extrinsic motivation. On the other hand, the amount of output seems to be the most salient information for attributions about a person's intrinsic motivation.

The Task Itself

Rewards and output provide salient information for a person to use in making attributions of intrinsic and extrinsic motivation. In the studies reported above where these factors were varied, the task was always constant. It was probably considered by subjects to be a reasonably interesting activity, though there are no clear-cut data on this. In making attributions of intrinsic and extrinsic motivation, the task itself would undoubtedly constitute very relevant information. An observer would have some assessment of how intrinsically interesting an activity is, regardless of whether or not there were rewards, output, or whatever.

Imagine a situation in which the intrinsic interest of an activity is either high or low. Then let us look at the question of how output and rewards affect attributions of intrinsic and extrinsic motivation.

When the task is interesting, there should be two main effects, as was found by Deci, Benware, and Landy. High output on an interesting task suggests that it is even more interesting. Low output suggests that it is not quite so interesting as it looks. Output is related directly to attributions of intrinsic motivation. Rewards, on the other hand, are a facilitating external force, so they tend to discount attributions of intrinsic motivation; hence, rewards would be inversely related to attributions of intrinsic motivation.

However, if the task is boring, the attributions of intrinsic motivation would be different. The observer begins by knowing that it is dull and boring. So, if the rewards were high, that would provide a very adequate account of the behavior. It is extrinsically motivated: Intrinsic motivation would be discounted. As for output, since it is so clearly an extrinsically motivated behavior, high output would not necessarily make the observer think the actor is intrinsically motivated. More likely, in fact, he'd see the actor as working hard to earn the high pay. High pay is the objective he has in performing the activity, so the more output, the more he is working for the money, i.e., the more extrinsically, and less intrinsically, motivated the actor must be.

If pay is low, then it does not provide an adequate account of the behavior. Since the actor is producing a lot, but isn't getting much pay, he must like the task. He is not doing it for pay, so internal forces have to be inferred.

In sum, when the task is dull and boring, if rewards are high there should be an inverse relationship between output and attributions of intrinsic motivation, whereas, if rewards are low, there should be a direct relationship. In other words, I am predicting an interaction between output and rewards when the task is dull and boring and two main effects when the task is ambiguous or interesting.

Now let us consider the data which relate to the above predictions. In the Deci, Benware, and Landy study, the predictions for an interesting task were upheld, that is, there were main effects for output and rewards. The higher the output, the higher the intrinsic attributions, and the higher the rewards, the lower the intrinsic attributions. The task in the Deci, Benware, and Landy study was ambiguous in terms of its interest value, though it was clearly not dull and boring, so it does seem like a reasonable test of the predictions for more interesting tasks.

I know of no study which has directly tested the predictions for a boring task. However, Bem (1967) has reported a study which has important relevance. In his study (which was essentially an inter-personal replication of the well known Festinger & Carlsmith, 1959, study), subjects listened to a tape recording of a person who had engaged in two dull and boring motor tasks. The listener heard the person on the tape (i.e., the actor) explain to another person that the tasks were fun and enjoyable, although, in fact, they were really quite uninteresting. In two conditions the person used several imaginative arguments to try to persuade the other that the task were interesting, and in the other two, he used fewer and less imaginative arguments. Although the number of arguments is not really output, it bears substantial similarity to it. Hence we will think of the number of arguments as the quantity of output. So, two of the conditions had high output (many imaginative arguments) and two of the conditions had low output (fewer, less imaginative arguments).

Further, in one high output and one low output condition the actor was said to have received $1 for trying to convince the other person, and in the remaining two conditions he was said to have received $20. So here too, as in the Deci, Benware, and Landy experiment, high and low rewards cross with high and low output. The primary difference between the two studies is that in one case (Bem) the task was dull and boring, whereas in the other (Deci, Benware, and Landy) it was somewhat interesting.

The results of the Bem study indicated that when rewards were low $1, the higher the output (i.e., the more arguments), the more the actor was seen to like the task. However, in the high reward conditions ($20), the higher the output, the less he was seen to like the task. Bem suggested that it may have been perceived that the highly paid person with many arguments "doth protest too much." The results, then, did show the predicted interaction between rewards and output when the task was dull and boring.

Of course, these results are only suggestive and do not test the proposition directly. Contrasting the Bem study with the Deci *et al.* study is problematic in that the former considered the attribution of attitudes rather than intrinsic motivation. Further, the monetary rewards were much different and the experimental paradigm was somewhat different. Still, the results suggest that the predictions may be reasonable and indicate that a more precise test of the derivations would be appropriate.

The Process of Making Attributions

In a real world situation, an observer experiences an event and makes attributions. When he hears a politician make a speech, he may make attributions about the speaker's honesty. When he sees an auto accident, he may make attributions about responsibility. When he observes a worker, he may make attributions about intrinsic motivation.

But how does he actually go about doing it? This question has not received a great deal of attention in the literature on attribution. In research studies, subjects are generally presented with a situation (either by written descriptions, taped accounts, acted performances, etc.) and then asked to rate the level of the actor's "belief in the topic," "amount of intrinsic interest," etc. In other words, the dimension is chosen for the observer. He responds to someone else's dimension, rather than selecting his own, and using that dimension, he processes information to arrive at an attribution. This procedure, however, raises questions about whether we are studying attribution as it goes on in the real world, or have created a special kind of situation.

Formal models of attribution (e.g., Jones & Davis, 1965, Kelley, 1971) begin with behaviors and their effects and proceed logically to attributions. The attributional dimensions (e.g., strength of attitude) are not selected, *per se*, but rather "fall out of " the analysis. In other words, they are the end product. Hence, someone listening to a speaker might not, according to the theories, even make an attribution about his honesty, or about the intrinsic motivation of a worker. Yet, in research studies, these dimensions are given to the subjects by the researcher's questions. Therefore, these studies may to some extent be confusing the larger questions of when and how people make attributions in real life situations. I shall, in the next several pages, outline a general approach to understanding the question of how attributions are made in actual situations.

Phenomenal or Causal

Heider (1958) distinguished between phenomenal and causal descriptions of perception. He proposed that attributions are phenomenal or immediate, and that there is not an elaborate cognitive processing involved in making attributions. He stated, "[In] person perception [the observer] not only perceives people as having certain spatial and physical properties, but also can grasp even such intangibles as their wishes, needs, and emotions by some form of *immediate apprehensions*" (Heider, 1958, p. 22, italics added). On the other hand, the model presented by Kelley (1967), for example, is much more analytical and is an example of what Heider called causal descriptions of perception.

Hence, we are left with two extremes on the question of how people make attributions. Heider suggested that it's phenomenal, and Kelley and others suggested that it's an elaborate, rational, cognitive process.

I am now suggesting that it may be both, as well as various versions in between. People may differ in the way they make attributions, depending on the situation. In some situations people will be very involved and very interested in the actor, so their attributions will be more elaborate and carefully considered. At other times they may be more immediate. In some situations the observer may not even make attributions. As one walks down a tree-lined street and notices a twig fall onto the lawn beside him, he may not even bother to make an attribution. He observes the event and it passes. On the other hand, a very paranoid person would probably not only make an attribution, but would make a personal one (e.g., someone's after him).

Further, if someone is concerned with some issue in himself, for example, if he is concerned with dominance, power, honesty, or so on, he will undoubtedly question this in the other person. Substantial attention is paid to this notion in personality and clinical psychology. For example, the mechanism of projection involves a related process. Gestalt therapists (Perls, Hefferline, & Goodman, 1951) believe that when a person is concerned with a particular issue, this issue will continue to come into his foreground and will affect his perceptions. If this is the case, he may either engage in a more detailed causal analysis in an attempt to understand himself better, or he may defensively project his own issue onto the other person in a phenomenal way. In the Lowe (1975) model presented earlier, the term *involvement* which mediates the attribution process at several points relates to the points which have just been raised.

Heider has stated that the reason people engage in attribution is to understand their world. This relates closely to the basis of intrinsic motivation, namely, that people have a need to experience themselves as competent, effective and self-determining. It is quite reasonable, then, to assume that the attribution process is intrinsically motivated and that whether a person makes an attribution and how he makes it depends on his own intrinsic needs. Everyone will not be motivated to make attributions in all situations—everyone is not intrinsically motivated to do the same thing. On the other hand, there are commonalities among people in the way they make attributions. My point is simply that there is greater "personalness" to the attribution process than one might think from the formal attribution models.

In spite of the fact that there are individual differences in the attributional process, I will attempt to specify a general approach to the attributional process. This is not new; it is simply an attempt to draw together some of the existing literature.

External First

Much of the work in attribution theory suggests or implies that we look first to the environment to explain the causes of behavior. If there is an obvious impersonal environmental or circumstantial cause, this would be the attribution. If a downpour of rain starts suddenly and people begin to scurry, the attribution would be impersonal environmental, the observer would probably not go further in the attributional process. In Kelley's (1967) terms, there would be high consensus, high consistency, and high distinctiveness. However, in an actual situation people would not go through the elaborate process of assessing the behavior on these criteria; the attribution would be phenomenal. Kelley's (1967) model is a very rational, scientist-like analysis of causality. As such, it is useful for predictive purposes, but it probably does not describe the way people actually make attributions. In presenting the augmentation and discounting principles, Kelley (1971) suggested that people generally make attributions without complete information on those dimensions, suggesting, therefore, that the attribution process itself is generally not so rational and analytic as his early model implied. I am in complete accord with this. A scientist may use information on consensus, consistency, and distinctiveness, but people in everyday life are less likely to do so.

On the other hand, they may bring that information to the situation in the form of a preconceived set. For example, the observer may carry with him a set which states essentially, "When fully clothed people run in heavy rain, they are running because of the rain." This set may well have developed because of consensus, consistency, and distinctiveness. Hence, the attribution itself may be phenomenal, yet the observer is able to make phenomenal attributions, in part because of causal analysis in past experiences.

I suggest, then, that the observer looks first for impersonal environmental forces which are likely to be very apparent. In the absence of these, the next most apparent forces will be external forces which lead to environmentally caused intentions. Incentive payments are an example. In the Deci, Benware, and Landy studies, the money was the most apparent cause of the behavior and therefore the observers tended to attribute external causality and to discount internal causality. When the external force was very clear-cut (contingent payments), the attribution was very external and the internal cause was greatly discounted. However, when the external force was more ambiguous (noncontingent payments), the observer inferred less external causality and therefore discounted internal causality less.

In sum, people look first to impersonal causes, then to external (personal) causes, and finally, in the absence of these, internal personal causality is inferred. The simplest reason why people look first to external causes is that external forces are readily observable and therefore more reliable. Further, as we saw in Chapter 5, external rewards tend to lead readily to the perception of external causality. This may mean that our socialization process emphasizes external controls, so we look first to those causes.

The assertion that people look first to impersonal, then to external, and finally, if necessary, to internal forces to determine the cause of a behavior is just the broad outline of the attributional process. Within this framework observers may make quick attributions to only one cause (e.g., the rain caused the running) or they may make attributions to several dimensions (e.g., David is fairly extrinsically motivated to do typing but he also seems to be getting some intrinsic enjoyment from it). Further, they may consider only very little information or they might consider several pieces of information. This different information will also have differential relevance or "centrality" (Asch, 1946) and it may be processed by the use of either gross or specific units of comparison (Newtson, 1973). Whether the observer stops with one cause or makes several attributions, whether it's a phenomenal or a causal analysis, and whether he uses only one piece of information or many, are motivational questions. In short, the attributional process is motivated behavior on the part of the observer. Hence, I am asserting that the general outline of the attribution process is as described above, but the way that this is actually carried out (e.g., the number of attributions made, etc.) should be studied as a motivational question. We will consider this more fully below.

In attributing causality, observers may use information about consistency, consensus, and distinctiveness, either by considering it at the time or by utilizing it implicitly, as in the rain example mentioned above. They would be likely to make such a detailed analysis at the time only if for some reason they were motivated to do it in that situation.

Let us look more carefully at the attributional process. People look first to impersonal forces. If there is an adequate account in those forces there will be an impersonal attribution and the process will end. (Although, if there is some extrinsic or affective motivation, the process may continue.) If the impersonal forces don't provide a plausible account the person looks to external causes. If there are facilitative external forces (such as extrinsic rewards), he infers external causality. The external cause will be augmented if the behavior occurs in the presence of other environmental forces which inhibit it. The inference of external causality will lead to an attribution of a disposition (such as high extrinsic motivation). If for some reason the person is motivated to do so, he may go on to make an internal inference, also. In that case, the inferred external causality will produce a discounting of any possible internal cause.

Finally, if there is no plausible external cause the person will infer internal causality. This inference will be augmented if there are inhibiting environmental forces or inhibiting personal forces, and the inference will be discounted if there were plausible external causality. Then the internal causality, having been augmented and discounted, will lead to an attribution of a personal disposition (such as high intrinsic motivation).

The process just described is shown graphically in Figure 22. Let us now look at the intrinsic motivation studies by Deci, Landy, and Benware using the model. Since there was no information on impersonal environmental forces, the observer then considered external forces. Observing external forces (money), they made external inferences and subsequently dispositional attributions of extrinsic motivation. But they also discounted internal forces, then made internal inferences, and finally dispositional attributions of intrinsic motivation.

The information is processed serially but it is done very rapidly. Newell and Simon (1972) have demonstrated both that processing is done serially and that it is done at a rate of about seven "chucks" of information per second. While I will not discuss the specific meaning of that in terms of attribution, it simply means that the process is very rapid. Therefore, although the model in Figure 22 may seem complicated or analytical, it can be a very rapid, essentially phenomenal, process. On the other hand, if an observer is highly motivated or involved in the attribution process, it can be a much longer and more careful process.

Expectations

Observers often come to attribution situations with expectations. People may have preconceived notions about the honesty of a particular politician, or about the feelings of brand new fathers, or about the motivation of used-car salesmen. To the extent that this is

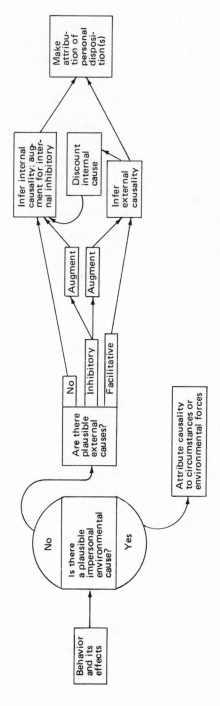

FIGURE 22. Basic elements of a general model of the attributional process.

so, it will have an important influence on the attribution process. This influence is made manifest when people are led through the attributional process just outlined in a way that selectively attends to the available data. If, for example, someone has expectations about a personal disposition of the actor, he is likely to speed through, perhaps even ignoring information on impersonal causes, and to look for confirmatory data.

Studies on attitude attribution have demonstrated the importance of expectations, and studies on order effects are also relevant to this question. These areas will be considered in turn. In the attitude attribution studies an actor generally espouses a position under some set of conditions, and an observer judges the extent to which he thinks the speaker believes the exposed attitude. If the espousal is caused primarily by the fact that the speaker believes the position, the locus of causality is internal. If it is caused by the money he's been paid, or the desire to please constituents, then the locus of causality is external. In either case, there is personal causality. Both would be intentional, voluntary, planned behaviors. The former case is analogous to intrinsically motivated behavior, the latter to extrinsically motivated behavior.

The general findings in the studies on attributions of attitudes (Jones & Harris, 1967; Jones, Worchel, Goethals, & Grumet, 1971) are that (1) the observer's expectations, (2) the actor's behavior, (3) the norm for that behavior, and (4) whether or not the actor had choice about the activity, all affect the attributions which the observer makes to the actor.

I suspect that in these situations the observer's expectation is the first factor he considers. If he expects the speaker to believe a certain thing, he looks for evidence to substantiate that belief. Only if the evidence is overwhelmingly contradictory to his expectations will he give up the expectation and its corresponding attributions. This phenomenon is what has generally been labelled a contrast effect; the evidence against the expectations is so strong that the observer is unable to assimilate the discrepant data, so he swings over to the new position and abandons his initial position. This will be elaborated more fully in the discussion of order effects.

The actual behavior is probably the most critical factor in overriding expectations, since, as Heider stated, "behavior engulfs the field." In other words, the behavior itself tends to be very important to the observer's attributions regardless of whether the actor had choice about the behavior, was paid for it, and so on. So behavior seems to be more relevant than factors of choice and norms, though less relevant in the observer's phenomenology than are his own expectations. This latter notion is supported by the evidence that when behavior and expectations are discrepant the behavior will be assimilated unless the composite of data is so clear-cut that it can't be.

If the behavior does not deviate drastically from the expectation, the expectation will be affirmed; if a discrepancy is present, the observer will then begin the process of making an attribution.

The observer also considers information related to the actor's freedom to engage in the behavior. In the Jones *et al.* study subjects either chose which position to espouse (free choice) or were assigned a position (no choice).

If the expectations and behavior were congruent, then choice is not of great significance; however, if the expectations and behaviors were discrepant, the role of choice would become much greater. If the actor were forced to engage in the behavior, then the discrepant behavior is readily assimilated into the expectation, but if there were choice, the evidence will be overwhelming, so the observer will abandon his expectation.

Order Effects

The effects of the order of presentation of information on attributions have been considered in great detail by Jones and Goethals (1971).

Typically, the order effects studies present the same pieces of information to a person in different sequences (generally one-way and then the reverse), to see whether or not the order in which a person receives information, in and of itself, affects the attribution.

In a classic study by Asch (1946) a list of adjectives was presented in such a way that half the subjects got the list in reverse order. This study showed a primacy effect; the early adjectives had the greatest effect on impressions, regardless of which adjectives came early. Asch suggested that the early traits influence later ones, in that the meaning of the later ones is modified somewhat to fit with the early ones.

Other studies have also produced primacy effects, though there have been other processes suggested as the cause of this effect (e.g., Bruner, Shapiro, & Tagiuri, 1958; Anderson, 1962, 1965, 1968).

Jones and Goethals (1971) have summarized these processes by saying that there seem to be three kinds of processes at work to produce primacy effects. The first is attention decrement; a person is unable to attend to later items, as well as early ones, because of his span of attention, so the earlier ones have more importance (this is supported by Hendrick & Costantini, 1970). The second process is discounting; a person discounts later information which is not consistent with early information (this is supported by Anderson). The final process is assimilation and is close to that suggested by Asch; a person assimilates later information into the set which was formed from early information. In other words, the meaning of later information is actually modified to fit with early information. This process differs from discounting, in that assimilation involves changing the meaning of discrepant information whereas discounting involves just giving less weight to discrepant information.

In short, early information seems to act in much the same way as expectations. Only when later information is too discrepant will the observer give up his "set." When this contrast occurs, we may observe a recency effect, that is, the later information will have more impact on attributions than early information.

Jones and Goethals pointed out two other situations in which one might expect recency effects. First, when long time periods elapse, causing problems of remembering early data, and second when the context suggests that later information is more relevant. This would happen, for example, when a person is warming up or improving through practice.

In sum, studies have shown both recency and primacy effects in impression formation, yet primacy effects seem to be most prevalent, at least when the time sequence is relatively short, and the context does not force a recency effect. The conditions for recency effects would seem to be relatively infrequent by comparison to situations likely to produce primacy effects.

The Motivation of Attribution

In the above discussion of the attributional process there was considerable attention paid to motivational factors. In general, the attributional process is motivated by the intrinsic need for feeling competent and self-determining, but it is also affected by extrinsic rewards, by expectations, and by other forms of involvement (Lowe, 1975). If a person is rewarded to do so he may be very careful and analytic about the process of attribution. For example, a behavioral scientist makes attributions as a major part of his occupation; he is extrinsically rewarded for doing so, and his attributions tend to be made only after very careful analyses of the possible causes. Kelley (1967) likened the attribution process to that of a good scientist who examines co-variation. I would say that this is so only when a person is motivated to make an attribution by some factor (whether intrinsic, extrinsic, or affective).

To consider further the question of motivating attribution, let us look at the termination of the attribution process. Attributions are sometimes made quickly to one cause and based on one piece of information. At other times, several attributions are made after consideration of much more information (the scientist being a case in point).

In general, I contend that the observer tends to stop the process when he has found a sufficient cause. If there is impersonal causality, he terminates the process. If not, he looks for external causality, and if he finds it he makes a corresponding attribution, and stops. If not, he infers internal causality, makes an attribution, and terminates. This is precisely what Simon (1967) referred to as "satisficing." When Judy observed David typing for pay, she probably considered the money, attributed extrinsic motivation, and left it at that, without going on to his intrinsic motivation.

However, although people often "satisfice," they sometimes make detailed analyses which result in very specific attributions on several dimensions. The termination process can be determined by the following considerations in addition to those already mentioned: (1) the set which the person brings to the situation, (2) the affect which is involved in the situation, and (3) relatively invariant individual differences.

The influence of set or expectations was discussed above. It can be further illustrated by the following example. In 1973 when the U.S. was in the middle of the so-called Watergate affair, many people had developed sets about the then President. When he gave televised speeches, and listeners were attributing such things as honesty to him, the process of making attributions may have been terminated very quickly. In fact, the attributions were brought to the situation and would have been changed only if there were overwhelming contradictory data.

The influence of affect works somewhat similarly. Consider this example. Shirley is angry with Charles, so she perceives a situation, and makes an attribution. The anger will essentially bias her attribution in such a way that she will (perhaps unconsciously) be "trying" to arrive at an unfavorable attribution. If the behavior allows her to say "he did it to annoy me" or "he did it because he really doesn't love me," she will terminate the process quickly. We see, then, that the perceiver's affect can influence the attributions, just as the actor's affect can influence his behavior.

Finally, there will be invariant individual differences which affect attributions, just as there are individual differences involved in any psychological process. People differ in the extent to which they consider relevant information before making any kind of decision. Some are more impulsive and quick to decide. Others are more thoughtful and slow and consider all information very carefully. This will lead to differential termination of the attribution process.

In sum, I have suggested that the attributional process is motivated. It is primarily intrinsically motivated but may be influenced or motivated by affect, set, or extrinsic rewards. People tend to terminate the attribution process when they have found a sufficient explanation for the behavior, and will go on only if they have a reason for doing so.

Summary

In this chapter we have considered the question of how observers make attributions about the causes of other people's behavior. We reviewed the theories or models of Heider, Jones and Davis, Kelley, and Lowe.

We distinguished between impersonal and personal causality, and further, between internal and external causality. Personal causality involves intention on the part of the actor, whereas impersonal causality does not. Both internal and external causality are personal and therefore lead to dispositional attributions. Internal causality exists when the desired effect of the behavior is the behavior itself and the accompanying internal feelings; in those situations there are personally caused intentions. External causality exists when the desired effect is an external event to which the behavior leads (for example, a monetary reward). In these situations there are environmentally caused intentions.

We also reviewed studies related to the attribution of intrinsic motivation, and we summarized a general model of attribution. This model asserts that people look first to impersonal causes, then to external causes, and finally, in the absence of these, infer internal causality. The model also suggests that the attributional process is motivated and is influenced by expectations, rewards, and affect. Further, it proposes that people's attributions differ in many ways as a function of situational factors and individual differences.

11

Perceiving Intrinsic Motivation in Oneself and Others

A substantial amount of recent literature on attribution has been concerned with the relationship between perception of oneself and of others. There is increasing evidence that there are similarities between phenomena which occur for actors and the inferences of those phenomena made by observers.

The Deci, Benware, and Landy studies (1974) presented in Chapter 10 reported an inverse relationship between extrinsic rewards paid to an actor and the observer's perceptions of the actor's intrinsic motivation. This relationship was very strong when rewards were contingent on performance and less apparent when rewards were noncontingent. The findings parallel quite closely the results reported in Chapter 5 which showed that, when actors were paid contingently, their intrinsic motivation decreased, whereas, when rewards were noncontingent, the actors' intrinsic motivation showed either no decrease or less decrease than when rewards were contingent.

Similarly, Bem (1967) reported interpersonal attribution findings which parallel the earlier findings of Festinger and Carlsmith (1959). In the Festinger and Carlsmith study, subjects received either $1 or $20 for telling another (bogus) subject that they had enjoyed a dull, boring task. Later, an attitude measure indicated that the $1 subjects had enjoyed the task more than had the $20 subjects. In Bem's experiment, subjects listened to a tape recording and made attitudinal attributions. The listeners reported that the person who had received $1 must have liked the task more than the one who received $20.

So, with self-attribution or interpersonal attribution, the amount of liking (presumably, therefore, the amount of intrinsic motivation) for a *dull, boring* activity is inversely related to the amount of extrinsic reward a person receives for engaging in the activity.

Calder *et al.* (1973) have reported results indicating striking similarities between the perceptions of actors and of observers. In this study which was described in detail in Chapter 6, actors engaged in a dull, boring task for low or high rewards, and had either choice or no choice about doing the task. When consequences were high, there was an interaction between choice and rewards. Under choice there was a dissonance effect (i.e., a negative relationship between rewards and liking for the task), whereas, under no choice, there was a reinforcement effect (i.e., a positive relationship between rewards and liking for the task). These findings were accurately predicted by observers. The interaction occurred for actors and was also attributed to them by observers.

There is not a great deal of evidence comparing what actually happens to actors' internal states with what observer's attribute to the actors' internal states. Yet the small amount of data which currently exists does indicate that there are important similarities, although, in addition to these clear parallels, we will see later in the chapter that there are some systematic differences which are easily accounted for by what we know about perceptual processes and motivation.

I am particularly concerned with the notable parallel between actor's perceptions and observer's perceptions of the inverse relationship between the amount of rewards an actor receives for an activity (whether it's a dull or interesting activity) and his intrinsic motivation for that activity.

There are at least two possible explanations for this similarity between the results of experiments on interpersonal attribution and self-attribution. One has been suggested by Bem (1967, 1972). The other explanation will be outlined here and is consistent with the theoretical perspective of this book.

Bem's self-perception theory asserts that people know their own internal states by making attributions to themselves which are based on their observations of their own behavior and the circumstances within which it occurs. In other words, people may infer their own internal states in the same way that they infer another's internal states, by using external cues. Bem's theory, then, looks at self-perception as a special case of interpersonal perception and ignores personal knowledge. Humans, according to Bem, come to know and understand themselves by observing their own behavior and making attributions, rather than by being aware of their internal states.

Self-attributions in situations where the activity was dull and boring would be as follows: A person observes himself doing a dull task and takes note of the external contingencies (e.g., the amount of reward). If there were not substantial extrinsic rewards, he would infer that he must have intrinsic motivation; otherwise, he'd have no account of why he engaged in the activity. "I did it without being paid; I must have liked it." If he received substantial extrinsic rewards he would assume that he did the task to get the rewards, so he would not need to attribute much intrinsic motivation to himself to account for the behavior.

Self-attributions in situations wherein the activity was intrinsically interesting would be somewhat similar (Bem, 1972; Nisbett & Valins, 1971). When a person sees himself doing an intrinsically interesting task for large payments he will infer that he is doing it for the money and will therefore attribute low intrinsic motivation to himself. As Bem (1972) pointed out, this requires the assumption that strongly apparent external contingencies will imply to the person that he did not want to do the task. On the other hand, when the person sees himself engaging in an interesting activity for low extrinsic rewards, he will infer that he must be intrinsically motivated or he wouldn't be doing the activity.

We see then, that in Bem's theory, the task itself is virtually irrelevant. One knows whether or not he likes an activity on the basis of whether or not he engages in it and whether or not there are readily apparent contingencies of reinforcement. The theory operates the same way for dull and boring activities as for intrinsically interesting ones. First, a person looks for extrinsic justification (i.e., contingencies of reinforcement); if he finds external justification he infers low intrinsic motivation, whereas if he does not find external justification he infers high intrinsic motivation for the activity.

The alternative explanation to Bem's begins with self-knowledge and asserts that people make interpersonal attributions partly on the basis of what they know about themselves. When one person observes another, he makes causal attributions to that other, primarily by attributing the same internal states to the other that he himself would have, if he were in that situation.

The self-knowledge explanation for the inverse relationship between an extrinsic justification, such as money (Festinger & Carlsmith, 1959) or threats (Aronson & Carlsmith, 1963), and intrinsic motivation for a dull, boring task involves cognitive dissonance reduction (Festinger, 1957). When a person does a dull, boring task and has substantial external justification, he feels no dissonance, since his justification for doing the task is the money or threat, so his intrinsic motivation for the activity remains low. He doesn't need to like it in order to justify doing it. However, if there is inadequate external justification, he will experience dissonance between the two cognitions, "the task is dull and boring," and "I don't have much justification for doing it." To reduce this dissonance he will imbue the task with additional intrinsic worth.

When one person makes an attribution to another, the process will work similarly. He will make an attribution to the other, essentially by putting himself in the other's place. This process need not be conscious, but he will attribute in accord with how he would be if he were in that situation.

Consider now the situation in which a person is doing an intrinsically interesting task and receiving various levels of extrinsic justification. In Chapter 5 I proposed a cognitive evaluation theory which asserted that there are two processes through which extrinsic rewards can affect intrinsic motivation. The first, involves a change in the perceived locus of causality (Heider, 1958, de Charms, 1968). When a person is intrinsically motivated to engage in an activity, the perceived locus of causality is within himself. He does the task because of the feelings of competence and self-determination which it affords him. However, when he begins to receive external rewards or controls (e.g., money or threats) for doing that task, he may become dependent on those rewards or controls. He loses intrinsic motivation, because he is now doing the task in order to get the external reward. His perceived locus of causality has switched from within himself to the external reward.

The second process by which intrinsic motivation can be affected involves a change in a person's sense of competence and self-determination through feedback. When someone receives positive information about his effectiveness, his sense of competence and self-determination will be enhanced, so he will be more likely to continue the activity without an external reward; in other words, his intrinsic motivation will have increased. However, if he receives negative feedback, his sense of competence and self-determination will be decreased; this will cause a decrease in his intrinsic motivation. Bem's theory can account for the phenomena caused by a change in perceived locus of causality, but it cannot readily account for the phenomena caused by a change in feelings of competence and self-determination.

When a person perceives another doing such a task for various levels of reward, he will make attributions which are consistent with the way that he himself would behave. Accordingly, Deci, Benware, and Landy found results showing that monetary rewards lead observers to attribute low intrinsic motivation, thereby paralleling the studies which actually showed that extrinsic rewards decrease intrinsic motivation. I do not know of a study which has investigated the effects of feedback on observer's attributions of intrinsic motivation, though such a study is certainly warranted.

De Charms (1968) and Bridgman (1959) have discussed the relationship between perceiving motivation in oneself and in others. Bridgman argued cogently that the process of verifying one's own motivation is a separate one from the process of inferring that someone else is motivated. One need have no observation of his own behavior in order to know that he's motivated, though observations are the basis of inferences about others' motivation. Bridgman pointed out that people may make observations of their own behavior and internal states, but that this is less common than knowing one's internal states from direct personal knowledge.

De Charms elaborated Bridgman's position by adding that personal knowledge may be useful in assessing others' internal states. We see, then, that the assertions I've made about the relationship between perceiving oneself and perceiving others derives from the positions of Bridgman and de Charms.

In sum, the difference between my position and Bem's is as follows: I am asserting that people have personal knowledge of their own internal states which is knowable only to them (unless they report it), and that they make attributions to others largely through knowing what their own internal states would probably be if they were in the position of the actor. Bem's position on the other hand asserts that people make attributions to others and to themselves by observing external cues and then inferring their internal states from their observations.

I am further asserting that, although self-attributions and attributions to others will generally be very similar, there will also be differences because internal processes, such as perceptual differences and motivational influences, will affect how one applies what he knows about himself to others. In Chapter 10, I said that the attribution process is motivated behavior. As such, it is influenced by affect, expectations, extrinsic rewards, etc.

In short, attributions about others will in many ways be similar to what would actually happen to the observer if he were in that situation. This is because he uses his own personal knowledge to make inferences about others. Further, however, there will be marked differences between self-perceptions and other percep-tions, but these differences will be systematic and predictable. Consideration of perceptual and motivational process should ultimately allow for an understanding of both the similarities and differences.

There has been substantial attention given in the experimental literature to the controversy over whether or not self-perception theory can adequately account for the cognitive dissonance phenomena. There is some support for the Bemian position (e.g., Bem & McConnell, 1970), yet several studies have shown convinc-ing refutations (e.g., Piliavin, Piliavin, Loewenton, McCauley, & Hammond, 1969; Freedman, 1969; Arrowood, Wood, & Ross, 1970; Ross & Shulman, 1973; Green, 1974).

The self-perception *vs.* dissonance controversy has focused primarily on forced compliance studies. Subjects argue for a position which is counter to their own, and have either sufficient or insufficient justification for doing so. Insufficient justification leads to a change in attitudes towards the espoused position.

Bem asserted that the reason for this is that people observe themselves performing an act for inadequate external reasons, so they infer that they must believe in what they said. In other words, they infer belief in the stated position because they stated it without adequate external justification.

Support for Bem's position came from interpersonal replications of counter-attitudinal studies. Bem (1967) showed that when observers hear someone espouse a position and know the circumstances within which the activity occurred, those observers are able to attribute correctly the post-espousal attitudes of the actors.

In order for this data to be construed as support for Bem's position, one must be willing to assume that after someone has engaged in a behavior such as essay writing he will have forgotten his prebehavioral attitude, so he will essentially be no better off than an observer. Neither the actor nor the observer will know the prebehavioral attitude, so both will be left to infer the current attitude from the behavior.

Jones, Linder, Kiesler, Zanna, and Brehm (1968) and Piliavin, Piliavin, Loewenton, McCauley, and Hammond (1969) criticized this assumption and showed that when observers were provided with data about the subjects' premanipulation attitudes they did not make attribution which replicated Bem's (1967) findings.

Bem (1968) and Bem and McConnell (1970) pointed out that, in fact, the Jones *et al.* and the Piliavin *et al.* data are not germane for refuting his position, since, in fact, subjects who engage in counterattitudinal advocacy do forget their pre-espousal attitudes. Bem and McConnell reported that when subjects whose attitudes were assessed and who then wrote counter-attitudinal essays were asked to recall their earlier attitudes, they were significantly wrong in their recollections. Therefore, Bem was able to respond adequately to the Jones *et al.* and Piliavin *et al.* critiques of his position.

However, data which are much more damaging to Bem's position have come from two recent studies (Ross & Shulman, 1973, & Green, 1974). If Bem's position were correct, then providing subjects with data about their premanipulation attitudes would eliminate any attitude change, just as providing observers with data about the subjects' premanipulation attitudes led to attributions of no attitude change. If either the actors or the observers knew the correct premanipulation attitudes, then there would be no reason to make "incorrect" attributions (whether self or other) following the counterattitudinal behavior. Hence, one would predict, using Bem's theory, that if premanipulation attitudes were made salient to the subjects following their counterattitudinal behavior, there would be no attitude change.

The dissonance prediction, however, is that making premanipulation attitudes salient by reminding the subjects of what they previously stated their attitudes to be would not eliminate attitude change. Indeed, it would make the dissonant cognitions of "believing one thing" and "doing another" quite apparent, so one would expect them to change their attitudes to reduce their dissonance.

Ross and Shulman (1973) reported data supporting the dissonance theory prediction. When the premanipulation attitudes of subjects were made salient to them after they wrote counterattitudinal essays, their attitudes still changed. In fact, there was a tendency for greater attitude change among subjects reminded of their previous attitudes than among subjects who were not reminded of their previous attitudes.

Further, Ross and Shulman showed that subjects who were reminded of their previous attitudes before stating their current attitude were, not surprisingly, able to recall correctly their earlier attitudes following their statements of their current attitudes. However, in line with what Bem and McConnell reported, Ross and Shulman found that subjects not reminded of their earlier attitudes could not correctly recall them. This is to be expected. If a person reduces dissonance by changing an attitude he will be in a state of greatest quiesence by forgetting that he even had a dissonant attitude. Therefore, the Bem and McConnell findings that subjects' misremembered their premanipulation attitudes were probably due to dissonance reduction.

Green (1974) has shown that dissonance theory is more accurate in its predictions about changes in subjects' motivational states than is self-perception theory. In his study subjects were either in a high-thirst or low-thirst condition (i.e., their initial position was either extreme or non-extreme) and were then asked to abstain from drinking for 24 hours. One group of extreme subjects and one group of non-extreme subjects was offered $5 for abstaining while one group of each was offered $20.

The dissonance theory prediction is that there would be greatest change in subjects' reported thirst for the extreme subjects with low justification, and that there would be a main effect for extremity of attitude across justification conditions. Self-perception theory pays no account to initial extremity of subjects' motivations or attitudes, so there is no basis for expecting a difference between extreme and nonextreme subjects.

The results of Green's study provide strong support for dissonance theory and none for self-perception theory. The dissonance predictions mentioned above were upheld on all three dependent measures used by Green.

In sum, Bem's theory has initiated considerable controversy, primarily in relation to its claim to provide an alternative interpretation of various cognitive dissonance phenomena. We have seen, however, from a review of the literature, that Bem's position has failed to receive convincing empirical validation. Instead, dissonance theory has been shown to be much more useful in predicting and explaining the experimental results.

Personal Knowledge and External Forces

It is important to note that my emphasis on personal knowledge does not imply that external forces are not important. Indeed, Chapters 5 and 6 dealt exclusively with how external forces can influence internal states. These internal states have a cognitive component, and this component is the mechanism through which external factors influences attitudes, emotions, and motivations. The thrust of the argument through Chapters 5 and 6 was precisely that cognitive factors influence intrinsic motivation.

The work of Schacter and his associates (e.g., Schacter, 1971a; Schacter & Singer, 1962; Valins, 1966) has emphasized the importance of cognitive, as well as physiological, factors in motivation and emotion.

The implication of all this work, however, is not that one infers his intrinsic motivation and other internal states from observations of his behavior and the external forces which are present, but rather that external forces will influence a person's internal states by affecting the cognitive component of those states.

The Actor and the Observer

Jones and Nisbett (1971) reviewed a number of studies to buttress their hypothesis—derived from Heider (1958)—that actors tend to attribute their behavior more to external than other causes, whereas observers tend to attribute the actor's behavior to his personal dispositions. The actor's account of his own behavior focuses on the initiating circumstances in the situation, whereas the observer's focuses on the stable dispositions of the actors. Jones and Nisbett suggested that this is due partly to the fact that the actor has more knowledge about himself, but even more importantly to the fact that there is a differential salience of information available to the actor and observer. For the observer, the behavior itself is of central importance. He is less likely to be aware of the various contingencies which are impinging on the actor. For him, therefore, the behavior is attributed to dispositions of the actor. However, the actor is aware primarily of the contingencies; he is responding to them. Therefore, since his focus is more on the contingencies than on the behavior itself, he is more likely to attribute external causality.

Thus, Jones and Nisbett have emphasized perceptual or attentional processes in explicating the differences between the perceptions of actors and observers. Two recent reports (Storms, 1973; Nisbett, Caputo, Legant, & Marecek, 1973) provide evidence in support of the Jones and Nisbett position.

Storms reported that when actors were shown videotapes of their own behavior, and observers were shown videotapes which focused on the actor's situation (i.e., focused on the person with whom the actor had been conversing), the actor's attributions were more personal than were those of the observers. In other words, changing the perspectives of the actor and observer led to a change in the attributions. This study, then, provides strong support for the Jones and Nisbett hypothesis.

Nisbett *et al.* (1973) reported three studies which provide further support. In the first study, observers predicted that in the future actors would behave the same way as they had in the past. Presumably this was because past behavior was attributed to dispositions which would continue to be present. However, actors' predictions of their future behavior were independent of their past behavior. Since they attributed past behavior to the situational cues, there was no reason to assume that future behavior would be the same if the situation were different. In the second study, subjects tended to attribute their choices of a major field of concentration and of a girl friend to properties of the field and of the girl friend. However, they attributed their best friend's choices to dispositional traits of the friend rather than to the properties of the field or of the girl friend. In the final study, subjects reported that they had fewer dispositional traits than had their friends.

In sum, the three studies by Nisbett *et al.* emphasize that observers are likely to see others' behavior as trait-determined, whereas they're likely to see their own behavior as situation-appropriate.

Although Jones and Nisbett focused on perceptual processes in investigating actor–observer differences, they did acknowledge that motivational processes may also be present. They suggested that the difference in perceptions may be accounted for by the fact that actors are quick to attribute their failures or reprehensible acts to the environment, whereas observers are quite willing to hold the actors accountable.

I agree with Jones and Nisbett that the need to see oneself in a favorable light will influence attributions. In fact, as we will see below, following this tack leads to the prediction that in some cases the actor will make more personal attributions than will the observer.

In general, people like to see themselves in favorable ways. In addition, they need to see themselves as being in control of themselves. When an event allows them to see themselves in a favorable way, they will tend to seize the opportunity to attribute the cause to a positive disposition in themselves. On the other hand, if the outcome is a negative one, they will tend to place greater causality on the environment (even though they are motivated, over all, to see themselves as being in control).

The observer is also motivated by his own best interest. Thus, when the actor fails (or is involved in some other unfortunate occurrence) the observer will need to hold the actor accountable. If the observer were to attribute the cause to an external situational factor, then the observer would be acknowledging that he (the observer) might soon fall prey to that force. Not wanting to see himself as susceptible to that, he'll attribute causality to the actor. On the other hand, if the outcome is a positive one, he will not see the actor as responsible, since he will tend to want to see the actor as less capable than he. This, then, predicts an interaction on attributions of causality between actor/observer and whether the outcome is favorable/unfavorable.

Consider the case of success and failure. If an actor succeeds at something, the motivational prediction would be that he'd attribute the behavior to himself, that is, he succeeded because he's very skilled or highly motivated. The observer, needing to see the actor as less capable than himself, would write off the successes to luck or facilitating environmental forces. With failure, the actor holds the situation responsible, whereas the observer needs to see the actor as responsible. Thus, a motivational prediction calls for an interaction between success/failure and actor/observer. With success the actor attributes personal factors and the observer attributes environmental ones, whereas with failure, the actor attributes environmental factors and the observer attributes personal ones.

This view, of course, does not explain the Jones and Nisbett hypothesis (unless one assumes that failure is more common than success). However I am not trying to explain their hypothesis in motivational terms, since I agree that differences in perceptual processes probably account for the tendency for actors to attribute causality to external forces, whereas observers attribute causality to internal forces. I am simply suggesting that motivational forces are also operative and that they, too, would cause systematic differences in attributions of actors and observers.

The prediction that a need to see oneself favorably leads to an interaction between success/failure and actor/observer has not been tested. Hence, it remains a speculation. Similarly, other motivational factors, such as dissonance reduction, reactance, etc., undoubtedly also influence the systematic difference in perceptions of oneself and others.

Summary

Studies have shown that there is a definite parallel between the effects of rewards on people's internal states and the attributions which observers make about the effects of rewards on these states. This chapter outlined two approaches which account for this similarity. One approach (Self-Perception Theory) asserted that people perceive themselves in the same way that they perceive others, that is, that they make inferences about their own and others' internal states on the basis of observation of external behavior. In other words, self-perception is just a special case of person perception. The other approach began with personal knowledge and asserted that people have awareness of their own internal states that is independent of whether or not they observe their own external behavior. Then, it asserted that people make attributions to others on the basis of what they know about themselves. In other words person perception is a special case of self-perception.

The second approach, which focused on personal knowledge, stated further that attributions to oneself will not always be the same as attributions to others. Perceptual and motivational processes will influence the attributions in systematic ways. So attributions to others will be based on what the observer knows about himself, but they will be mediated in predictable ways by motivational and perceptual processes.

References

ADAMS, J. S. Toward an understanding of inequity. *Journal of Abnormal and Social Psychology*, 1963, *67*, 422–436. (a)

ADAMS, J. S. Wage inequities, productivity, and work quality. *Industrial Relations*, 1963, *3*, 9–16. (b)

ADAMS, J. S. Inequity in social exchange. In L. Berkowitz (Ed.), *Advances in experimental social psychology*. (Vol. 2.) New York: Academic Press, 1965.

ADAMS, J. S., & JACOBSEN, P. R. Effects of wage inequities on work quality. *Journal of Abnormal and Social Psychology*, 1964, *69*, 19–25.

ADAMS, J. S., & ROSENBAUM, W. B. The relationship of worker productivity to cognitive dissonance about wage inequities. *Journal of Applied Psychology*, 1962, *46*, 161–164.

ALLPORT, G. W. *Personality: A psychological interpretation*. New York: Holt, 1937.

ALPER, T. G. Achievement motivation in college women: A now-you-see-it-now-you-don't phenomenon. *American Psychologist*, 1974, *29*, 194–203.

ANDERSON, N. H. Application of an additive model to impression formation. *Science*, 1962, *138*, 817–818.

ANDERSON, N. H. Primacy effects in personality impression formation using a generalized order effect paradigm. *Journal of Personality and Social Psychology*, 1965, *2*, 1–9.

ANDERSON, N. H. Application of a linear-serial model to a personality-impression task using serial presentation. *Journal of Personality and Social Psychology*, 1968, *18*, 354–362.

ANDREWS, I. R. Wage inequity and job performance: An experimental study. *Journal of Applied Psychology*, 1967, *51*, 39–45.

ANGYAL, A. *Foundations for a science of personality*. New York: Commonwealth Fund, 1941.

ARGYRIS, C. *Personality and organization*. New York: Harper, 1957.

ARGYRIS, C. Some unintended consequences of rigorous research. *Psychological Bulletin*, 1968, *70*, 185–197.

ARISTOTLE. *Metaphysico*, 980. Translated by W. D. Ross as *The works of Aristotle*. (Vol. 8). Oxford: Clarendon Press, 1924.

295

ARNOLD, M. *Emotion and personality.* *(Vol. I).* New York: Columbia University Press, 1960.

ARONFREED, J. *Conduct and conscience.* New York: Academic Press, 1968.

ARONSON, E. The psychology of insufficient justification: An analysis of some conflicting data. In S. Feldman (Ed.). *Cognitive consistency.* New York: Academic Press, 1966, pp. 109–133.

ARONSON, E. The theory of cognitive dissonance: A current perspective. In L. Berkowitz (Ed.), *Advances in experimental social psychology.* *(Vol. 4.)* New York: Academic Press, 1969, pp. 1–34.

ARONSON, E., & CARLSMITH, J. M. Effect of severity of threat on the devaluation of forbidden behavior. *Journal of Abnormal and Social Psychology,* 1963, *66,* 584–588.

ARONSON, E., & MILLS, J. The effect of severity of initiation on liking for a group. *Journal of Abnormal and Social Psychology,* 1959, *59,* 177–181.

ARROWOOD, A. J. Some effects on productivity of justified and unjustified levels of reward under public and private conditions. Unpublished doctoral dissertation, University of Minnesota, 1961.

ARROWOOD, A. J., WOOD, L., & ROSS, L. Dissonance, self-perception, and the perception of others: A study in *cognitive* cognitive dissonance. *Journal of Experimental Social Psychology,* 1970, *6,* 304–315.

ASCH, S. E. Forming impressions of personality. *Journal of Abnormal and Social Psychology,* 1946, 41, 258–290.

ATKINSON, J. W. Motivational determinants of risk taking behavior, *Psychological Review,* 1957, *64,* 359–372.

ATKINSON, J. W. Towards experimental analysis of human motivation in terms of motives, expectancies, and incentives. In J. W. Atkinson (Ed.), *Motives in fantasy, action and society.* Princeton, N. J.: van Nostrand, 1958, pp. 288–305.

ATKINSON, J. W. *An introduction to motivation.* Princeton, N. J.: van Nostrand, 1964.

ATKINSON, J. W., & FEATHER, N. T. (Eds.). *A theory of achievement motivation.* New York: Wiley, 1966.

AUSUBEL, N. (Ed.). Applied psychology. In *A treasury of Jewish folklore.* New York: Crown, 1948, pp. 440–441.

BALDWIN, A. L. *Theories of child development.* New York: Wiley, 1967.

BALDWIN, A. L. A cognitive theory of socialization. In D. A. Goslin (Ed.), *Handbook of socialization theory and research.* Chicago: Rand McNally, 1969, pp. 325–346.

BASSETT, G. A., & MEYER, H. H. Performance appraisal based on self-review. *Personnel Psychology,* 1968, *21,* 421–430.

BEM, D. J. Self-perception: An alternative interpretation of cognitive dissonance phenomena. *Psychological Review,* 1967, *74,* 183–200.

BEM, D. J. The epistemological status of interpersonal simulations: A reply to Jones, Linder, Kiesler, Zanna, and Brehm. *Journal of Experimental Social psychology,* 1968, *4,* 270–274.

BEM, D. J. Self-perception theory. In L. Berkowitz (Ed.), *Advances in experimental social psychology* (Vol. 6.). New York: Academic Press, 1972, pp. 1–62.

BEM, D. J., & MCCONNELL, H. K. Testing the self-perception explanation of dissonance phenomena: On the salience of pre-manipulation attitudes. *Journal of Personality and Social Psychology*, 1970, *14*, 23–31.

BENWARE, C. Quantitative and qualitative learning differences as a function of learning in order to teach another. Unpublished manuscript, University of Rochester, 1975.

BENWARE, C., & DECI, E. L. Attitude change as a function of the inducement for espousing a pro-attitudinal communication. *Journal of Experimental Social Psychology*, 1975, in press.

BERKOWITZ, L. *The development of motives and values in the child.* New York: Basic Books, 1964.

BERLYNE, D. E. Novelty and curiosity as determinants of exploratory behavior. *British Journal of Psychology*, 1950, *41*, 68–80.

BERLYNE, D. E. The arousal and satiation of perceptual curiosity in the rat. *Journal of Comparative and Physiological Psychology*, 1955, *48*, 238–246.

BERLYNE, D. E. *Conflict, arousal and curiosity.* New York: McGraw-Hill, 1960.

BERLYNE, D. E. Motivational problems raised by exploratory and epistemic behavior. In S. Koch (Ed.), *Psychology: A study of a science* (Vol. 5). New York: McGraw-Hill, 1963.

BERLYNE, D. E. Exploration and curiosity. *Science*, 1966, *153*, 25–33.

BERLYNE, D. E. Arousal and reinforcement. *Nebraska Symposium on Motivation*, 1967. *15*, 1–110.

BERLYNE, D. E. The reward-value of different stimulation. In J. T. Trapp (Ed.), *Reinforcement and behavior.* New York: Academic Press, 1969.

BERLYNE, D. E. What next? Concluding summary. In H. I. Day, D. E. Berlyne, & D. E. Hunt (Eds.), *Intrinsic motivation: A new direction in education.* Toronto: Holt Rinehart, and Winston of Canada, 1971, pp. 186–196. (a)

BERLYNE, D. E. *Aesthetics and psychobiology.* New York: Appleton-Century-Crofts, 1971. (b)

BERLYNE, D. E. The vicissitudes of aplopathematic and thelematoscopic pneumatology (or the hydrography of hedonism). In D. E. Berlyne and K. B. Madsen (Eds.), *Pleasure, reward, and preference.* New York: Academic Press, 1973, pp. 1–33.

BEXTON, W. H., HERON, W., & SCOTT, T. H. Effects of decreased variation in the sensory environment. *Canadian Journal of Psychology*, 1954, *8*, 70–76.

BINDRA, D. *Motivation: A systematic reinterpretation.* New York: Ronald, 1959.

BOGART, K., LOEB, A., & RUTMAN, I. D. *A dissonance approach to behavior modification.* Paper presented at the meeting of the Eastern Psychological Association, Philadelphia, April, 1969.

BOSTROM, R. VLANDIS, J., & ROSENBAUM, M. Grades as reinforcing contingencies and attitude change. *Journal of Educational psychology*, 1961, *52*, 112–115.

BRAYFIELD, A. H., & CROCKETT, W. H. Employee attitudes and employee performance. *Psychological Bulletin*, 1955, *52*, 396–424.

BREHM, J. W. Motivational effects of cognitive dissonance. *Nebraska Symposium on Motivation*, 1962, *10*, 51–77.

BREHM, J. W. *A theory of psychological reactance.* New York: Academic Press, 1966.

BREHM, J. W. *Responses to loss of freedom: A theory of psychological reactance.* Morristown, New Jersey: General Learning Press, Module Series, 1972.

BREHM, M. L., BACK, K. W., & BOGDONOFF, M. D. A physiological effect of cognitive dissonance under stress and deprivation. *Journal of Abnormal and Social Psychology,* 1964, *69,* 303–310.

BREHM, J. W., & SENSENIG, J. Social influence as a function of attempted and implied usurpation of choice. *Journal of Personality and Social Psychology,* 1966, *4,* 703–707.

BRIDGMAN, P. W. *The way things are.* Cambridge, Mass.: Harvard University Press, 1959.

BROCK, T. C., & BLACKWOOD, J. E. Dissonance reduction, social comparison, and modification of other's opinions. *Journal of Abnormal and Social Psychology,* 1962, *65,* 319–324.

BROCK, T. C., & GRANT, L. D. Dissonance, awareness, and motivation. *Journal of Abnormal and Social Psychology,* 1963, *67,* 53–60.

BRODEN, M., HALL, R. V., DUNLAP, A., & CLARK, R. Effects of teacher attention and a token reinforcement system in a junior high school special education class. *Exceptional Children,* 1970, *36,* 341–349.

BROWN, J. S. *The motivation of behavior.* New York: McGraw-Hill, 1961.

BRUNER, J. *On knowing: Essays for the left hand.* Cambridge, Mass.: Harvard University Press, 1962.

BRUNER, J. S., SHAPIRO, D., & TAGIURI, R. The meaning of traits in isolation and in combination. In R. Tagiuri, & L. Petrullo (Eds.), *Person perception and interpersonal behavior.* Stanford: Stanford University Press, 1958.

BUHLER, C. & ALLEN, M. *Introduction to humanistic psychology.* Monterey, Cal.: Brooks-Cole, 1972.

BUTLER, R. A. Discrimination learning by rhesus monkeys to visual exploration motivation. *Journal of Comparative and Physiological Psychology,* 1953, *46,* 95–98.

BUTLER, R. A. Incentive conditions which influence visual exploration. *Journal of Experimental Psychology,* 1954, *48,* 19–23.

BUTLER, R. A. The effect of deprivation of visual incentives on visual exploration motivation in monkeys. *Journal of Comparative and Physiological psychology,* 1957, *50,* 177–179.

BUTLER, R. A. The differential effect of visual and auditory incentives on the performance of monkeys. *American Journal of Psychology,* 1958, *71,* 591–593.

BUTLER, R. A., & HARLOW, H. F., Discrimination learning and learning sets to visual exploration incentives. *Journal of Genetic Psychology,* 1957, *57,* 257–264.

CALDER, B. J., ROSS, M., & INSKO, C. A. Attitude change and attitude attribution: Effects of incentive, choice, and consequences. *Journal of Personality and Social Psychology,* 1973, *25,* 84–99.

CALDER, B. J. & STAW, B. M. The self-perception of intrinsic and extrinsic motivation. Unpublished manuscript, 1973.

CALDER, B. J. & STAW, B. M. The interaction of intrinsic and extrinsic motivation: Some methodological notes. *Journal of Personality and Social Psychology*, 1975, *31*, 76–80.

CARLSMITH, J. M., COLLINS, B. E., & HELMREICH, R. L. Studies in forced compliance: I. The effect of pressure for compliance on attitude change produced by face to face role playing and anonymous essay writing. *Journal of Personality and Social Psychology*, 1966, *4*, 1–13.

CHAPANIS, N. P., & CHAPANIS, A. Cognitive dissonance: Five years later. *Psychological Bulletin*, 1964, *61*, 1–22.

CHASE, T. C. Attitude change in the advocate as a function of attitude change in the audience and being seen by the audience as sincere: A clarification of the effect of reward for counter attitudinal advocacy. Unpublished doctoral dissertation, University of Texas. 1970.

CHILD, I. L., STORM, T., & VEROFF, J. Achievement themes in folk tales related to socialization practice. In J. W. Atkinson (Ed.), *Motives in fantasy, action and society*. Princeton, N. J.: Nostrand, 1958, pp. 479–494.

CIALDINA, R. B. Attitudinal advocacy in the verbal conditioner. *Journal of Personality and Social Psychology*, 1971, *17*, 350–358.

COHEN, A. R. An experiment on small rewards for discrepant compliance and attitude change. In J. W. Brehm & A. R. Cohen, *Explorations in cognitive dissonance*. New York: Wiley, 1962, pp. 73–78.

COLLINS, B. E. The effect of monetary inducements on the amount of attitude change produced by forced compliance. In A. C. Elms (Ed.), *Role-playing, reward, and attitude change*. New York: van Nostrand, 1969.

COLLINS, B. E., & HOYT, M. F. Personal responsibility for consequences: An integration and extension of the "forced compliance" literature. *Journal of Experimental Social Psychology*, 1972, *8*, 558–593.

COOPER, J., & WORCHEL, S. Role of undesired consequences in arousing cognitive dissonance. *Journal of Personality and Social Psychology*, 1970, *16*, 199–206.

COOPER, J., ZANNA, M. P., & GOETHALS, G. R. Mistreatment of an esteemed other as a consequence affecting dissonance reduction. *Journal of Experimental Social Psychology*, 1974, *10*, 224–233.

DARLEY, J. M., & ARONSON, E. Self-evaluation *vs.* direct anxiety reduction as determinants of the fear-affiliation relationship. *Journal of Experimental Social Psychology*, 1966, (Supplement 1), 66–79.

DASHIELL, J. F. A quantitative demonstration of animal drive. *Journal of Comparative Psychology*, 1925, *5*, 205–208.

DAVIS, R. T., SETTLAGE, P. H., & HARLOW, H. F. Performance of normal and brain-operated monkeys on mechanical puzzles with and without food incentive. *Journal of Genetic Psychology*, 1950, *77*, 305–311.

DE CHARMS, R. *Personal causation: The internal affective determinants of behavior.* New York: Academic Press, 1968.

DECI, E. L. Effects of externally mediated rewards on intrinsic motivation. *Journal of Personality and Social Psychology*, 1971, *18*, 105–115.

DECI, E. L. Intrinsic motivation, extrinsic reinforcement and inequity. *Journal of Personality and Social Psychology*, 1972, *22*, 113–120. (a)

DECI, E. L. Effects of contingent and non-contingent rewards and controls on intrinsic motivation. *Organizational Behavior and Human Performance*, 1972, *8*, 217–229. (b)

DECI, E. L., BENWARE, C., & LANDY, D. A. *Money talks: So does output in attributing motivation.* Paper presented at the meeting of the American Psychological Association, Montreal, 1973.

DECI, E. L., BENWARE, C. & LANDY, D. The attribution of motivation as a function of output and rewards. *Journal of Personality*, 1974, *42*, 652–667.

DECI, E. L., & CASCIO, W. F. *Changes in intrinsic motivation as a function of negative feedback and threats.* Paper presented at the meeting of the Eastern Psychological Association, Boston, April, 1972.

DECI, E. L., CASCIO, W. F., & KRUSELL, J. *Sex differences, verbal reinforcement, and intrinsic motivation.* Paper presented at the meeting of the Eastern Psychological Association, Washington, D.C., May, 1973.

DECI, E. L., CASCIO, W. F., & KRUSELL, J. Cognitive evaluation theory and some comments on the Calder Staw critique. *Journal of Personality and Social Psychology*, 1975, *31*, 81–85.

DEMBER, W. N., & EARL, R. W. Analysis of exploratory, manipulatory, and curiosity behaviors. *Psychological Review*, 1957, *64*, 91–96.

DOLLARD, J., DOOB, L. W., MILLER, N. E., MOWRER, O. H., & SEARS, R. R. *Frustration and aggression.* New Haven: Yale University Press, 1939.

DORNBUSCH, S. M., HASTORF, A. H., RICHARDSON, S. A., MUZZY, R. E. & VREELAND, R. S. The perceiver and the perceived: Their relative influence on the categories of interpersonal cognition. *Journal of Personality and Social Psychology*, 1965, *1*, 434–440.

DRISCOLL J. M., & LANZETTA, J. T. Effects of problem uncertainty and prior arousal on predecisional information search. *Psychological Reports*, 1964, *14*, 975–988.

EISENBERGER, R. Explanation of rewards that do not reduce tissue needs. *Psychological Bulletin*, 1972, *77*, 319–339.

ELKIND, D. Cognitive growth cycles in mental development. *Nebraska symposium on motivation*, 1971, *19*, 1–31.

ELMS, A. C., & JANIS, I. L. Counter-norm attitudes induced by consonant versus dissonant conditions of role playing. *Journal of Experimental Research in Personality*, 1965, *1*, 50–60.

ENZEL, M. E., HANSEN, R. D., & LOWE, C. A. Causal attribution in the mixed motive game: Effects of facilitory and inhibitory environmental forces. *Journal of Personality and Social Psychology*, 1975, *31*, 50–54.

EVAN, W. M., & SIMMONS, R. G. Organizational effects of inequitable rewards: Two experiments in status inconsistency. *Administrative Science Quarterly*, 1969, *14*, 224–237.

FEATHER, N. T. The relationship of persistence at a task to expectations of success and achievement related motives. *Journal of Abnormal and Social Psychology*, 1961, *63*, 552–561.

FEATHER, N. T. Effects of prior success and failure on expectations of success and subsequent performance. *Journal of Personality and Social Psychology*, 1966, *3*, 287–298.

FEATHER, N. T. Change in confidence following success or failure as a predictor of subsequent performance. *Journal of Personality and Social Psychology*, 1968, *9*, 38–46.

FEATHER, N. T., & SAVILLE, M. R. Effects of amount of prior success and subsequent task performance. *Journal of Personality and Social Psychology*, 1967, *5*, 226–232.

FESTINGER, L. *A theory of cognitive dissonance*. Evanston, Ill: Row, Peterson, 1957.

FESTINGER, L. The psychological effects of insufficient rewards. *American Psychologist*, 1961, *16*, 1–11.

FESTINGER, L. The effect of compensation on cognitive processes. Paper presented at the meeting of the McKinsey Foundation on Managerial Compensation, Tarrytown, N. Y., March, 1967.

FESTINGER, L., & CARLSMITH, J. M. Cognitive consequences of forced compliance. *Journal of Abnormal and Social Psychology*, 1959, *58*, 203–210.

FISKE, D. W., & MADDI, S. R. *Functions of varied experience*. Homewood, Ill.: Dorsey, 1961.

FLAVELL, J. H., & WOHLWILL, J. F. Formal and functional aspects of cognitive development. In D. Elkind & J. H. Flavell (Eds.), *Studies in cognitive development: Essays in honor of Jean Piaget*. New York: Oxford University Press, 1969.

FOWLER, H. *Curiosity and exploratory behavior*. New York: Macmillan, 1965.

FOWLER, H. Satiation and curiosity. In K. W. Spence, & J. T. Spence (Eds.), *Psychology of learning and motivation*. (Vol. 1). New York: Academic Press, 1967, pp. 157–227.

FREEDMAN, J. L. Attitudinal effects of inadequate justification. *Journal of Personality*, 1963, *31*, 371–385.

FREEDMAN, J. L. Long-term cognitive dissonance. *Journal of Experimental Social Psychology*, 1965, *1*, 145–155.

FREEDMAN, J. L. Role playing: Psychology by consensus. *Journal of Personality and Social Psychology*, 1969, *13*, 107–114.

GALBRAITH, J., & CUMMINGS, L. L. An empirical investigation of the motivational determinants of task performance. *Organizational Behavior and Human Performance*, 1967, *2*. 237–257.

GATELY, M. J. Manipulation drive in experimentally naive rhesus monkeys. Unpublished master's thesis, University of Wisconsin, 1950.

GEORGOPOULOS, B. S., MAHONEY, G. M., & JONES, N. W. A path goal approach to productivity. *Journal of Applied Psychology*, 1957, *41*, 345–353.

GERARD, H., & MATHEWSON, G., The effects of severity of initiation on liking for a group: A replication. *Journal of Experimental Social Psychology*, 1966, *2*, 278–287.

GIORGI, A. *Psychology as a human science*. New York: Harper & Row, 1970.

GLANZER, M. Stimulus satiation: An explanation of spontaneous alternation and related phenomena. *Psychological Review*, 1953, *60*, 257–268.

GLANZER, M. Curiosity, exploratory drive, and stimulus satiation. *Psychological Bulletin*, 1958, *55*, 302–315.

GOETHALS, G. R., & COOPER, J. Role of intention and postbehavioral consequence in the arousal of cognitive dissonance. *Journal of Personality and Social Psychology*, 1972, *23*, 293–301.

GOLDSTEIN, K. *The organism*. New York: American Book Co., 1939.

GOODMAN, P. S., & FRIEDMAN, A. An examination of the effect of wage inequity in the hourly condition. *Organizational Behavior and Human Performance*, 1968, *3*, 340–352.

GOODMAN, P. S., & FRIEDMAN, A. An examination of quantity and quality of performance under conditions of overpayment in piece rate. *Organizational Behavior and Human Performance*, 1969, *4*, 365–374.

GOODMAN, P. S., & FRIEDMAN, A. An examination of Adam's theory of inequity. *Administrative Science Quarterly*, 1971, *16*, 271–288.

GREEN, D. Dissonance and self-perception analyses of "forced compliance": When two theories make competing predictions. *Journal of Personality and Social Psychology*, 1974, *29*, 819–828.

GREENE, D. Immediate and subsequent effects of differential reward systems on intrinsic motivation in public school classrooms. Unpublished doctoral dissertation, Stanford University, 1974.

GREENE, D. & LEPPER, M. R. Effects of extrinsic rewards on children's subsequent intrinsic interest. *Child Development*, 1974, *45*, 1141–1145.

GREENWALD, A. G. Nuttin's neglected critique of the Law of Effect. *Psychological Bulletin*, 1966, *65*, 199–205.

GROSSMAN, S. P. *A textbook of physiological psychology*. New York: Wiley, 1967.

HABER, R. N. Discrepancy from adaptation level as a source of affect. *Journal of Experimental Psychology*, 1958, *56*, 370–375.

HARLOW, H. F. Learning and satiation of response in intrinsically motivated complex puzzle performance by monkeys. *Journal of Comparative and Physiological Psychology*, 1950, *43*, 289–294.

HARLOW, H. F. Motivation as a factor in the acquisition of new responses. *Nebraska symposium on motivation*, 1953, *1*, 24–49. (a)

HARLOW, H. F. Mice, monkeys, men, and motives. *Psychological Review*, 1953, *60*, 23–32. (b)

HARLOW, H. F., HARLOW, M. K., & MEYER, D. R. Learning motivated by a manipulation drive. *Journal of Experimental Psychology*, 1950, *40*, 228–234.

HAWKINS, C. K., & LANZETTA, J. T. Uncertainty, importance, and arousal as determinants of predecisional information search. *Psychological Reports*, 1965, *17*, 791–800.

HEBB, D. O. The forms and conditions of chimpanzee anger. *Bulletin of the Canadian Psychological Association*, 1945, *5*, 32–35.

HEBB, D. O. Emotion in man and animal: An analysis of the intuitive processes of recognition. *Psychological Review*, 1946, *53*, 88–106. (a)

HEBB, D. O. On the nature of fear. *Psychological Review*, 1946, *53*, 259–276. (b)

HEBB, D. O. *The organization of behavior*. New York: Wiley, 1949.

HEBB, D. O. Drives and the c.n.s. (conceptual nervous system). *Psychological Review*, 1955, *62*, 243–254.

HEBB, D. O, & RIESEN, A. H. The genesis of irrational fears. *Bulletin of the Canadian Psychological Association*, 1943, *3*, 49–50.

HEBB, D. O., & THOMPSON, W. R. The social significance of animal studies. In G. Lindzey (Ed.), *Handbook of Social Psychology.* (Vol. 1). Reading, Mass.: Addison-Wesley, 1954. pp. 532–561.

HEIDER, F. *The psychology of interpersonal relations.* New York: Wiley, 1958.

HEIDER, F. The Gestalt theory of motivation. In *Nebraska Symposium on Motivation,* 1960, *8,* 145–172.

HELSON, H. *Adaptation-level theory.* New York: Harper & Row, 1964.

HENDRICK, C., & CONSTANTINI, A. F. Effects of varying trait inconsistency and response requirements on the primacy effect in impression formation. *Journal of Personality and Social Psychology,* 1970, *15,* 158–164.

HENDRICK, I. Instinct and the ego during infancy. *Psychoanalytic Quarterly,* 1942, *11,* 33–58.

HENDRICK, I. The discussion of the "instinct to master." *Psychoanalytic Quarterly,* 1943, *12,* 561–566.

HERON, W., DOANE, B. K., & SCOTT, T. H. Visual disturbances after prolonged isolation. *Canadian Journal of Psychology,* 1956, *10,* 13–18.

HOLMES, J. G., & STRICKLAND, L. H. Choice freedom and confirmation of incentive expectancy as determinants of attitude change. *Journal of Personality and Social Psychology,* 1970, *14,* 39–45.

HOLT, J. *How children fail.* New York: Dell, 1964.

HOMANS, G. C. *The human group.* New York: Harcourt, Brace, 1950.

HOMANS, G. C. *Social behavior: Its elementary forms.* New York: Harcourt, Brace, 1961.

HORNER, M. S. Sex differences in achievement motivation and performance in competitive and non-competitive situations. Unpublished doctoral dissertation, University of Michigan, 1968.

HORNER, M. S. Femininity and successful achievement: A basic inconsistency. In J. Bardwick, E. M. Douvan, M. S. Horner & D, Gutmann (Eds.), *Feminine personality and conflict.* Belmont, Calif: Brooks-Cole, 1970.

HORNER, M. S. The psychological significance of success in competitive achievement situations: A threat as well as a promise. In H. I. Day, D. E. Berlyne, & D. E. Hunt (Eds.), *Intrinsic motivation: A new direction in education.* Toronto: Holt, Rinehart, and Winston of Canada, 1971. pp. 46–60.

HORNER, M. S. Toward an understanding of achievement-related conflicts in women. *Journal of Social Issues,* 1972, *28* (2), 157–175.

HOVLAND, C. I., JANIS, I. L., & KELLEY, H. H. *Communication and persuasion.* New Haven: Yale University Press, 1953.

HOYT, M. F., HENLEY, M. D., & COLLINS, B. E. Studies in forced compliance: The confluence of choice and consequences on attitude change. *Journal of Personality and Social Psychology,* 1972, *23,* 205–210.

HULL, C. L. Knowledge and purpose as habit mechanisms. *Psychological Review,* 1930, *37,* 511–525.

HULL, C. L. *Principles of behavior.* New York: Appleton–Century, 1943.

HUNT, J. McV. Motivation inherent in information processing and action. In O. J. Harvey (Ed.), *Motivation and social interaction.* New York: Ronald, 1963. pp. 35–94.

HUNT, J. MCV. Intrinsic motivation and its role in psychological development. *Nebraska symposium on motivation,* 1965, *13,* 189–282.

HUNT, J. MCV. Toward a history of intrinsic motivation. In H. I. Day, D. E. Berlyne, & D. E. Hunt (Eds.), *Intrinsic motivation: A new direction in education.* Toronto: Holt, Rinehart, and Winston of Canada, 1971, pp. 1–32. (a)

HUNT, J. MCV. Intrinsic motivation: Information and circumstances. Also Intrinsic motivation and psychological development. In H. M. Schroder, & P. Suedfeld (Eds.), *Personality theory and information processing.* New York: Ronald, 1971. pp. 85–117. (b)

IRWIN, F. W. *Intentional behavior and motivation: A cognitive theory,* New York: Lippincott, 1971.

ISAAC, W. Evidence for a sensory drive in monkeys. *Psychological Reports,* 1962, *11,* 175–181.

JACQUES, E. *Equitable payment.* New York: Wiley, 1961.

JAMES, W. What is emotion? *Mind,* 1884, *9,* 188–205.

JAMES, W. *The principles of psychology. (Vols. I and II).* New York: Holt, 1890.

JANIS, I. L., & GILMORE, J. B. The influence of incentive conditions on the success of role playing in modifying attitudes. *Journal of Personality and Social Psychology,* 1965, *1,* 145–155.

JONES, A. Supplementary report: Information deprivation and irrelevant drive as determiners of an instrumental response. *Journal of Experimental Psychology,* 1961, *62,* 310–311.

JONES, A., WILKINSON, H. J., & BRADEN, I. Information deprivation as a motivational variable. *Journal of Experimental Psychology,* 1961, *62,* 126–137.

JONES, E. E., & DAVIS, K. E. From acts to dispositions. In L. Berkowitz (Ed.) *Advances in experimental social psychology.* (Vol. 2). New York: Academic Press, 1965, pp. 219–266.

JONES, E. E., & GOETHALS, G. R. *Order effects in impression formation: Attribution context and the nature of the entity.* New York: General Learning Press, Module Series, 1971.

JONES, E. E., & HARRIS, V. A. The attribution of attitudes. *Journal of Experimental Social Psychology,* 1967, *3,* 1–24.

JONES, E. E., & NISBETT, R. E. *The actor and the observer: Divergent perceptions of the causes of behavior.* New York: General Learning Press, Module series, 1971.

JONES, E. E., WORCHEL, S., GOETHALS, G. R., & GRUMET, J. F., Prior expectancy and behavioral extremity as determinants of attitude attribution. *Journal of Experimental Social Psychology,* 1971, *7,* 59–80.

JONES, R. A., LINDER, D. E., KIESLER, C. A., ZANNA, M. P., & BREHM, J. W. Internal states or external stimuli: Observers' attitude judgements and the dissonance theory—self-persuasion controversy. *Journal of Experimental Social Psychology,* 1968, *4,* 247–269.

JOURARD, S. M. *Self-disclosure: An experimental analysis of the transparent self.* New York: Wiley, 1971.

KAGAN, J. Motives and development. *Journal of Personality and Social Psychology,* 1972, *22,* 51–66.

KAHN, R. L. Productivity and job satisfaction. *Personnel Psychology,* 1960, *13,* 275–287.

KAZDIN, A. E., & BOOTZIN, R. R. The token economy: An evaluative review. *Journal of Applied Behavior Analysis (Monograph no. 1)*, 1972, *5*, (3).

KELLER, F. S. *Learning: Reinforcement theory* (2nd. ed.). New York: Random House, 1969.

KELLEY, H. H. Attribution Theory in Social Psychology. *Nebraska Symposium on Motivation*, 1967, *15*, 192–238.

KELLEY, H. H. *Attribution in social interaction.* New York: General Learning Press, Module Series, 1971.

KIESLER, C. A., NISBETT, R. E., & ZANNA, M. P. On inferring one's beliefs from one's behavior. *Journal of Personality and Social Psychology*, 1969, *11*, 321–327.

KIESLER, C. A., & SAKUMURA, J. A test for a model for commitment. *Journal of Personality and Social Psychology*, 1966, *3*, 349–353.

KITE, W. R. Attribution of causality as a function of the use of reward and punishment. Doctoral dissertation, Stanford University, 1964.

KOCH, S. Behavior as "intrinsically" regulated: Work notes toward a pre-theory of phenomena called "motivational." *Nebraska symposium on motivation*, 1956, *4*, 42–87.

KOCH, S. Psychological science *vs.* the science-humanism antinomy: Intimations of a significant science of man. *American Psychologist*, 1961, *16*, 629–639.

KOLB, D. A. Achievement motivation training for underachieving high-school boys. *Journal of Personality and Social Psychology*, 1965, *2*, 783–792.

KORNHAUSER, A. W. *Mental health of the industrial worker: A Detroit Study.* New York: Wiley, 1965.

KRUGLANSKI, A. W., ALON, S., & LEWIS, T. Retrospective misattribution and task enjoyment. *Journal of Experimental Social Psychology*, 1972, *8*, 493–501.

KRUGLANSKI, A. W., FREEDMAN, I., & ZEEVI, G. The effects of extrinsic incentive on some qualitative aspects of task performance. *Journal of Personality*, 1971, *39*, 606–617.

KRUSELL, J. L. Attribution of responsibility for performance outcomes of males and females. Unpublished doctoral dissertation, University of Rochester, 1973.

KUN, A., & WEINER, B. Necessary *vs.* sufficient causal schemata for success and failure. *Journal of Research in Personality*, 1973, *7*, 197–207.

KUYPERS, D. S., BECKER, W. C., & O'LEARY, K. D. How to make a token system fail. *Exceptional Children*, 1968, *35*, 101–109.

LAING, R. D. *The politics of experience.* New York: Ballentine Books, 1967.

LANGE, C. G. *Om Sindsbevaegelser et psyko. fysiolog. studie.* Copenhagen: Krønar, 1885.

LANZETTA, J. T. Information acquisition in decision making. In O. J. Harvey (Ed.), *Motivation and social interaction.* New York: Ronald Press, 1963, pp. 239–265.

LANZETTA, J. T. The motivational properties of uncertainty. In H. I. Day, D. E. Berlyne, & D. E. Hunt (Eds.), *Intrinsic motivation: A new direction in education.* Toronto: Holt, Rinehart, and Winston of Canada, 1971, pp. 134–147.

LASKER, H. M. Factors affecting responses to achievement motivation training in India. Unpublished honors thesis, Harvard University, 1966. Cited in de Charms, 1968.

LAWLER, E. E. Equity theory as a predictor of productivity and work quality. *Psychological Bulletin,* 1968, *70,* 596–610.

LAWLER, E. E. Job design and employee motivation. *Personnel Psychology,* 1969, *22,* 426–435.

LAWLER, E. E. *Pay and organizational effectiveness: A psychological view.* New York: McGraw-Hill, 1971.

LAWLER, E. E. *Motivation in work organizations.* Monterey, California: Brooks-Cole, 1973.

LAWLER, E. E., KOPLIN, C. A., YOUNG, T. F., & FADEM, J. A. Inequity reduction over time in an induced overpayment situation. *Organizational Behavior and Human Performance,* 1968, *3,* 253–268.

LAWLER, E. E., & O'GARA, P. W. Effects of inequity produced by underpayment on work output, work quality, and attitudes toward the work. *Journal of Applied Psychology,* 1967, *51,* 403–410.

LEAVITT, H. J. Unhuman Organizations. *Harvard Business Review,* 1962, *40,* 90–98.

LEEPER, R. W. A motivational theory of emotion to replace 'emotion as disorganized response.' *Psychological Review,* 1948, *55,* 5–21.

LEPPER, M. R., & GREENE, D. Turning play into work: Effects of adult surveillance and extrinsic rewards on children's intrinsic motivation. *Journal of Personality and Social Psychology,* in press.

LEPPER, M. R., GREENE, D. & NISBETT, R. E. Undermining children's intrinsic interest with extrinsic rewards: A test of the "overjustification" hypothesis. *Journal of Personality and Social Psychology,* 1973, *28,* 129–137.

LEUBA, C. Toward some integration of learning theories: The concept of optimal stimulation. *Psychological Reports,* 1955, *1,* 27–33.

LEWIN, K. *Principles of topological psychology.* New York: McGraw-Hill, 1936.

LEWIN, K. *The conceptual representation and measurement of psychological forces.* Durham, N.C.: University Press, 1938.

LEWIN, K. *Field theory in social science.* New York: Harper, 1951.

LIKERT, R. *New patterns of management.* New York: McGraw-Hill, 1961.

LIKERT, R. *The human organization.* New York: McGraw-Hill, 1967.

LINDER, D. E., COOPER, J., & JONES, E. E. Decision freedom as a determinant of the role of incentive magnitude in attitude change. *Journal of Personality and Social Psychology,* 1967, *6,* 245–254.

LOCKE, E. A. Toward a theory of task motivation and incentives. *Organizational Behavior and Human Performance,* 1968, *3,* 157–189.

LOWE, C. A. *Flattery vs. honesty: The biasing effects of being a target.* Unpublished manuscript, 1975.

LOWE, C. A., & ENZEL, M. E. *Status and intent as determinants of attraction to the source of benefits and harm, and an unexpected normative effect on reciprocity.* Unpublished manuscript, 1974.

MADDI, S. R. The search for meaning. *Nebraska Symposium on Motivation,* 1970, *18,* 137–186.

MALCOLM, N. Behaviorism as a philosophy of psychology. In T. W. Wann (Ed.), *Behaviorism and phenomenology.* Chicago: University of Chicago Press, 1964, pp. 141–155.

MANSSON, H. H. *The cognitive control of thirst motivation: A dissonance approach.* Unpublished doctoral dissertation. New York University, 1965.

MARTIN, M., BURKHOLDER, R., ROSENTHAL, R. L., THARP, R. G., & THORNE, G. L. Programming behavior change and reintegration into school milieux of extreme adolescent deviates. *Behavior Research and Therapy,* 1968, *6,* 371–383.

MARROW, A. J., BOWERS, D. G., & SEASHORE, S. E. *Management by participation.* New York: Harper, 1967.

MASLOW, A. H. A theory of human motivation. *Psychological Review,* 1943, *50,* 370–396.

MASLOW, A. H. *Motivation and personality.* New York: Harper, 1954.

MASLOW, A. H. Deficiency motivation and growth motivation. *Nebraska Symposium on Motivation,* 1955, *3,* 1–30.

MASLOW, A. H. *Eupsychion management.* Homewood, Ill.: Irwin–Dorsey, 1965.

MASLOW, A. H. *Toward a psychology of being.* New York: van Nostrand Reinhold, 1968.

MASLOW, A. H. *Motivation and personality* (2nd ed.). New York: Harper & Row, 1970.

McCLELLAND, D. C. Risk taking in children with high and low need for achievement. In J. W. Atkinson (Ed.), *Motives in fantasy action and society.* Princeton, N.J.: van Nostrand, 1958.

McCLELLAND, D. C. *The achieving society.* Princeton, N.J.: van Nostrand, 1961.

McCLELLAND, D. C. Toward a theory of motive acquisition. *American Psychologist,* 1965, *20,* 321–333.

McCLELLAND, D. C., ATKINSON, J. W., CLARK, R. W., & LOWELL, E. L. *The achievement motive.* New York: Appleton-Century-Crofts, 1953.

McCLELLAND, D. C., & FRIEDMAN, G. A. A cross-cultural study of the relationship between child-training practices and achievement motivation appearing in folk tales. In G. E. Swanson, T. M. Newcomb, & E. L. Hartley (Eds.), *Readings in Social Psychology.* New York: Holt, 1952.

McDOUGAL, W. *Social psychology.* New York: Luce & Co., 1908.

McGREGOR, D. *The human side of enterprise.* New York: McGraw-Hill, 1960

MEEHL, P. E. On the circularity of the Law of Effect. *Psychological Bulletin,* 1950, *47,* 52–75.

MEICHENBAUM, D. H., BOWERS, K. S., & ROSS, R. R. Modification of classroom behavior of institutionalized female adolescent offenders. *Behavior Research and Theory,* 1968, *6,* 343–353.

MERLEAU-PONTY, M. *The structure of behavior.* Barton: Beacon Press, 1963.

MILLER, G. A., GALANTER, E., & PRIBRAM, K. H. *Plans and the structure of behavior.* New York: Holt, 1960.

MILLER, M. B. Intrinsic motivation: Unlearned, learned, and modifiable. In H. I. Day, D. E. Berlyne, and D. E. Hunt (Eds.), *Intrinsic motivation: A new direction in education.* Toronto: Holt, Rinehart and Winston of Canada, 1971, pp. 171–185.

MILLER, N. E. Liberalization of basic S–R concepts: Extensions to conflict behavior, motivation, and social learning. In S. Koch (Ed.), *Psychology: A study of a science.* (Vol. 2). New York: McGraw-Hill, 1959, pp. 196–292.

MILLER, N. E., & DOLLARD, J. *Social learning and imitation.* New Haven: Yale University Press, 1941.

MISCHEL, T. Piaget: Cognitive conflict and the motivation of thought. In T. Mischel (Ed.), *Cognitive development and epistomology.* New York: Academic Press, 1971, pp. 311–355.

MONTESSORI, M. *The discovery of the child.* New York: Ballantine, 1967.

MONTGOMERY, K. C. A test of two explanations of spontaneous alternation. *Journal of Comparative and Physiological Psychology,* 1952, *45,* 287–293.

MONTGOMERY, K. C. Exploratory behavior as a function of "similarity" of stimulus situations. *Journal of Comparative and Physiological Psychology,* 1953, *46,* 129–133.

MONTGOMERY, K. C. The role of exploratory drive in learning. *Journal of Comparative and Physiological Psychology,* 1954, *47,* 60–64.

MONTGOMERY, K. C. The relation between fear induced by novel stimulation and exploratory behavior. *Journal of Comparative and physiological Psychology,* 1955, *48,* 254–260.

MONTGOMERY, K. C., & SEGALL, M. Discrimination learning based upon the exploratory drive. *Journal of Comparative and Physiological Psychology,* 1955, *48,* 225–228.

MOSS, H. A., & KAGAN, J. Stability of achievement and recognition seeking behaviors from early childhood through adulthood. *Journal of Abnormal and Social psychology,* 1961, *62,* 504–513.

MOWRER, O. H. *Learning theory and behavior.* New York: Wiley, 1960.

MURRAY, H. A. *Thematic Apperception Test manual.* Cambridge: Harvard University Press, 1943.

MYERS, A. K., & MILLER, N. E., Failure to find a learned drive based on hunger: Evidence for learning motivated by "exploration." *Journal of Comparative and Physiological Psychology,* 1954, *47,* 428–436.

MYERS, M. S. *Every employee a manager.* New York: McGraw-Hill, 1970.

NAGEL, E. *The structure of science.* New York: Harcourt, Brace, and World, 1961.

NEILL, A. S. *Summerhill: A radical approach to child rearing.* New York: Hart, 1960.

NEL, E., HELMREICH, R. L., & ARONSON, E. Opinion change in the advocate as a function of the persuadability of his audience: A clarification of the meaning of dissonance. *Journal of Personality and Social Psychology,* 1969, *12,* 117–124.

NEMETH, C. Effects of free *vs.* constrained behavior on attraction between people. *Journal of Personality and Social Psychology,* 1970, *15,* 302–311.

NEWELL, A., & SIMON, H. A. *Human problem solving.* Englewood Cliffs, N.J.: Prentice-Hall, 1972.

NEWTSON, D. Attribution and the unit of perception of ongoing behavior. *Journal of Personality and Social Psychology,* 1973, *28,* 28–38.

NISBETT, R. E. CAPUTO, C., LEGANT, P., & MARECEK, J. Behavior as seen by the actor and as seen by the observer. *Journal of Personality and Social Psychology,* 1973, *27,* 154–164.

NISBETT, R. E., & VALINS, S. *Perceiving the causes of one's own behavior.* New York: General Learning Press, Module Series, 1971.

NISSEN, H. W. A study of exploratory behavior in the white rat by means of the obstruction method. *Journal of Genetic Psychology*, 1930, *37*, 361–376.

NUTTIN, J. M. Dissonant evidence about dissonance theory. Second Conference of Experimental Social Psychologists in Europe, 1964.

OLDS, J., & OLDS, M. Drives, rewards, and the brain. In T. Newcomb (Ed.), *New directions in psychology, II*. New York: Holt, Rinehart, & Winston, 1965.

O'LEARY, K. D., & BECKER, W. C. Behavior modification of an adjustment class: A token reinforcement program. *Exceptional Children*, 1967, *9*, 637–642.

O'LEARY, K. D., BECKER, W. C., EVANS, M. B., & SAUDARGAS, R. A. A token reinforcement program in a public school: A replication and systematic analysis. *Journal of Applied Behavior Analysis*, 1969, *2*, 3–13.

O'LEARY, K. D., & DRABMAN, R. Token reinforcement programs in the classroom: A review. *Psychological Bulletin*, 1971, *75*, 379–398.

O'LEARY, K. D., DRABMAN, R., & KASS, R. E. Maintenance of appropriate behavior in a token program. *Journal of Abnormal Child Psychology*, 1973.

OPSAHL, R. L., & DUNNETTE, M. D. The role of financial compensation in industrial motivation. *Psychological Bulletin*, 1966, *66*, 94–118.

ORNE, M. T. On the social psychology of the psychological experiment: With particular reference to demand characteristics and their implications. *American Psychologist*, 1962, *17*, 776–783.

OSGOOD, C. E. *Methods and theory in experimental psychology*. New York: Oxford Univ. Press, 1953.

PATCHEN, M. *The choice of wage comparisons*, Englewood Cliffs, N.J.: Prentice-Hall, 1961.

PEAK, H. Attitude and motivation. *Nebraska Symposium on Motivation*, 1955, *3*, 149–189.

PERLS, F., HEFFERLINE, R. F., & GOODMAN, P. *Gestalt therapy*. New York: Delta, 1951.

PIAGET, J. *Play, dreams, and imitation in childhood*. New York: Norton, 1951.

PIAGET, J. *The origins of intelligence in children*. New York: International Universities Press, 1952.

PIAGET, J. *Les relations entre l'affectivite et l'intelligence dans le developpment mental de l'enfant*. Paris: Centre de Documentation Univ., 1954. Extensively cited in Mischel (1971).

PIAGET, J. Apprentissage et conaissance. In P. Greco & J. Piaget (Eds.), *Apprentissage et conaissance*. Etudes d'epistemologie genetique, 7. Paris: Presses Université de France, 1959. Cited in Mischel (1971).

PIAGET, J. *Six psychological studies*. D. Elkind (Ed.). New York: Random House, 1967.

PILIAVIN, J. A., PILIAVIN, I. M., LOEWENTON, E. P., McCAULEY, C., & HAMMOND, P. On observers' reproductions of dissonance effects: The right answers for the wrong reasons? *Journal of Personality and Social Psychology*, 1969, *13*, 98–106.

POLANYI, M. *Personal knowledge*. Chicago: University of Chicago Press, 1958.

PORTER, L. W., & LAWLER, E. E. *Managerial attitudes and performance*. Homewood, Ill.: Irwin–Dorsey, 1968.

POSTMAN, L. The history and present status of the Law of Effect. *Psychological Bulletin*, 1947, *44*, 489–563.

POSTMAN, L. Rewards and punishments in human learning. In L. Postman (Ed.), *Psychology in the making.* New York: Knopf, 1962, pp. 331–401.

PREMACK, D. Toward empirical behavior laws: 1. Positive reinforcement. *Psychological Review*, 1959, *66*, 219–233.

PREMACK, D. Reversibility of the reinforcement relation. *Science*, 1962, *136*, 255–257.

PREMACK, D. Rate differential reinforcement in monkey manipulation. *Journal of the Experimental Analysis of Behavior*, 1963, *6*, 81–89.

PRITCHARD, R. D. Equity theory: A review and critique. *Organizational Behavior and Human Performance*, 1969, *4*, 176–211.

PRITCHARD, R. D., DUNNETTE, M. D., & JORGENSON, D. O. Effects of perceptions of equity and inequity on worker performance and satisfaction. *Journal of Applied Psychology Monograph*, 1972 (Feb.), *56*, (No. 1), 75–94.

RAPAPORT, D. *Emotions and memory.* New York: Science Editions, 1961.

REIS, H. *The role of communication and contact in mediating self-interest, equity, and equality in social exchange.* Unpublished doctoral dissertation, New York University, 1975.

RICKERS-OVSIANKINA, M. Die Wiederaufnahme unterbrochenes Handlunger. *Psychologische Forschung*, 1928, *11*, 302–375.

ROGERS, C. R. *On becoming a person.* Boston: Houghton–Mifflin, 1961.

ROSEN, B. C. Race, ethnicity, and the achievement syndrome. *American Sociological Review*, 1959, *24*, 47–60.

ROSEN, B. C., & D.'ANDRADE, R. The psychosocial origins of achievement motivation. *Sociometry*, 1959, *22*, 185–218.

ROSENBERG, M. J. When dissonance fails: On eliminating evaluation apprehension from attitude measurement. *Journal of Personality and Social Psychology*, 1965, *1*, 28–42.

ROSENTHAL, R. *Experimenter effects in behavior research.* New York: Appleton-Century-Crofts, 1966.

ROSS, I. C., & ZANDER, A. Need satisfaction and employee turnover. *Personnel Psychology*, 1957, *10*, 327–338.

ROSS, M. Salience of reward and intrinsic motivation. *Journal of Personality and Social Psychology*, in press.

ROSS, M., & SHULMAN, R. F. Increasing the salience of initial attitudes: Dissonance *vs.* self-perception theory. *Journal of Personality and Social Psychology*, 1973, *28*, 138–144.

ROTTER, J. B. *Social learning and clinical psychology.* Englewood Cliffs, N.J.: Prentice-Hall, 1954.

ROTTER, J. B. Generalized expectancies for internal *vs.* external control of reinforcement. *Psychological Monographs*, 1966. *80* (1), Whole no. 609, pp. 1–28.

RYCKMAN, R. M., GOLD, J. A., & RODDA, W. C. Confidence rating shifts and performance as a function of locus of control, self-esteem, and task experience. *Journal of Personality and Social Psychology*, 1971, *18*, 305–310.

SARTRE, J.-P. *Existentialism and human emotion.* New York: Wisdom Library, 1957.

SAYLES, L. R. *Behavior of industrial work groups: Prediction and Control.* New York: Wiley, 1958.

SCHACTER, S. *The psychology of affiliation.* Stanford, Cal.: Stanford University Press, 1959.

SCHACTER, S. Some extraordinary facts about obese humans and rats. *American Psychologist,* 1971, *26,* 129–144. (a)

SCHACTER, S. *Emotion, obesity and crime.* New York: Academic Press, 1971. (b)

SCHACTER, S., & SINGER, J. Cognitive, social and physiological determinants of emotional states. *Psychological Review,* 1962, *69,* 379–399.

SCHLACHET, P. J. The effect of dissonance arousal on the recall of failure stimuli. *Journal of Personality,* 1965, *33,* 443–461.

SCHLOSBERG, H. Three dimensions of emotion. *Psychological Review,* 1954, *61,* 81–88.

SCOTT, W. Attitude change by response reinforcement: Replication and extension. *Sociometry,* 1959, *22,* 328–335.

SENSENIG, J., & BREHM, J. W. Attitude change from an implied threat to attitude freedom. *Journal of Personality and Social Psychology,* 1968, *8,* 324–330.

SHERMAN, S. J. Effects of choice and incentive on attitude change in a discrepant behavior situation. *Journal of Personality and Social Psychology,* 1970, *15,* 245–252.

SIMON, H. A. Motivational and emotional controls of cognition. *Psychological Review,* 1967, *74,* 29–39.

SKINNER, B. F. *Science and human behavior.* New York: Free Press, 1953.

SKINNER, B. F. *Beyond freedom and dignity.* New York: Knopf, 1971.

SMITH, E. E. The power of dissonance techniques to change attitudes. *Public Opinion Quarterly,* 1961, *25,* 626–639.

SMITH, M. B. Competence and "mental health": Problems in conceptualizing human effectiveness. In S. B. Sells (Ed.), *The definition and measurement of mental health: A symposium.* Washington, D.C.: National Center for Health Statistics, USPHS, 1969.

SMITH, M. B. Normality: For an abnormal age. In D. Offer and D. X. Freedman (Eds.), *Modern psychiatry and clinical research: Essays in honor of Roy R. Grinkes, Sr.* New York: Basic Books, 1972.

SMITH, M. B. On self-actualization: A transambivalent examination of a focal theme in Maslow's psychology. *Journal of Humanistic Psychology,* 1973, *13,* (2), 17–33.

SOKOLOV, E. N. Neural models and the orienting reflex. In M. A. B. Brazier (Ed.), *The central nervous system and behavior.* New York: Josiah Macy, Jr. Foundation, 1960.

SOKOLOV, E. N. Higher nervous functions: The orienting reflex. *Annual Review of Physiology,* 1963, *25,* 545–580.

STEIN, A. H., & BAILEY, M. M. The socialization of achievement orientation in females. *Psychological Bulletin,* 1973, *80,* 345–366.

STORMS, M. D. Videotape and the attribution process: Reversing actors' and observers' points of view. *Journal of Personality and Social Psychology*, 1973, *27*, 165–175.

TAYLOR, D. W. Toward an information processing theory of motivation, *Nebraska Symposium on Motivation*, 1960, *8*, 59–79.

TAYLOR, F. W. *Principles of scientific management.* New York: Harper, 1911.

THIBAUT, J. W., & RIECKEN, H. W. Some determinants and consequences of the perception of social causality. *Journal of Personality*, 1955, *24*, 113–133.

THORNDIKE, E. L. *The psychology of learning.* New York: Teacher's College, Columbia University, 1913.

TOLMAN, E. C. *Purpose behavior in animals and men.* New York: Century, 1932.

TOLMAN, E. C. Principles of purposive behavior. In S. Koch (Ed.), *Psychology: A study of a science.* (Vol. II). New York: McGraw-Hill, 1959, pp. 92–157.

TURNER, E. A., & WRIGHT, J. C. Effects of severity of threat and perceived availability on the attractiveness of objects. *Journal of Personality and Social Psychology*, 1965, *2*, 128–132.

VALINS, S. Cognitive effects of false heart-rate feedback. *Journal of Personality and Social Psychology*, 1966, *4*, 400–408.

VON BERTALANFFY, L. The theory of open systems in physics and biology. *Science*, 1950, *111*, 23–28.

VROOM, V. H. *Work and motivation.* New York: Wiley, 1964.

VROOM, V. H., & DECI, E. L. (Eds.) *Management and motivation.* London: Penguin, 1970.

WALKER, E. L. Psychological complexity as a basis for a theory of motivation and choice. *Nebraska Symposium on Motivation*, 1964, *13*, 47–95.

WALKER, E. L. Psychological complexity and preference: A hedgehog theory of behavior. In D. E. Berlyne, & K. B. Madsen (Eds.), *Pleasure, reward, preference.* New York: Academic Press, 1973, pp. 65–97.

WALSTER, E., BERSCHEID, E., & WALSTER, G. W. The exploited: Justice or justification? In J. McCauley, & L. Berkowitz (Eds.), *Altruism and helping behavior.* New York: Academic Press, 1970, pp. 179–204.

WALSTER, E., BERSCHEID, E., & WALSTER, G. W. New directions in equity research. *Journal of Personality and Social Psychology*, 1973, *25*, 151–176.

WATSON, J. B. Psychology as the behaviorist views its. *Psychological Review*, 1913, *20*, 158–177.

WEICK, K. E. Reduction of cognitive dissonance through task enhancement and effort expenditure. *Journal of Abnormal and Social Psychology*, 1964, *68*, 533–539.

WEINER, B. *Theories of motivation: From mechanism to cognition.* Chicago: Markham, 1972.

WEINER, B., FRIEZE, I., KUKLA, A., REED, L., REST, S., & ROSENBAUM, R. M. *Perceiving the causes of success and failure.* New York: General Learning Press, Module Series, 1971.

WELKER, W. L. Some determinants of play and exploration in chimpanzees. *Journal of Comparative and Physiological Psychology*, 1956, *49*, 84–89. (a)

WELKER, W. L. Effects of age and experience on play and exploration of young chimpanzees. *Journal of Comparative and Physiological Psychology*, 1956, *49*, 223–226. (b)

WHITE, R. W. Motivation reconsidered: The concept of competence. *Psychological Review*, 1959, *66*, 297–333.

WHITE, R. W. Competence and the psychosexual stages of development. *Nebraska Symposium on Motivation*, 1960, *8*, 97–141.

WINTERBOTTOM, M. R. The relation of need for achievement to learning experiences in independence and mastery. In J. W. Atkinson (Ed.), *Motives in fantasy, action, and society*. Princeton, N.J.: van Nostrand 1958, pp. 453–478.

WOOD, I., & LAWLER, E. E. Effects of piece rate overpayment on'productivity. *Journal of Applied Psychology*, 1970, *54*, 234–238.

WOODWORTH, R. S. *Dynamic psychology*. New York: Columbia University Press, 1918.

WOODWORTH, R. S. *Dynamics of behavior*. New York: Holt, 1958.

WUNDT, W. *Grundzuge der physiologischen Psychologie*. Leipzig: Englemann, 1874.

YERKES, R. M., & DODSON, J. D. The relation of strength of stimulus to rapidity of habit-formation. *Journal of Comparative and Neurological Psychology*, 1908, *18*, 459–482.

YOUNG, P. T. *Emotion in man and animal: Its nature and relation to attitude and motive*. New York: Wiley, 1943.

YOUNG, P. T. *Motivation and emotion*. New York: Wiley, 1961.

ZANNA, M. P., LEPPER, M. R., & ABELSON, R. P. Attentional mechanisms in children's devaluation of a forbidden activity in a forced-compliance situation. *Journal of personality and Social Psychology*, 1973, *28*, 355–359.

ZEIGARNIK, B. Das behalten erledigter und unerledigter handlungen. *Psychologische Forschung*, 1927, *9*, 1–85.

ZIMBARDO, P. G. The effect of effort and improvisation on self-persuasion produced by role-playing. *Journal of Experimental Social Psychology*, 1965, *1*, 103–120.

ZIMBARDO, P. G. (Ed.). *The cognitive control of motivation: The consequences of choice and dissonance*. Glenview, Ill.: Scott, Foresman, 1969.

ZIMBARDO, P. G., & FORMICA, R. Emotional comparison and self-esteem as determinants of affiliation. *Journal of Personality*, 1963, *31*, 141–162.

ZIMBARDO, P. G., & MILLER, N. E. Facilitation of exploration by hunger in rats. *Journal of Comparative and Physiological Psychology*, 1958, *51*, 43–46.

ZIMBARDO, P. G., WEISENBERG, M., FIRESTONE, I., & LEVY, B. Communicator effectiveness in producing public conformity and private attitude change. *Journal of Personality*, 1965, *33*, 233–255.

Author
Index

Likert, R., 222–224, 227,
306
Linder, D. E., 174,
176–177, 180, 205, 287,
296, 304, 306
Locke, E. A., 115–117, 306
Loeb, A., 167, 297
Loewenton, E. P.,
286–287, 309
Lowe, C. A., 247, 251,
254, 270, 278, 280, 300,
306
Lowell, E. L., 14, 33, 307

Maddi, S. R., 33, 44–45,
47, 49, 58, 60, 87–90,
92, 301, 306
Madsen, K. B., 297
Mahoney, G. M., 106, 301
Malcolm, N., 20, 306
Mansson, H. H., 184, 307
Marecek, J., 290, 308
Marrow, A. J., 222, 224,
227, 307
Martin, M., 214, 307
Maslow, A. H., 17, 57–58,
76, 82–87, 92, 95,
222–223, 227, 307
Mathewson, G., 172, 301
McCauley, C., 286–287,
309
McCauley, J., 312
McClelland, D. C., 14,
33–36, 44, 51, 58,
76–80, 82, 92, 104,
107–109, 116, 307
McConnell, H. K.,
286–288, 297
McCullers, J. C., 159
McDougall, W., 25, 28,
307
McGraw, K., 159
McGregor, D., 220, 222,
307
Meehl, P. E., 11, 307

Meichenbaum, D. H.,
214–215, 307
Merleau-Ponty, M., 19,
307
Meyer, D. R., 28, 131, 302
Meyer, H. H., 226–227,
296
Miller, G. A., 37, 120, 307
Miller, M. B., 82, 307
Miller, N. E., 6, 13,
27–29, 39, 58, 173, 300,
307–308, 313
Mills, J., 172, 296
Mischel, T., 66, 67, 69,
308–309
Montessori, M., 212, 308
Montgomery, K. C.,
26–29, 58, 308
Moss, H. A., 78, 308
Mowrer, O. H., 6, 39, 300,
308
Murray, H. A., 107, 308
Muzzy, R. E., 19, 300
Myers, A. K., 27–29, 58,
308
Myers, M. S., 223, 227,
308

Nagel, E., 124, 308
Neill, A. S., 211–212, 308
Nel, E., 177, 180, 308
Nemeth, C., 254, 308
Newell, A., 273, 308
Newtson, D., 272, 308
Nisbett, R. E., 140, 188,
235, 254, 283, 290–291,
304–306, 308
Nissen, H. W., 26, 309
Nuttin, J. M., 172, 309

O'Gara, P. W., 200–201,
204, 306
Olds, J., 50, 60, 309
Olds, M., 50, 60, 309
O'Leary, K. D., 214–215,
219, 305, 309

Opsahl, R. L., 201, 309
Orne, M. T., 203, 309
Osgood, C. E., 6, 309

Patchen, M., 189, 309
Patty, R., 149
Peak, H., 105, 309
Perls, F., 270, 309
Piaget, J., 13, 66–69, 71,
84, 92, 116, 156, 309
Piliavin, I. M., 286–287,
309
Piliavin, J. A., 286–287,
309
Pinder, C. C., 159
Polanyi, M., 19, 309
Porac, J., 159
Porter, L. W., 107, 224,
309
Postman, L., 11, 310
Premack, D., 28, 310
Pribram, K. H., 37, 120,
307
Pritchard, R. D., 190–195,
200–201, 310

Rapaport, D., 185, 310
Reed, L., 242, 312
Reis, H., 194, 310
Rest, S., 242, 312
Richardson, S. A., 19, 300
Rickers-Ovsiankina, M.,
38, 310
Riecken, H. W., 254, 312
Riesen, A. H., 32, 302
Riter, A., 159
Rodda, W. C., 146, 310
Rogers, C. R., 89, 310
Rosen, B. C., 78, 79, 310
Rosenbaum, M., 173, 297
Rosenbaum, R. M., 242,
312
Rosenbaum, W. B.,
192–193, 195, 295
Rosenberg, M. J.,
173–174, 176, 203, 310

Subject
Index